Domesticating the West

Women in the West

Domesticating the West

The Re-creation of the
Nineteenth-Century
American Middle Class

BRENDA K. JACKSON

UNIVERSITY OF NEBRASKA PRESS
LINCOLN ❖ LONDON

© 2005
by the Board of Regents of the
University of Nebraska
All rights reserved
Manufactured in the
United States of America

⊗

Library of Congress
Cataloging-in-Publication Data
Jackson, Brenda K.
Domesticating the West: the re-creation
of the nineteenth-century American
middle class / Brenda K. Jackson.
p. cm.—(Women in the West)
Includes bibliographical
references and index.
ISBN-13: 978-0-8032-2602-9
(cloth : alk. paper)
ISBN-10: 0-8032-2602-0 (cloth : alk. paper)
ISBN-13: 978-0-8032-5105-2 (electronic)
ISBN-10: 0-8032-5105-X (electronic)
1. Tannatt, Thomas, 1833–1913.   2. Tannatt,
Elizabeth F. (Elizabeth Forster), 1837–1920.
3. Pioneers—West (U.S.)—Biography.
4. Middle class—West (U.S.)—Biography.
5. Frontier and pioneer life—West
(U.S.).   6. Community life—West.
(U.S.)—History—19th century.
7. West (U.S.)—Social conditions—19th
century.   8. West (U.S.)—Social Life
and customs—19th century.   9. Inland
Empire—History—19th century.
10. Inland Empire—Biography.
I. Title.   II. Series.
F590.5.J33 2005
978'.02'092—dc22
2005009944

Set in Minion by Kim Essman.
Designed by Ray Boeche.
Printed by Thomson-Shore, Inc.

To the memory of
Clara Leona Cummings Sanders
(1915–2000)

Contents

Illustrations

Acknowledgments

When Thomas and Elizabeth Tannatt entered my life in the fall of 1997, the thought of turning a dissertation crafted from a study of their lives into a book was the furthest thing from my mind. As research continued, however, and it became increasingly clear that Thomas and Elizabeth provided the perfect representation of members of the nineteenth-century middle class, the need to tell their story became paramount. Middle-class studies have taken on a new urgency in recent years, and the Tannatts' story, complete with their East Coast upbringings, post–Civil War wanderlust and eventual migration, reestablishment in the West, and assumption of community leadership roles, adds a vital chapter to the growing collection of community and regional studies aimed at an eventual nineteenth-century middle-class synthesis. The story that follows is theirs—and the pleasure to tell it is mine.

A project of this magnitude is impossible to accomplish without the assistance and expertise of others, and I have benefited from the talents and knowledge of many wonderful people. Laila Miletic-Vejzovic and Trevor Bond, from Manuscripts, Archives, and Special Collections (MASC) at Washington State University, not only employed me while I was a graduate student but made the WSU archives, and the Tannatt collections and other collections housed there, readily available to me. Lawrence Stark, MASC's assistant archivist, with his vast wealth of knowledge on the Pacific Northwest in general and Washington State University in particular, proved to be an invaluable personal resource. I thank them all for their unselfish contributions of time and knowledge to this project, and for their friendship. Receipt of the Pettyjohn Graduate Research Fellowship, awarded by the department of history at Washington State University, and a WSU graduate school travel grant allowed me to conduct research in Massachusetts, and I am most appreciative of the interest and confidence in this project held by both the university and its history department. The staffs at the Manchester Historical Society and Manchester Public Library in Manchester-by-the-Sea opened their offices and Tappan collections to me, and I am particularly grateful for Esther "Slim" Proctor's wealth of knowledge on all things Manchester. Dorothy Jodice, the society's executive director, introduced me to its headquarters, the beautiful Trask House, where I began to develop an understanding of and appreciation for the eighteenth- and nineteenth-century Manchester that molded the personalities and characters of Thomas and Elizabeth Tannatt.

My association with the Manchester Historical Society allowed me to make the acquaintance of C. P. Weaver, a Tappan descendant and now a close and special friend. Kitty traveled from her home in Virginia to meet with me in Manchester and to share Tappan family stories and lore. Kitty, a descendant of Samuel F. Tappan, Elizabeth's first cousin, introduced me to Manchester proper, and together we visited the 1661 cemetery, Singing Beach, the many Tappan homes in town, the town square, and countless other Manchester landmarks. I cannot thank her enough for sharing so much of herself and her Tappan records with me, and I look forward to visiting her soon in Manchester, where she now resides in a Tappan family home. The archivists at the U.S. Military Academy at West Point, the Northwest Museum of Arts and Culture in Spokane, and the National Archives Administration in Washington DC were also very generous with their collections, for which I thank them.

There is no doubt that the individual who held the most confidence in this project from its inception was my mentor at Washington State University, Sue Armitage. For five years she listened to, consoled, defended, and advised me on every aspect of this project, and on a host of others, and in the process we became very dear friends. I will never forget the day of my doctoral defense when Sue insisted that this project was ready to submit for publication. I was enormously humbled by her confidence but not at all convinced of the publishability of this work. As usual, though, Sue was right. I am a better and more thoughtful historian because of the time and interest Sue has invested in me, and for her unwavering support I will be forever grateful. John Kicza and Richard Hume, of Washington State University's history department, and Janice Rutherford, now affiliated with the museum studies department at the University of Oregon, all gave this work careful and constructive readings in its initial stage, and I am appreciative of their advice and support. The careful and thorough readings of this study by Ruth Moyhihan and Mary Murphy have strengthened it considerably, and I thank them both for their kind words, encouragement, and thoughtful suggestions. I have had the good fortune to work with a wonderful editor at the University of Nebraska Press, Elizabeth Demers, and I am thankful and appreciative for her staunch and unwavering confidence in this project and in me as its author.

Friends and family become particularly important during the self-imposed isolation of writing, especially during long, dark Pullman, Washington, winters when it seemed as though neither the season nor the project itself would ever end. My Pullman graduate school friends deserve a huge thank you, and maybe a parade, for listening to endless Tannatt stories and anecdotes, when any other topic would probably have been preferable, and with the patience only fellow historians could muster. I'm reminded in particular of the countless times I pointed out the Steptoe Monument to my friend and colleague Jeff Crane, who, after awhile, began pointing the monument out to me! Elizabeth Van Beek, my professor at San Jose State University, once told me that the best friendships are forged in graduate school. She was right—and to Michelle Tabit, Carli Schiffner, John Mann, Kevin Marsh, Steve Shay, Andrew Duffin, Suzanne Julin, Mee-Ae Kim, Sara Ewert—and Jeff Crane—without whom I never would have survived Pullman, or completed this project, I thank you all so much for your friendships. Thank you, too, to my parents, Dick and Shirley Jackson, and to my brothers and their families—Loren, Malea, Alex, and Matt, and Kevin, Mary, Drew, and Rachel—for their unwavering support.

My colleagues at Belmont University in Nashville, Tennessee, have been enormously supportive and encouraging during this year of revisions and rewrites, while at the same time helping me adjust to a new school and my new life in the South. I am thankful for the friendships I have made both at Belmont and in Nashville, and I am particularly grateful for the support of Jeff Coker, my friend and colleague during this period of transition and revision. Jennifer Coker, out of the goodness of her heart, and because of our friendship, indexed this manuscript—a project I couldn't even imagine taking on myself—and I thank her so much. To Jack Abernathy: thank you for keeping me on task during my "revision summer," and especially for coming into my life.

My grandmother, Clara Leona Cummings Sanders, has influenced me enormously throughout my life. She loved history and was very enthusiastic about this project, and particularly about my planned research trip to Massachusetts in the summer of 2000. She died while I was in Manchester, but somehow she knows this manuscript is now completed. She was my friend, my confidante, and my role model. For these reasons, and many more, this telling of Thomas and Elizabeth's story is dedicated to her memory.

Domesticating the West

Thomas Redding Tannatt, ca.
1880. *Courtesy of Manuscripts,*
Archives, and Special Collections,
Washington State University
Libraries, Pullman.

Elizabeth Tappan Tannatt, ca.
1880. *Courtesy of Manuscripts,*
Archives, and Special Collections,
Washington State University
Libraries, Pullman.

In 1881, Thomas and Elizabeth Tannatt said a final good-bye to Massachusetts and the eastern seaboard, where they had spent the majority of their lives, and moved west, as had so many American pioneers before them. Here, however, the similarities end, for the Tannatts undertook their journey in the years following the Civil War, more than a generation after the great migrations of the 1840s and 1850s. And unlike the agricultural and speculative motivations that drove pioneers during the first half of the century, middle-class travelers of the postwar era sought roles in the West as leaders, philanthropists, and community builders, opportunities that social and economic change wrought by war had rendered unattainable in many of their eastern hometowns.

The United States celebrated the fiftieth anniversary of its independence in 1826, just a decade prior to the births of Thomas and Elizabeth in the 1830s. In the years that followed the country experienced an era of exceptional development and transformation as it grew from a young and largely agricultural nation to one perched on the brink of industrial explosion. The transportation revolution succeeded in connecting the eastern seaboard with the Ohio Valley and points west, and this shift of attention from the Atlantic coast to the heartland brought about a new sense of American pride and growth of a national spirit, witnessed in part by the 1828 presidential victory of "upstart" Andrew Jackson over incumbent John Quincy Adams.

The events of the century's early decades disrupted many aspects of American society, in particular the class system, in place since the earliest days of colonization. Borrowed from the European model, the American social ladder included the wealthy at one end, the laboring poor, destitute, and enslaved at the other, and in between those loosely referred to as the "middling sort." Prior to the mid-nineteenth century, this "natural" order remained largely unchallenged, for, despite the success of the few who did improve their social standing, the opportunities from which they benefited remained unavailable to the majority of the population.

The early nineteenth century's transportation revolution produced a burst of technology, manufacture, and growth in the United States, all of which expanded in response to burgeoning national and international markets demanding large quantities of goods and services for rapidly expanding "consumer" populations. This era, often referred to as the Market Revolution, greatly upset the traditional class structure as it introduced the concept of upward mobility: the notion that individuals could move up the social ladder through diligence and hard work. "Ours is a country where men start from an humble origin, and from small beginnings rise gradually in the world, as the reward of merit and industry," declared Rev. Calvin Colton early in the nineteenth century.[1] This rhetoric appealed to members of the growing and expanding middle class: the "white collar" workers employed as bank tellers, clerks, bookkeepers, farmers, mechanics, and manual laborers who hoped to improve their social and financial situations, or at least lay the groundwork that would allow their children to experience upward mobility.[2]

The Market Revolution intensified the impact of capitalism on American citizens, for as historian Harry Watson has stated, "every new mill created opportunities for time clerks, bookkeepers, foremen, superintendents, engineers, and other management personnel," and "the same was true for every railroad company, canal company, bank, insurance firm, or mercantile house that flourished in the new commercial environment."[3] Simply put, the system of industrial capitalism that originated during the early decades of the nineteenth century created a need for a management tier theretofore absent in American society. The Market Revolution led to the creation of the American middle class.

These increased career opportunities and possibilities for social advancement did not, however, extend evenly throughout the population. The advent of the factory system and mass production adversely affected members of the artisan class, traditionally among the "middling sort," who found their standing reduced from that of fine craftsmen to ordinary laborers and wage earners.[4] At the same time, the northern concentration of factories and mills created an enormous discrepancy between the industrial capabilities of the North and the South and, as a result, hindered the development of a strong southern middle class. This lack of industrial strength would plague the South in the upcoming Civil War and lead to regional classifications and characterizations that endured into the late nineteenth century and beyond. Burton Bledstein has suggested that northern observers paid a great deal of attention to the ways in which the South lagged behind the North in industrialization, transportation, and immigration, noting that these discrepancies were magnified by the inadequacies of southern transit and port facilities and the preference of many European immigrants to avoid the South altogether.[5]

The Tannatts' story is a nineteenth-century middle-class study, and it is worth telling for many reasons. Thomas and Elizabeth represent a segment of the population often absent from historical study, since traditional scholarship has focused much of its attention on the accomplishments of history's "great men," and recent studies have been devoted in large part to the laboring poor and minorities. As a result, according to Melanie Archer and Judith Blau, "the middle class is the least studied segment of nineteenth-century American society."[6] In recent years this neglect has become a regular topic of discussion, with historians taking one another to task for disregarding this portion of the population. In his work on the development of the American middle class, Stuart Blumin addresses this lack of attention and reveals that problems associated with the identification and classification of a "middle class" plagued historians throughout the twentieth century and that mid-nineteenth-century writers and journalists opted to deny the very existence of an American middle class. According to Blumin, "writers of the nineteenth century ignored middling folk because they did not know how to deal with them" and also because the extremes represented by the very rich and the very poor, particularly in New York, Philadelphia, and other large cities, provided the sensationalism that appealed to the reading public.[7] "There are but two classes in the city—the poor and the rich," wrote New Yorker James Dabney McCabe in 1868, and more than a century later, in 1984, Peter Buckley discussed the "two cultural axes" and the "two distinct idioms" at work during the city's 1849 Astor Place riot. Neither addressed the presence of a nineteenth-century New York middle class; in fact, McCabe insisted that "the middle class, which is so numerous in other cities, hardly exists at all here."[8] According to Sean Wilentz, however, "no study of New York workers, particularly not one that tries to analyze working-class beliefs as well as behavior, can leave these people out," and he has insisted that "the middle class merits respectful study."[9]

In his recent work on late-nineteenth-century New York, Sven Beckert opted to use the term "bourgeoisie" instead of "middle class" to identify his study's focus on "a particular kind of elite whose power . . . derived from the ownership of capital rather than birthright, status, or kinship." Use of "middle class" seemed unsuitable to Beckert as he interpreted popular usage of the term to "stand either for all Americans, past and present, who are neither extremely wealthy nor homeless, or for a distinct social group that corresponds somewhat with the European notion of the 'petite bourgeoisie'—artisans, shop owners, and lesser professionals."[10] For Maris Vinovskis, the term "middle class" is simply problematic, as "it refers not only to one's occupational or economic circumstances but also to one's goals and life style," a combination that renders the term, as well as those encompassed by it, difficult to pinpoint and identify.[11]

These problems of identification have led historians and others to ask if the specific composition of the middle class is important enough to warrant concern and generate discussion, and the answer, according to Beckert, is a resounding "yes," "because the confused use of the term 'middle class' has made it very difficult to come to terms with central issues in American history." Beckert sees the term as "confused" because, by its inclusion of all except the very rich and the very poor, "the specific beliefs, gender roles, and politics of the nation's bankers, industrialists, shopkeepers, artisans, and professionals have become . . . harder to grasp since they were all subsumed into the great middle class."[12] He suggests that by distinguishing among the various groups of nineteenth-century property-holding Americans the "confusion" of the middle class would begin to untangle. Bledstein has echoed Beckert's sentiments, with the added proviso that "those who care about the working classes put understanding at risk by not taking an interest in the history of the middle classes, since these histories are intrinsically related."[13]

The questions, concerns, and indecision that continue to plague contemporary historians and researchers did not seem to trouble members of the nineteenth-century middle class at all. These individuals knew precisely who they were. More accurately stated, perhaps, they knew who they were not. In colonial America, the "middling sort" developed through the efforts of tradesmen, merchants, and artisans who wished to distinguish themselves from the lower, or common, classes, composed of the nonpropertied, the poor, and the destitute. By the nineteenth century, as the concept of "rank" fell from favor, middling sorts became the "middle class" and, in American society, a lifestyle. According to Bledstein, the idea of "middle class" appealed to nineteenth-century Americans, for unlike Karl Marx's "bourgeoisie" and "proletariat" (respectively, those who own the means of production and those who labor), "the middle-class person in America owns an acquired skill or cultivated talent" that was not looked upon "as a commodity, an external resource, like the means of production or manual labor."[14] In sum, in mid- to late-nineteenth-century America anyone could aspire to the "middle class," for rather than classifying the individual, it epitomized "a way of doing things, a display of selective *characteristics*, . . . [and] a matter of discerning emphasis and attention."[15] Thomas and Elizabeth Tannatt knew they belonged to the middle class, and they spent their lives striving for the top rung of this social classification.

This telling of the Tannatts' story seeks to provide the largely undifferentiated nineteenth-century American middle class with a face and an identity. At the same time, this account sheds light on a chapter in American history that has been not only neglected but essentially ignored: the postwar lives of Civil War veterans and their families. It is a common misconception that, for northerners, few hardships resulted from the war, and that they were far outweighed by the wealth and opportunity to be gleaned at the expense of the devastated South. A renewed interest in scholarship of the period has challenged these perceptions, however, and recent studies reveal that—though certainly not to the extent experienced in the South—northern cities suffered severe, often permanent economic setbacks as a result of the war, and numerous New England towns, and their citizens, witnessed significant drops in the rate of industrialization and the accumulation of personal wealth.[16] Elizabeth's hometown of Manchester, Massachusetts, numbered among these, and its factories never recovered the productivity and success they enjoyed in the century prior to the war.[17] In addition, and in response to the prospect of greatly diminished opportunities, countless individuals, particularly young men, abandoned their northern hometowns in the postwar years to seek livelihoods elsewhere, thus accelerating township decline through population losses and the resultant reduction in birthrates.

Civil War scholarship has flourished without interruption since the war's end, and thousands of publications have chronicled the victories and defeats of such leaders as Ulysses S. Grant, Thomas "Stonewall" Jackson, and Robert E. Lee. In recent years, research has focused on wartime reform and benevolent efforts and has added women's names to the list of Civil War heroes, among them Dorothea Dix, Harriet Tubman, and Clara Barton. It is surprising that this vast outpouring of scholarship has avoided inquiry into the long-term effects of the war on those who fought its battles and on the families who suffered and persevered with them. In 1989, Maris Vinovskis lamented that "we do not know much about the effects of the Civil War on everyday life in the United States . . . and almost nothing is available on the postwar life course of Civil War veterans."[18] In the past decade a few historians have undertaken this formidable task, and the Tannatts' story adds an important piece to this emerging scholarship on yet another segment of America's nineteenth-century middle class.

The story of Thomas Redding Tannatt and Elizabeth Tappan Tannatt begins more than a century before their births, across the Atlantic Ocean in the British Isles. Chapter 1 introduces Thomas's and Elizabeth's forebears and their reasons for migrating to North America, and reveals that while Thomas's roots extend deep into the houses of Scottish and Welsh gentry, Elizabeth's English ancestors enjoyed modest successes as "middling sorts." During the years following their migration, however, and for a number of reasons, the social standings of these families shifted, and as the Tappans rose to claim positions of prestige in their New England communities, the Tannatts experienced a decline in social status.

The chapters that follow examine the Tannatts' lives chronologically, and while their activities frequently intertwine, Thomas and Elizabeth are often discussed independently of one another. Chapter 1 examines their childhood and adolescent years, their educational experiences in the 1850s, and their marriage and relocation from New England to a distant military post in the Dakota Territory. Chapter 2 begins with the Tannatts' recall from the frontier in 1861, as hostilities erupted in the East. Their official Civil War experience ended in 1864, when Thomas suffered a severe head wound during the Battle of Petersburg, and chapter 3 examines his ensuing postwar restlessness and wanderlust that took the family first to the mining districts of Colorado and then to Reconstruction-era Tennessee before returning them to Manchester in 1876.

By the mid-1870s, lack of professional opportunity, partly a result of the economic depression gripping the nation, forced Thomas to look far beyond New England and the East for his livelihood, and chapter 4 chronicles the early years of his association with railroad magnate Henry Villard. The opportunities Villard made available to Thomas not only led to the family's permanent relocation to the Pacific Northwest but helped restore in Thomas the sense of purpose he had sought since his separation from the army at the end of the Civil War. As Thomas negotiated with Villard and endeavored to reestablish himself professionally, Elizabeth took advantage of the family's sojourn in Manchester to become involved with several women's organizations emerging in late-nineteenth-century Massachusetts. From the late 1870s until her death in 1920, Elizabeth devoted a good deal of her time and energy to issues of reform, benevolence, and civic commemoration.

The early 1880s found the Tannatts firmly established in eastern Washington Territory, a region known as the Inland Empire, and chapter 5 focuses on their civic involvement in the towns of Walla Walla, Farmington, and environs. This period witnessed Thomas's election as mayor of Walla Walla and Elizabeth's role in the establishment of the region's first Woman's Christian Temperance Union chapters. It is clear that these years represent the happiest in the Tannatts' lives, as they provided them not only with their first permanent home but also with a great deal of fulfillment and satisfaction. Finally, chapter 6 chronicles the Tannatts' "retirement" years, though this should not suggest that the couple withdrew from active participation in civic and community affairs. Rather, these years witnessed Thomas's tenure as a member of the board of regents of Washington's land-grant college, the Washington Agriculture College and School of Science (now Washington State University), his growing interest and dedication as an orchardist, and Elizabeth's involvement as a founding member of the Spokane chapter of the Daughters of the American Revolution.

Thomas's entry into the business world during the postwar years coincided with the development of the American corporate system and the emergence of the middle manager, another feature of the nineteenth-century middle class. Historian Alfred Chandler has suggested that modern management techniques originated with the growth of the railroads, which "caused entrepreneurs to integrate and subdivide their business activities and to hire salaried managers to monitor and coordinate the flow of goods through their enlarged enterprises."[19] In *The Visible Hand*, Chandler reveals the tier system that resulted from this experiment in corporate organization and its placement of executive officers and their staffs on a top tier, with a number of autonomous divisions located on the tiers below, each dedicated to a specific function, such as manufacturing, selling, and purchasing.[20] Thomas certainly participated in this "integration and subdivision" through his affiliation with Colorado mining conglomerates and, more particularly, during his association with Villard's transportation empire in the West. The positions Thomas filled were typical of those undertaken by nineteenth-century middle-class professionals, and as the details of his personal experiences will make clear, the value of these middle managers to the corporations and conglomerates that hired them was immeasurable.[21]

Similarly, the concept of community volunteerism gained momentum in the mid-nineteenth century with such middle-class organizations as the Military Order of the Loyal Legion of the United States (founded 1865), the Woman's Christian Temperance Union (1874), and the Daughters of the American Revolution (1890). Through the efforts of the middle-class membership base of these organizations and others like them, benevolent societies, reform movements, and commemorative efforts became an important aspect of American culture. As historian Don Harrison Doyle has suggested, however, "the expansion of local public institutions sprang from two interlocking concerns: community leaders' growing interest in the safety and aesthetics of the town's physical order, and nineteenth-century reformers' interest in the control of moral behavior through manipulation of the environment."[22] These concerns, united in a community's dedication to "grow" its region both physically and economically, separated the emerging midwestern and frontier middle classes from their established urban counterparts.

Recent attention to the nineteenth-century middle-class has generated a series of new questions about its formation and development across the country. Historians now ask whether or not the middle class was "created equally" and how its advent and involvement in rural, agricultural, and frontier regions differed from that found in the urban centers in the East. In his epilogue to *The Emergence of the Middle Class*, Blumin asks whether "big-city social patterns and identities [were] replicated in any way in smaller communities," wondering, "Can we speak of class, and more specifically of the middle class, in small-town and rural America?"[23] Doyle answers these queries in the affirmative in his study on nineteenth-century Jacksonville, Illinois, and at the same time clearly differentiates between the rise of a middle class in established, eastern urban centers and the arrival of a middle-class to rural and frontier areas. Doyle suggests that the difficulties of community building separate the various aspects of the middle class, since "the problem of building new communities was social as well as economic." Members of the rural and frontier middle class, for instance, dealt with "the early difficulty of defining status and leadership in an unformed social structure," issues long resolved in the established East. Doyle further asserts that "for community leaders and property-owners, the problems of social disorder were ultimately intertwined with the overriding concerns of promoting the town's economic future."[24] And despite the assertion of Archer and Blau that "the success of organized philanthropy, consumer products, and leisure institutions . . . was less applicable to rural populations," these cultural traits and social and economic issues set forth by Doyle as defining Jacksonville's middle-class at midcentury do apply to the Tannatts and the late-nineteenth-century eastern Washington frontier.[25] In Walla Walla, Farmington, and other Inland Empire towns and burgeoning cities, middle-class Washingtonians clearly and purposefully used their professions, their associations, and their affiliations to develop and shape the social, political, and economic characteristics of their communities and to create unique places for themselves within them.

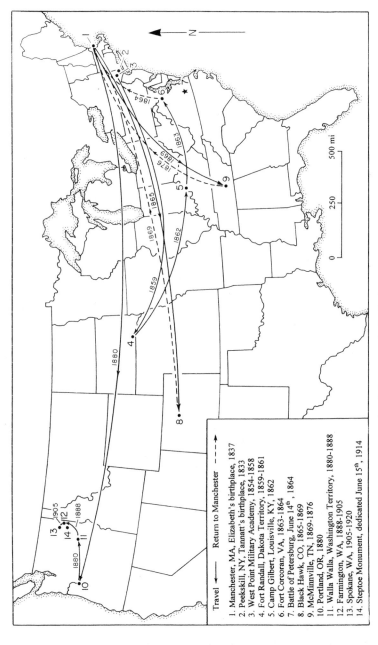

Travels of Thomas and Elizabeth Tannatt, 1833–1920

Travel ⟶   Return to Manchester - - - ⟶

1. Manchester, MA, Elizabeth's birthplace, 1837
2. Peekskill, NY, Tannatt's birthplace, 1833
3. West Point Military Academy, 1854–1858
4. Fort Randall, Dakota Territory, 1859–1861
5. Camp Gilbert, Louisville, KY, 1862
6. Fort Corcoran, VA, 1863-1864
7. Battle of Petersburg, June 14th, 1864
8. Black Hawk, CO, 1865-1869
9. McMinnville, TN, 1869-1876
10. Portland, OR, 1880
11. Walla Walla, Washington Territory, 1880-1888
12. Farmington, WA, 1888-1905
13. Spokane, WA, 1905-1920
14. Steptoe Monument, dedicated June 15th, 1914

1. The Early Years, 1833–1861

Elizabeth's Girlhood and the Tappans of Manchester, Massachusetts

At the busy store located on Central Street in Manchester-by-the-Sea, Massachusetts, early-nineteenth-century customers often asked after the son of the proprietor, to which Ebenezer Tappan responded, "Which son? Do you want Colonel Eben, Lieutenant-Colonel Israel, Major Ben, or Captain Sam?"[1] A patriot who served in both the American Revolution and the War of 1812, and Manchester's longest-surviving veteran of the former at his death in 1849, at eighty-eight years of age, Ebenezer could not conceal his pride in the four sons who had served their country in time of war.[2] He was also proud to belong to the large and distinguished Tappan family that numbered among its members his nephews Lewis and Arthur Tappan, the noted abolitionists.[3]

The Tappans, or Toppans, as they were known in their native England, took part in the Great Migration to the American colonies between 1630 and the outbreak of the English Civil War in 1642. The "Register of the names of such persons who are twenty-one years and upwards, and have license to passe into forraign parts from March 1637 to the 29th of September, by vertu of a Commission to Mr Thomas Mayhew, gentleman" is housed in London's Public Records Office, and on that list are the names of Abraham Toppan, his wife, Susannah Taylor, their two children, Peter and Elizabeth, and one "mayd" servant, Anne Goodlin, all of whom set sail from Yarmouth on May 10, 1637, aboard the *Mary Ann*.[4]

The party arrived in New England in the fall of 1637, a scant seven years following the settling of Boston in 1630 and just seventeen years after the Pilgrims landed at Plymouth in 1620. "Abraham Toppan being licensed by John Endicott, Esq. To live in this jurisdiction, was received into the town of Newbury as an inhabitant thereof," read his October 16 town admission, "and hath here promised under his hand to be subject to any lawful order that shall be made by the towne."[5] Over the next several years, Abraham acquired a number of land grants in Newbury and built a home there for his growing family. Procurement of these tracts of land required a considerable outlay of capital, and it appears that Abraham may have made his living as a merchant seaman. He certainly took to the sea on numerous occasions and made several trips to Barbados, "returning with sugar, cotton, wool and molasses with great profit."[6] It is apparent that some of the seafaring Toppans and Tappans remained in Barbados and either made the journey with their families or started families while on the island, for churchyards there contain a number of gravestones inscribed with the family names.[7]

Abraham and Susannah Toppan belong to that group of early American immigrants that migration historian Virginia DeJohn Anderson has labeled "families in process." These individuals generally made the Atlantic voyage to the American colonies in complete family groups consisting of mother, father, and children, but as most were less than halfway through their reproductive years, the families were incomplete. The American-born children of these immigrants constituted the rapid increase in population experienced by the colonies during the first decades of settlement. Following this typical process, Abraham and Susannah added five children to the family after settling in Massachusetts.[8]

The line to Elizabeth and the Manchester Tappans passes through Abraham and Susannah's eldest son, Peter, just three years old when he accompanied his parents on the ocean voyage to America. Peter became a physician and Newbury's third-largest sheep owner, and in keeping with the family tradition, he "traded at sea." He resided in Newbury until his death in 1707.[9] Peter's third son, Samuel, spent all of his eighty years—from his birth in 1670 to his death in 1750—in Newbury. It was his fourth son, Benjamin, who left the family settlement, changed the spelling of the family name, and established the Manchester Tappans.[10]

Benjamin Tappan was born at Newbury on February 28, 1720. He studied divinity at Harvard College, graduated in 1742, and in the summer of 1745 received an "invitation" from Manchester to fill the recently vacated position of town minister. He accepted the offer, which included an annual salary of "one hundred and forty Eight Ounces of Silver, or Bills of Public Credit equal to 148 ounces," £450 for "settling," use and improvement of all ministry lands, sufficient firewood for his family's use, and the house, barn, orchard, and all land within the ministry fence.[11]

According to tradition, Manchester's first meeting of public worship took place in the late 1620s at the time of the town's settlement. Gathering "beneath the branches of a tree at 'Gales Point,' near the site of an ancient wharf," the Manchester faithful enjoyed neither the services of a permanent, full-time minister nor the benefit of their own church structure until the town fathers engaged Rev. Amos Cheever in 1716. On September 17, 1745, Rev. Benjamin Tappan succeeded the esteemed and admired Cheever, became the second permanent minister of Manchester's Congregational Church, and began a term of service that lasted forty-five years, until his death in 1790 at the age of seventy.[12]

Manchester, so named by the General Court of the Massachusetts Bay Colony in May 1645, celebrated its centennial the same year Reverend Tappan stepped into its pulpit, and he soon realized that while the sea attracted settlers and provided their livelihoods, it also delivered a great deal of heartache to the harbor town.[13] Manchester, Gloucester, Rockport, and the other seaside towns that made up the northern Massachusetts coastal region known as Cape Ann "began with men taking fish from the sea," and as a consequence the sea took many of Manchester's fishermen and sailors.[14] In his history of the town, written in the late 1880s, William Henry Tappan noted that "since 1749 the hungry waves have engulfed no less than ninety-seven of the inhabitants of this little town."[15]

Elizabeth's ties to Manchester predated those of her Tappan relations by a full seventy-five years. Her mother's family, the Hoopers, had taken up residence in the town as early as 1670.[16] The Hooper men numbered among those Manchester citizens who earned their livelihoods at sea, and no fewer than five of Elizabeth's Hooper relations, including her grandfather William Hooper, served as masters of seagoing vessels embarked upon foreign voyages. "They encountered savages, pirates' and enemies' fleets, typhoons in the China seas, icebergs in the Atlantic, doldrums and tidal waves," wrote Rev. D. F. Lamson in an 1895 tribute to Manchester's sailors. In spite of the challenges and adversities they faced, they "built up a commerce which was once our national pride and the envy of the world."[17]

Reverend Tappan and Elizabeth Marsh, of neighboring Marblehead, Massachusetts, married in the fall of 1746, and by the following October welcomed the first of their twelve children, a son named Benjamin.[18] The couple's eighth child, Ebenezer, was born in 1761, and he and his younger brother, Michael, caused great consternation for Benjamin and Elizabeth when, still in their teens, they joined George Washington's Continental army.[19] The Revolution presented Reverend Tappan with professional as well as personal challenges, for he was "a patriot of the most unyielding type." British warships made regular raids on coastal colonial towns and villages in attempts to frighten the idea of independence out of the local populace, and Benjamin exemplified his dedication to both country and parishioners by implementing safety measures to protect Manchester's townspeople as they traveled about town and to and from worship. He encouraged them to carry their arms and ammunition with them to church, just as he carried "his own musket to the pulpit stairs," and he often quoted Scripture from the book of Luke that advocated "he that hath no sword let him sell his garment and buy one."[20]

Although British vessels never landed at Manchester harbor, the town and its people did suffer the lingering hardships of war. Payment of the taxes needed to supply the Continental army with men and provisions proved particularly difficult for a population whose principal means of livelihood, the sea, had become a battlefield, and the situation only worsened as the Continental Congress levied fines for nonpayment. Financial conditions in many American colonial towns deteriorated further in the postwar years, as provisions granted under the Treaty of Paris allowed British creditors to collect on accounts accrued in the years prior to independence. Soldiers who returned to Manchester after the war found family and friends deep in debt and the town's commerce ruined as vessels making up the fishing fleet were either destroyed in battle or decayed beyond usefulness after years of neglect.[21] As a result, the driving force of the Manchester economy shifted away from the sea, with woodworking—cabinetry in particular—emerging as the primary occupation of the town's craftsmen.[22]

More elaborate and finely crafted homes replaced Manchester's rough, timber-framed dwellings in the mid-eighteenth century, and their inhabitants required furnishings of a higher quality as well. In response to this demand, Moses Dodge pioneered Manchester's cabinetry trade from his workshop on School Street, where he sought "to provide Manchesterites with sturdy, reasonably priced, everyday furniture."[23] Even prior to the Revolutionary War and the ensuing boycotts of English products, the cost of importing furniture from Europe was prohibitive to all but the wealthiest of America's colonists. Dodge's introduction of American-produced cabinetry not only furnished Manchester's homes but established the industry that rescued the town from its economic doldrums and sustained it for almost a century.

In the years following the war, a number of cabinetry shops opened in Manchester, and Ebenezer Tappan, who learned the trade in the prewar years apprenticing for his uncle Wigglesworth Tappan in Portland, Maine, was "among the first to set up."[24] By the early 1820s, output by Manchester's craftsmen exceeded regional demand, and factory owners sought new and untapped markets. John Allen, engaged in the cabinetry business since 1805 or 1806, first promoted Manchester craftsmanship beyond the Cape Ann region and, in order to determine demand and marketability of his product, shipped samples, including fine mahogany bureaus, to Boston and New York. Deemed a great success, Allen's experiment resulted in numerous orders for Manchester-crafted furniture, and at substantially higher prices than those customarily paid by Cape Ann locals.[25]

The growth of the Manchester cabinetry trade occurred during the era referred to by historians as the Market Revolution. The early nineteenth century witnessed severe shifts in methods of industrial production, and the implementation of systems of mass production redefined the American artisan as it diminished the value of his labor and often reduced him from independent craftsman to permanent wage earner.[26] In Manchester, a seemingly endless flood of furniture orders and the resultant shortage of skilled craftsmen caused factory owners to experiment with time- and labor-saving devices such as the veneering saw, capable of cutting a four-inch plank into one hundred separate veneers. Prior to the installation of these saws in Manchester cabinetry shops, craftsmen hand-cut wood veneer, one painstaking plank at a time. Veneering saws, the turning lathe, and other pieces of machinery developed to speed up production and more effectively meet demand also hastened the demise of the skilled craftsman, dedicated to creating one unique piece of fine cabinetry at a time, and increased the number of unskilled laborers and equipment operators necessary for mass production of uniformly produced pieces.[27] John Allen's workforce grew to over one hundred men by the early 1830s as he strove to meet the increasing demand. By the 1840s the reputation of Manchester-produced cabinetry extended far beyond New England into the southern markets of New Orleans, Mobile, and Charleston, and in the years leading to the Civil War at least thirteen separate factories operated in Manchester.[28]

Ebenezer Tappan, Manchester cabinetmaker and leading citizen of the town, operated a general store in the front of the building on Central Street that housed his cabinetry shop in the rear, and he served his many customers "ever quick with twinkling eyes and practical jokes."[29] His wealth was not limited to these enterprises, however, and according to Daniel Langdon Tappan's history of the family, he owned a number of large boats that he docked in Manchester's harbor. While Ebenezer used these ships primarily for the transportation of goods from markets in Boston and elsewhere, his schooner, the *Nancy*, became the target of a British man-of-war during the War of 1812.[30] Ebenezer's second son, Maj. Ben Tappan, a sailor on the *Nancy*'s crew, left a lively account of the episode and recalled that as the ship sailed toward Manchester, a cannon shot glanced her bow. Capt. Jerry Danforth beached the vessel just south of Manchester at neighboring Beverly, and Ben quickly made his way to Manchester to gather reinforcements, among them his brother, Col. Eben Tappan. Although the Manchester men arrived at Beverly to find the *Nancy* and its cargo ablaze, they did succeed, without casualty, in driving the British out of Cape Ann and rescuing the schooner.[31]

The eldest of Ebenezer and Elizabeth Forster Tappan's seven children, Eben Tappan Jr. lived his entire life in Manchester and earned the moniker "Colonel" for his service with Capt. Joseph Hooper's company during the War of 1812.[32] Born in 1792, Eben possessed an inquisitive mind that launched him into a lifetime of manufacture and invention. He is credited with building the first continuous-action turning lathe used in the manufacture of cabinetry in Manchester, and the town purchased his most noteworthy creation, a suction fire engine, in the 1830s.[33] Nicknamed "The Torrent," Eben's fire engine held approximately 125 gallons of water and emptied in about a minute by "throwing a column of water a distance of 103 feet."[34] The Torrent performed so well that Manchester's fire company kept it in service until 1885. On November 12, 1814, Eben Tappan and Sarah Hooper, daughter of William Hooper, "were lawfully published" and established their family, which would eventually number eight children.[35] The youngest, Elizabeth

Forster Tappan, named for her paternal grandmother, was born on December 10, 1837.

Elizabeth Tappan grew up at 39 Central Street in Manchester, in a home her grandfather Hooper had built in 1805 and sold to her father twenty years later. In addition to the house, the property contained a large barn her father used as a workshop, where he designed and built the Torrent.[36] Elizabeth's childhood was typical for a girl belonging to a leading family in a nineteenth-century New England town, and with grandparents and countless aunts, uncles, and cousins in Manchester, she never lacked for company or attention. She attended the Congregational Church, where her great-grandfather had preached for more than forty years, and sat in the ever-increasing block of Tappan family pews. As early as 1647, the General Court had made provision for the education of the colony's children, setting forth that "where any towne shall increase to ye numbr of 100 families or householdrs, they shall set up a grammar schoole."[37] Elizabeth no doubt began her educational endeavors in one of these primary schools.

As an adolescent, Elizabeth attended Manchester's Chapel School, established in 1836. The catalog for 1855 advertised the school as "remarkably healthy, free from noise, bustle, and temptations to idleness and dissipation," and described Manchester society as "characterized by a high moral tone," able to provide its young male and female scholars with "facilities for uninterrupted study [which] may well compare with those of any other school throughout the state."[38] During the academic year ending in May 1855, seventeen-year-old Elizabeth excelled in the school's French branch, which cost her parents an additional $1.50 after the regular $4 tuition for a twelve-week term. She attended school with a number of her local cousins, Bethiah Tappan and Eliza and Ellen Hooper among them, but the student body also included individuals from distant San Francisco, Brooklyn, and Aux Cayes, Santo Domingo.[39] Such diversity in the student populations of nineteenth-century academies and private schools became quite common, for in addition to their exemplary academic reputations, many were located in small towns and drew significant boarding populations. Sarah Pierce's Litchfield, Connecticut, academy, for instance, boasted students from Georgia, New York, Massachusetts, New Hampshire, and the West Indies, as well as from Connecticut.[40]

The opportunity for young, middle-class women to attain formal educations grew substantially in late-eighteenth- and early-nineteenth-century America, particularly in the nation's northern regions. In the years following the American Revolution, common rhetoric held that the strength and survival of the Republic depended solely on the virtue of its citizens, and in order to produce and raise virtuous citizens, future mothers "needed to be well informed and decently educated."[41] This led not only to the expansion of "in-home" education for girls as well as boys but to the formation of day schools and summer schools, the integration of private boys' schools, and eventually the establishment of women's academies and colleges. It is clear that motivation to admit young women into existing male academies was, at least in part, financially driven, for headmasters such as New Haven's William Woodbridge and Boston's Caleb Bingham were unlikely to turn away middle-class parents who were ready to pay full tuition for their daughters' academic and scientific education.[42]

Academy and private school education for women remained largely a middle- and upper-class privilege throughout much of the nineteenth century, and those able to educate their female children in this manner also elevated themselves in terms of class and status. At the same time, however, many of these newly educated women became educators themselves, and in the middle decades of the century such women as Mary Lyon and Emma Willard established women's academies and colleges, while countless others expanded the reach and breadth of education to individuals of all classes, nationalities, and backgrounds in America's frontier schoolhouses.[43]

After completing her studies at the Chapel School, Elizabeth attended the Charlestown Female Seminary. The program printed for the celebration of the institution's twenty-sixth anniversary, held on July 10, 1857, indicates that she participated in the Original French Colloquy portion of the program.[44] Performances other than her own clearly did not hold Elizabeth's attention or that of the friend seated next to her, for Elizabeth's program is covered with penciled notes the girls wrote to each other throughout the evening. "Lewis is more social to day than usual," the friend wrote, to which Elizabeth answered, "Didn't I tell you you would like him better after you had seen 1 or twice."[45] The Lewis referred to here is certainly Elizabeth's brother, six years her senior and the sibling to whom she was closest.

With her education complete, Elizabeth turned her attention to perfecting her domestic skills, and in the spring of 1858, at twenty years of age, she accepted the marriage proposal of West Point cadet Thomas Redding Tannatt.

Thomas's Youth: The Hudson River Valley and Beyond

Born on September 27, 1833, at Verplanck Point, near the town of Peekskill on New York's Hudson River, Thomas Tannatt belonged to the first generation of his mother's family born in America. Mary Gilmour, a descendant of Sir John Gilmour and a member of the Morrison clan from the Isle of Lewis, was born in 1802 at Craigmillar Castle, near Edinburgh, Scotland.[46] In about 1818, after securing large tracts of land in Canada, Mary Gilmour's family sailed for North America and settled the town of Paisley in the province of Upper Canada that later, in 1867, was renamed Ontario.[47]

The genealogy of Thomas Tannatt's family is not as complete as that of Elizabeth Tappan, though some interesting details have come to light. The name "Tannatt" is derived from the river Tanad, or Tannat, in Montgomeryshire, Wales, and was taken in the sixteenth century by members of the gentry as their family name.[48] James Tannatt, a descendant of these Welsh Tannatts, traveled to America on a hunting excursion, though the decade in which he did so and his exact relationship to Thomas's father, James S. Tannatt, are unknown. It does appear, however, that "Tannatt the Hunter," or his descendants, settled in America, for young James was born in Boston in about 1800. The Tannatts left the United States soon thereafter and spent a number of years traveling abroad. James returned some years later and met and married Mary Gilmour, probably in the mid-1820s. James worked as an editor in New York City and spent several years with the *Highland Democrat* newspaper.[49] At some point for a period of about four years he held the position of purveyor at the Brooklyn Navy Yard, the construction site for Robert Fulton's steam frigate and many famous American warships.[50]

By the early 1830s the family had relocated from Brooklyn to Peekskill, where James was involved with the operation of steamship lines on the Hudson River and may have been in partnership with Isaac Depew, father of New York politician and railroad entrepreneur Chauncey Depew.[51] On August 23, 1845, at about the age of forty-five, James Tannatt, a staunch Whig supporter during Henry Clay's presidential campaigns of 1824 and 1832, died suddenly of unknown causes.[52]

Determining the makeup of Thomas Tannatt's immediate family is also difficult, since no documentation, such as a family Bible, has been discovered. The census for Westchester County, New York, does indicate that a rather large family headed by "James Tannatt" resided in Peekskill in 1840. The record reveals a household comprising two males under the age of five years, one male and one female between the ages of five and ten (this male would be Thomas Tannatt who was seven years old in 1840), one female between ten and fifteen, one female between fifteen and twenty, two males between twenty and thirty, one male and one female between thirty and forty (Mary Gilmour Tannatt, born in 1802 and thirty-eight years old in 1840), and one male between forty and fifty. James S. Tannatt could fall into either of the last two categories, as he was about forty at the time of the census.[53] In summary, identified members of Thomas Tannatt's family in 1840 include his parents, James S. and Mary Gilmour Tannatt; his younger brothers, John G. Tannatt and Henry Tannatt; and himself. The five other members of the household may have been children from previous marriages or individuals employed by the Tannatts. It appears the census taker did not include Kate Tannatt, born in 1838 and just two years old at the time of the census, though she would become the family's most recognized member.

The youngest of James S. and Mary Gilmour Tannatt's children, Kate was born in Peekskill on December 20, 1838. She was educated at the Peekskill Seminary until the family left the area following her father's death in 1845. She taught in the public schools in Salem, Massachusetts, for a time and later married George H. Woods, a Salem native and graduate of Brown University and Harvard Law School. At the outbreak of the Civil War, George raised a company for the First Minnesota Regiment and was sworn into service as first lieutenant. When the First Minnesota received its orders, Kate and their children accompanied George to the front, and with other camp wives she nursed and cared for the sick and wounded. Though permanently debilitated by injuries received in battle, George outlived the war by nineteen years. After his death, Kate embarked upon a writing career and contributed articles to such publications as *Harper's Bazaar, Ladies' Home Journal*, and the *Boston Globe*, and penned, among others, the juvenile novels *Hester Hepworth* and *A Fair Maid of Marblehead*. She served among the first officers of the General Federation of Women's Clubs and as the organization's first auditor, numbered among the founders of the Massachusetts State Federation of Women's Clubs, was a founder of the Thought and Work Clubs of Salem, and served as vice president of the Women's National Press Association. She died in 1910 in Falmouth, Massachusetts, at the age of seventy-two.[54]

Thomas Tannatt spent his first twelve years in Peekskill, and by all indications he engaged in activities typical of a nineteenth-century boy. In the late 1870s or early 1880s, more than thirty years after leaving Peekskill, Thomas drew from memory a map of his hometown, identifying locations associated with boyhood activities and pranks. "This street leads out to a Creek where I went fishing," and "this street was where we boys went out to old Fort," he wrote of the roadways passing in front of Mr. Sutton's shop and the Nelson home, respectively. Of course, young boys require nourishment during their long days of fun and play, and on his map Thomas drew an orchard near the fort, inscribed with the words, "have stolen apples here." Many of the homes and businesses Thomas remembered are noted on the map, including "Mrs. Tannatt's Bake Shop" and two residences identified as "Mrs. Tannatt." At the bottom of his map, Thomas wrote, "Note. Dr. Stewarts should be close enough to Mrs Tannatts to permit boys and girls to crawl from garret to garret."[55] There is no doubt that Thomas enjoyed these early boyhood years in Peekskill, brought sadly to a premature close by his father's sudden death.

Barber and Howe's *Historical Collections of the State of New York*, published in 1841 when Thomas was eight years old, describes Peekskill as a busy and bustling village. Incorporated in 1826, just fifteen years later it contained a bank, printing offices, iron foundries, several churches, and more than two hundred dwellings. In addition, the village boasted a ferry that ran from Peekskill to Caldwell's landing, two miles away and on the opposite side of the river, and to landmarks commemorating the recent American Revolution, including Verplanck's point and Continental village. The authors paid particular attention to the Peekskill Academy, describing it as "a large edifice, situated on a commanding eminence at the south [and] erected by subscription, at an expense of $7,000."[56] The town boasted a public school as early as 1820, but James and Mary Tannatt opted to send their children to private schools—the boys to the Peekskill Academy, whose curriculum would have more closely followed that found in Boston's preparatory schools, and Kate to the Peekskill Seminary. This ability to educate their children in private academies would have placed the Tannatts firmly among the desired ranks of Peekskill's middle class.[57] Thomas identified Peekskill Academy on the map he drew decades later, but none of his reminiscences of it remain. Chauncey Depew, one of Thomas's classmates at the academy, referred to it in his memoirs as the "dominant educational institution" of the region at the time, attracting students not only from Peekskill but from distant villages and towns as well. The purpose of the academy was to prepare its students for university, and Depew remembered it as "a character-making institution" whose "graduates entering into the professions or business had an unusual record of success in life." Depew was most specific in his definition of successful graduates and described them as not necessarily wealthy but as individuals who had "acquired independence and were prominent and useful citizens in all localities where they settled."[58] Thomas Tannatt would certainly fit Depew's definition of having had "success in life."

After the death of her husband in 1845, Mary Tannatt moved the family to New England. It appears that either she or James had been married prior to their marriage to each other, since after leaving Peekskill she and the children moved into the New Hampshire home of an older, married daughter, identified in Willard and Livermore's A Woman of the Century as "a half-sister of Kate." When the husband of this "half-sister" relocated his medical practice to Manchester-by-the-Sea, Mary and most of the children went along. Their stay in Manchester was short, however, as she soon moved the family to the Essex County seat of Salem.[59]

It is likely that Thomas Tannatt and Elizabeth Tappan made their first acquaintance while Thomas's mother resided in Manchester, though he did not live there during these years. The 1850 census for Manchester-by-the-Sea lists four Tannatts, most likely Mary and her children, though there appear to be a number of errors in the recording of ages and places of birth. Mary Tannatt, born in Scotland, is listed as forty-three years of age. Mary

Gilmour Tannatt would have been forty-eight years of age at the 1850 census. Catharane Tannatt is listed as being fourteen years of age. This is probably Kate Tannatt, who would have been twelve years old in 1850. John G. Tannatt, age twelve, and Henry Tannatt, age eleven, are also listed, and their ages are probably incorrect as well, as Kate Tannatt Woods's biographical entries never list her as being a twin. John and Henry are most likely the two males between zero and five years of age listed on the 1840 census for Westchester County, New York.[60]

The reasons behind Mary Tannatt's moves from Peekskill to New Hampshire to Manchester to Salem, and eventually to Springfield, Massachusetts, are undocumented, though motivating factors may have included her desire to live in closer proximity to other family members and to provide better social and educational opportunities for her children. The record also fails to reveal whether financial need caused her to enter into an occupation to support herself and the children after James's death. Since she resided in the homes of family members for only short periods of time, she likely had sufficient funds on which to live, but the family was by no means wealthy. Mary and James both came from well-connected families, but it appears, with James's frequent career changes, that the family's status declined somewhat during the years of their marriage. Never, however, did it sink below that invisible line separating the "middle class" from those beneath it. This dip in social status seems to have made a particular impression on Thomas, just twelve years old at the time of his father's death but cognizant of the changes to the family's style of living resulting from that event. Throughout his lifetime, Thomas worked diligently to maintain position and status and to not allow himself to be dislodged from the place he coveted in America's nineteenth-century "middle class."

At the time of Mary Tannatt's first relocation, to New Hampshire, she arranged for Thomas to board with either friends or relatives there, and he spent the next six years farming during the summer and attending school in the winter months. Later, in about 1851, Thomas began a three-year apprenticeship in Salem, where he learned construction and bridge building and acquired an interest in engineering. For the final two of these years he attended school three evenings a week and studied mathematics, drawing, and civil engineering. A comparison of the educational and apprenticeship opportunities available to Thomas Tannatt and to the Tappan brothers reveals the vast difference in the economic resources and social standings of these two families by the 1850s, though both considered themselves members of the "middle class." While Thomas spent half of each year earning his room and board through agricultural labor, Elizabeth's brothers attended school throughout the year, their early training under the watchful eye of "Master" John Price, who taught in Manchester from 1828 until 1872. The apprenticeship experiences available to the young men differed dramatically as well, for while Thomas labored at construction and bridge building and studied the technical aspects of engineering only through evening school, the Tappan brothers apprenticed at trades more appropriate to their standing in the community. Elizabeth's brothers traveled to Boston, the cultural and intellectual center of Massachusetts, where Eben III, and later George, engaged in printing and lithography, Lewis learned the manufacture of jewelry, and William Henry became a draftsman and artist, engaged by the noted naturalist Louis Agassiz to provide illustrations for some of his books.[61]

In late 1853 or early 1854, with his apprenticeship and education completed, Thomas Tannatt accepted a position with the Jersey City Water Works, though his term of employment there would be very short-lived.[62]

A West Point Cadet

In March 1854, Rep. Charles Upham of the Sixth Congressional District of Massachusetts penned a short letter to Secretary of War Jefferson Davis in Washington: "I hereby nominate to fill the vacancy in my district, as represented at West Point, Thomas R. Tannatt of Salem, Mass."[63] Thus began the journey, and the training, that guided and directed Thomas throughout his life. The War Department immediately issued a conditional appointment as a West Point cadet, which Thomas accepted on March 17, and on July 1, at almost twenty-one years of age, Thomas Tannatt officially entered the United States Military Academy at West Point as cadet number 1804.[64] Congress formalized the prevailing custom of annually admitting one cadet from each congressional district and ten "at large" cadets, appointed by the president and representing the District of Columbia, the army, and the navy, in 1843, and while the details of the acquaintance between Thomas and Representative Upham are unknown, the history of the academy makes Thomas's reasons for seeking admission very clear.[65]

The necessity for the establishment of a military academy first came under discussion in the fall of 1776, due to the lack of preparation and training of Continental soldiers and a shortage of suitable officers. West Point, New York, the perceived "key to the United States," appeared to be the natural location for the institution.[66] One of the more interesting stories associated with West Point's location concerns the Secret Committee, on which sat a Maj. C. Tappan, appointed by the Provincial Convention on July 16, 1776. The convention charged the committee with the task of devising methods to obstruct the channel leading to the Hudson River, or at least making the task of entry difficult for enemy British ships. The committee recommended stringing strong iron chains and booms across the river at four strategic locations, and the work, which included construction of military posts at West Point and Forts Clinton, Montgomery, and Independence, commenced in early 1778.[67] On March 16, 1802, Congress signed into the law "An Act fixing the military Peace Establishment of the United States," thus officially creating the U.S. Military Academy at West Point.[68]

Bvt.-Maj. Sylvanus Thayer, an early graduate of the academy and distinguished veteran of the War of 1812, assumed the position of West Point superintendent in 1817 and is credited with establishing the academy's first entrance requirements. Seeking to instill order and discipline within the ranks, Thayer organized the cadets into a Battalion of Companies, divided the classes into sections, implemented the weekly submission of class reports and publication of the *Annual Register*, and established a code of regulations for cadets.[69] Thayer also became aware of the woeful lack of trained engineers in the United States in the early nineteenth century and, in order to meet the demand generated by the nation's rapidly expanding transportation system, established a four-year curriculum at West Point specifically designed to provide trained officers to the army's Corps of Engineers and other branches. Thayer's curriculum included a civilian component, and as the engineers it produced received more civil than military engineering training, the point was made to an American society resentful of military expenditure of the ease with which engineering skills could be transferred between the nation's military and civilian sectors.

The result of Thayer's efforts was the creation of the first college-level institution to offer engineering training, and for the next fifty years West Point graduates played a leading role in the construction of the nation's new railways, bridges, and roads.[70] By the time Thomas Tannatt entered West Point, numerous other American military academies and universities offered engineering instruction, the Virginia Military Institute and the Citadel among them, but certainly the opportunity to gain scientific engineering training from the nation's foremost engineering school prompted Thomas to seek admission.

During Thomas's first year at West Point, Captain of Engineers John C. Barnard assumed the role of superintendent from Col. Robert E. Lee, who had been promoted to the cavalry. Barnard embarked upon an extensive building campaign, which included construction of a $22,000 riding hall, at the time the largest building in the United States built specifically for the purpose of equestrian exercises.[71] Barnard might have remained as superintendent for an extended term had Maj. Richard Delafield not desired a return to the position he had held from 1838 to 1845.[72]

As was typical for many of the academy's students, Thomas's marks rose progressively and dramatically over his four years at West Point. In his first year he placed in the bottom third of his class in academic subjects, though he accumulated only thirty-four demerits for the entire year, fewer than did most of his classmates. The next year Thomas moved to the middle of his class in all academic areas, and reduced his demerits even further, to twenty. In his third year he raised his academic standing to sixth in the class, and again he lowered the number of demerits accumulated during the year, to thirteen. Thomas completed his final year at West Point with a very respectable academic standing of seventh in his class and an amazingly low five demerits for the entire year. He and his classmate Samuel McKee seem to have had an ongoing competition throughout their West Point years, for both numbered among the top three in fewest demerits, with McKee edging Thomas out in each of the first three years. Finally, in his fourth year, Thomas finished ahead of McKee and the rest of the class in this category.[73]

Few of Thomas's letters have survived from his years at West Point, but one, written to Elizabeth in the spring of 1858, describes the "public" nature of his upcoming examinations. "Just think of it in one week I must pass seven separate examinations open to all; reporters not excepted," he wrote with a bit of anxiety. The tone of the letter then turned reflective, and typical of those Thomas wrote throughout his adult life, as he questioned the academy's guidelines for the "success" or "failure" of its cadets. "Notoriety is of little worth in this world," he continued; "*better men* than myself are minus chevrons & why? simply because dame nature has not given the good voices, forms, & command, alike to all her sons."[74] This early letter reveals a number of things about Thomas's nature and character. First, he acknowledges that physical attributes are not "distributed" equally. Second, he recognizes that such attributes do not necessarily denote the "better" man. And third, despite the fact that some men might be deemed "better" than he, Thomas believes that he possesses the attributes needed to lead and command. These revelations concerning the importance of the attributes of men would serve Thomas well in the years ahead, for in 1858, as he wrote this letter to Elizabeth, the clouds of civil war had begun to gather.

Thomas's romance with Elizabeth, and their upcoming marriage, may have been one of the reasons for his self-discipline and dedication to study, but certainly there were others as well. With the exception of a few cases of apple pilfering in his youth, Thomas was a serious and conscientious person. The loss of his father at such a young age, and the perceived loss of the rest of his family when Thomas entered into apprenticeship at age twelve or thirteen, may have intensified this seriousness and cemented his desire always to think and act righteously. Thomas's deep religious conviction helped to keep him focused at West Point as well, and he wrote to Elizabeth with enthusiasm of the religious dedication he had observed in the region and of its importance to the cadets residing there. "There is much religious interest in this section of the country and ere this I trust Henry [most likely Thomas's younger brother] has chosen the good part. Oh!" he continued, "that we could feel the workings of the Holy Spirit in our body of young men so soon to be scattered throughout the land."[75] It is apparent that classmates and friends both understood and were concerned by the somberness of Thomas's nature. A letter received the summer following his graduation from former classmate M. H. Knight reminded him "to lead a consistent Christian life" but at the same time to remain "cheerful, cultivate pleasant, cheerful acquaintances—& of all things beware of melancholy habits."[76]

This reserved and cautious manner did not extend to all aspects of Thomas's life, however, and his letters to Elizabeth during their courtship reveal a sense of romance and his growing love for her. "T'is a recreation to get a pen in my hand and scratch a line or two to some person gifted with charity enough to read what I write," he wrote on March 19, 1858.[77] In another letter, probably penned that same spring and seemingly following an argument or some other misunderstanding, Thomas closed a newsy and chatty letter with "I am as confident in your love as if you were telling me it all with your own lips & sealing it with a kiss. . . . Yours in much love, Thomas."[78] Thomas had promised to bring his uniform home while on furlough in the spring of his last year at West Point so that Elizabeth might "see a live cadet in uniform." It is a shame that the picture he intended to have taken for her either was not taken or has not survived, for the young cadet in full dress must have been a sight to behold.[79]

Upon his graduation from the academy on July 1, 1858, Thomas received promotion to brevet second lieutenant of artillery and, after a ninety-day furlough, reported on September 26 to Fort Monroe, Virginia. His military records list him on sick leave from February 1859 to February 1860. Somehow, on July 6, 1859, in the midst of this extended leave, he received promotion to second lieutenant, Fourth Artillery. The medical report that later accompanied his resignation from the army noted that this twelve-month period of sick leave was brought on by "a severe attack of amaurosis." Thomas probably suffered from vasospastic amaurosis fugax, which causes episodic vision loss and is brought on by constriction of the retinal veins and sluggish flow in the retinal bed. The condition generally corrects itself within a short period of time, but it usually reoccurs and was probably one of the causes of the health problems—particularly the severe headaches—that plagued Thomas throughout his lifetime. At the time of his diagnosis, no treatment for this condition existed other than complete rest for the eyes, hence the lengthy period of sick leave.[80] Sufficiently recovered in February 1860, Thomas reported to Fort Columbus, New York, and in the late spring of 1860 to Fort Randall, Dakota Territory, for frontier duty.[81]

Newlyweds on the Frontier

Thomas and Elizabeth's wedding took place in Manchester-by-the-Sea on April 18, 1860, and shortly thereafter the newlyweds departed for Fort Randall in the Dakota Territory. Although details of Thomas's reaction to the vastness and "wildness" of the plains has not survived, Elizabeth's first trip to the West seemed to delight her immeasurably. "Today has been a very interesting one to me," she wrote to her mother on May 25 as the traveling party rested thirty miles or so from Fort Randall. "Saw many Indians, went ashore, shook hands with the chief and many distinguished old indians. . . . They took a great deal of notice of me, and . . . one indian kept throwing kisses T. said, when my back was turned."[82] Despite the fact that nothing in Elizabeth's middle-class New England upbringing had prepared her for life on the frontier, by all accounts she embraced the experience wholeheartedly, admirably performing the duties expected of her as an officer's wife while stationed at Fort Randall.

Demand for the expanded, permanent presence of military personnel that delivered the Tannatts to the Dakota frontier grew, in part, from an event that occurred in August 1854. Early that year the army dispatched Lt. John L. Grattan, a recent West Point graduate and novice in Indian affairs, and twenty-nine men to Nebraska—later Dakota—Territory to apprehend members of the Brulé and Minneconjou Sioux accused of stealing oxen from an immigrant wagon. The soldiers found more than a thousand Sioux in camp on the Platte River near Fort Laramie, and Grattan saw it as his duty to take them to task. When leaders of the band refused to surrender those accused of the theft, Grattan sounded the order to fire. In the ensuing battle, the Sioux killed Grattan and all twenty-nine of his men in what became known as the Grattan Massacre. The number of Sioux killed remains unrecorded. Later that year, in response to the Grattan affair and other attacks against soldiers and civilians alike, the army assigned Bvt. Brig. Gen. William S. Harney the task of establishing a new military fort near the confluence of the Missouri and Niobrara rivers.[83]

General Harney's distinguished military career, his status as a decorated veteran of the Blackhawk and Mexican wars, and his understanding of the ways and cultures of Indians, including his proven ability to earn their respect, qualified him for the task at hand.[84] The Post Return for June 26, 1856, reports that "Lieut. Stanley, one Sergt. & 100 Recruits joined, and garrisoned the new Post . . . by order of Gen. Harney" and that the structures it comprised amounted to portable buildings, collapsed at the recently abandoned Fort Pierre and reassembled at the new location.[85] In August, Companies C and I of the Second Infantry and Companies D, E, H, and K of the Second Dragoons joined the troops already in residence, their combined strength constituting the fort's first garrison.[86] As the final task in establishing the new post, Harney requested that it be named Fort Randall, in honor of the late Col. Daniel Randall, former deputy paymaster general.[87]

The new military reservation occupied 175,000 acres, 10,000 of which provided timber needed for building and fuel, sufficient grazing lands, and the fort located on the west bank of the Missouri River in Nebraska Territory, thirty miles above the mouth of the Niobrara River.[88] An 1861 newspaper account described the post's location as "a beautiful plateau descending gradually to the river" and the officers' quarters and enlisted men's barracks as "commodious" and "sufficient," respectively.[89] The newest of the western military forts in 1856, Fort Randall represented the last link in a chain of posts that encircled the northwest frontier and assisted westward-bound pioneers. It was also the first of the new forts built along the Missouri as a deterrent to conflict between white settlers and Indians.[90]

The Tannatts settled into junior officer quarters at Fort Randall, although unforeseen circumstances soon shortened their stay in Dakota Territory. Few of Elizabeth's records from the frontier have survived, but the wives of other officers, living on army posts at approximately the same time, left detailed descriptions of their frontier experiences. Frances Roe recorded the events of a dance given by the post commander while her husband was stationed at Fort Lyon, Colorado Territory, in 1871. She described the evening as "most enjoyable. . . . The girls East may have better music to dance by, and polished waxed floors to slip down upon, but they cannot have the excellent partners one has at an army post and I choose the partners!"[91] In 1873, when her husband's regiment was reassigned to the "dreaded" Camp Supply in the Indian Territory, Roe wrote of the strength and perseverance exhibited by the frontier army wife. "Her very presence has often a refining and restraining influence over the entire garrison," she wrote. "No one can as quickly grasp the possibilities of comfort in quarters like these, or as bravely busy herself to fix them up. . . . [H]owever discouraging its condition may be, for his sake she pluckily . . . performs miracles."[92] The greatest compliment paid to these women came from Gen. Philippe Regis Denis de Keredern de Trobriand, Civil War hero and military commander in Louisiana, who stated that "no one could adapt oneself more resolutely to circumstances, accommodate oneself better to adventures, nor brave with such humor the harshness of military life upon the frontier."[93] This recognition of both the hardships they endured and the contributions they made to frontier military life certainly would have pleased Elizabeth and her middle-class cohorts.

The duties performed by soldiers stationed at frontier posts fell into two distinct categories. The more monotonous tasks, including military preparedness and post maintenance, seldom warranted a mention in the Post Returns, although the December 1861 return reveals that the Iowa Volunteers spent their early weeks at the post "employed mostly in drilling and procuring a supply of fuel for winter."[94] Settling conflicts between the Brulé Sioux and their more peaceful neighbors, the Yankton and Ponca, and providing escort to the supply and mail trains that traveled west from Sioux City constituted the most critical of these soldiers' duties, and the Post Returns reveal that Fort Randall's commanding officers regularly deployed companies throughout the region for these purposes.

In January 1858, three companies of the Second Infantry left Fort Randall for detached service south of the post "in consequence of small depredations by the Ponca Indians, and serious threats by the same nation."[95] Many of the entries in the Fort Randall Post Returns are cryptic in their accounts of troop movements to and from the post, but from time to time a particularly articulate commanding officer recorded the reasons for troop deployment in great detail. Thomas Tannatt, first lieutenant of the Fourth Artillery and acting commanding officer in late 1861, was one of these, and in the September 1861 Post Return he recorded that "upon the call of the agent of the Yancton [sic] Indians it was deemed requisite that troops should be sent to his aid. Accordingly, on the 29th of September 38 men from company 'M' immediately sent to the assistance of the agent making a forced march of 18 miles in three hours. The troops returned to this post Oct 3rd the trouble having been adjusted."[96] Thomas did not elaborate on the nature of the "adjustment."

The personnel makeup at Fort Randall began to change significantly in the spring of 1861 as the firing by Confederate troops on Union forces stationed at Fort Sumter, South Carolina, catapulted the nation into civil war and prompted a number of soldiers from southern states to desert the frontier post and return to the South.[97] Capt. J. A. Brown, commanding officer at Fort Randall, left the post without orders or authorization to join the Confederate forces. Although it has been suggested that his southern-born wife persuaded him, "against his own inclinations, to cast his fortunes with the Confederacy," the fact remains that Brown was not heard from again until his resignation, posted from a southern city, reached the War Department in July 1861.[98]

Captain Brown's departure left Thomas, the only commissioned officer still in residence, in command of Fort Randall.[99] Despite his youth and junior status, the Yankton community embraced both Thomas and Elizabeth, who seems to have had no reservation about stepping into the role of post hostess. "Lieut. Tannatt and lady passed down on Tuesday—the lady to go East, and the Lieutenant to return in a few days to Fort Randall," the *Dakotian* reported on June 6, 1861. "He is an accomplished officer, and although quite young in the service, has by recent resignations, been promoted to be 1st Lieutenant. Long may he wave!"[100] Elizabeth's journey east took her to Manchester for a visit with family and friends, and by October Thomas missed her deeply. "I have needed you very much lately," he wrote just weeks before they reunited at Fort Randall, "for reasons that you will understand when you come to know all."[101] While Thomas certainly missed the romantic aspects of his relationship with Elizabeth during her absences, he also missed the opportunity to discuss day-to-day concerns and events with her. Over the years, he grew to rely and depend upon her strength and determination, and it is apparent that this reliance began in the first year of their marriage.

The number of desertions from military posts increased dramatically in the first half of 1861, and frontier settlers feared that a depleted military presence would encourage hostile activities by Indians in the region. By June the situation had garnered the attention of local authorities in the Fort Randall area, and the *Dakotian* reported that Capt. D. McLaughlin from Dakota City had engaged in enlisting volunteers to serve as Home Guards and that "the companies raised in Nebraska for this purpose, will, in case of the withdrawal of the regular U.S. troops, occupy Forts Kearney and Randall, and afford efficient protection to the country commanded by these posts."[102] By late 1861, all regular army troops located on the frontier received orders to return to the East to fight for the Union cause, and Capt. John Pattee and 299 members of the Fourteenth Iowa Volunteer Infantry were ordered to Fort Randall to relieve the troops there. Arriving on December 4, 1861, Pattee found "two companies of the 4th U.S. artillery at Fort Randall under the command of First Lieutenant Thomas Tennant [*sic*], a bright and agreeable gentleman." Pleased to find the post in good order, he noted that Thomas had "the papers all made out and the transfer of the stores was commenced and hurried through in the shortest time possible so that the two companies which had been ordered to Kentucky could begin their long overland march to St. Joseph, Missouri."[103]

Elizabeth's journal entries for the next several days reflect the speed with which military relocations occurred on the frontier. Her entry for Saturday, November 30, 1861, notes the arrival in camp of a Lieutenant Reiton, the weather report (cold and windy), and that the mails brought no particular news of importance.[104] Less than a week later, on Friday, December 6, Elizabeth spent the day "packing, running to the door, receiving callers etc.,"[105] and on Saturday, December 7, she "rose at reveille," said her good-byes, and departed Fort Randall for the East in the company of the regiment. The first day of the journey witnessed the trials and tribulations of frontier travel as chains connecting teams to wagons broke and horses became mired in quicksand. Through it all, however, Elizabeth's spirits remained high, and after setting up camp that first afternoon she "superintended" preparation of the evening meal, which, she confided to her journal, she would have enjoyed more fully had she been less tired. All the same, Elizabeth closed her journal entry for this frantic day with the words "very pleasant."[106]

As Thomas and Elizabeth left the Dakota frontier for battlefields in the East, it is unlikely that they paused long enough to consider either the qualities that had brought them together or the circumstances that would soon deliver them to a war zone. The differences in their upbringing might portend marital problems for some, but the young army lieutenant and the privileged New England schoolgirl proved to be remarkably well suited. They enjoyed the same deep, religious convictions and soon became each other's greatest confidants. Thomas and Elizabeth would be required to utilize the inner strength these qualities provided on numerous occasions in the months and years immediately ahead as they faced the first challenge in their married life, the Civil War.

2. The Civil War, 1861–1864

Return from the Frontier

Thomas and Elizabeth Tannatt first encountered evidence of the Civil War in December 1861 as they traveled east from the Dakota frontier. On the road between Savannah and St. Joseph, Missouri, Elizabeth observed and recorded the war damages sustained by one small town. "Passed a court house in Fillmore nearly demolished," she wrote, "every paine [sic] of glass broken and bullet holes in the brick fronts, union & secession."[1] Despite the increased potential for trouble these damages represented, neither Thomas nor Elizabeth showed signs of apprehension as they continued the march toward Louisville, Kentucky, Thomas commanding his troops and Elizabeth recording their movements. Thomas had long trained for a military career, and surviving letters and journals give no indication that he felt anything but prepared for the battle and leadership tasks that lay ahead. As for Elizabeth, formative years in Republican-dominated Manchester and family gatherings attended by her abolitionist cousins Lewis and Arthur Tappan had provided her with a good deal of political knowledge, and she strongly supported the Northern-based objective of preserving the Union.[2] She appeared neither surprised nor shaken at the onset of civil war, taking in stride both Thomas's obligations as an army officer and hers as an army wife as they traveled toward the eastern battlefront.

Relocation of the men, animals, and equipment that made up the Fourth Artillery required a good deal of planning, organization, and leadership, and these duties fell to Thomas as the troop's sole ranking officer. The four-week overland march commenced in December 1861, as pleasant and mild autumn days were replaced by the rain, slush, and snow of winter, conditions that often caused a reduction in daily progress from the usual fifteen miles to as few as five. Elizabeth was left to her own devices, and she spent at least part of most days walking alongside the teams, enjoying the sights provided by the plains, and escaping the closeness and staleness of the wagon. "I walked . . . in advance of the command," she recorded in her journal on December 16 after setting out at a quarter past six in the morning, and "saw the moon set behind me and the sun rise before me."[3]

At the midway point of the journey, represented by the Kansas-Missouri border, the party was advised by the wagon master that a group of five hundred "jay hawkers"—free-state guerilla fighters who had opposed the pro-slavery "border ruffians" in the struggle over Kansas prior to the war— had bivouacked in the area less than a week before.[4] Thomas shared the anti-slavery and pro-Union sentiments of the jayhawkers, and their recent presence in the region did not particularly alarm him. It did, however, almost guarantee that the "border ruffians" would not be far behind, and for this reason he issued the order "muskets ready." This episode reveals one of the few when Elizabeth felt pangs of anxiety, and she admitted that she spent a rather fitful night armed with just "an umbrella, *broken musket* & sword and a feather pillow" while Thomas dealt with regimental matters. [5] Her trepidation was short-lived, however, and after a night without incident the troop resumed its eastward march at daybreak.

Elizabeth kept journals intermittently throughout her lifetime, and her entries provide the personal details that enhance this study of the Tannatts' lives in particular but also contribute to the growing scholarship on the nineteenth-century middle class in general. Her journals represent the only surviving documentation for a number of periods and episodes in the Tannatts' lives, and it is fortunate that she both enjoyed recording the details surrounding the people, places, and events that touched her and also appreciated the value of preserving the past. To the casual observer some of Elizabeth's entries may seem very bland, perhaps meaningless and not at all worthwhile, but closer scrutiny reveals a plethora of valuable information scattered throughout the often cryptic entries. Those made during the journey from Fort Randall to Louisville, for instance, provide a clear record of the distance covered each day by the assemblage. "Miles made—5," "Miles 22," "Miles 16," Elizabeth noted at the end of a day's entry, tracking their progress toward the east, and at the same time confirming that weather and road conditions often hampered their progress. The welfare and outfitting of the soldiers seem to have particularly concerned her, and many entries include the phrase "men without overcoats." [6] In addition to their value in telling the Tannatts' story, Elizabeth's journal entries make a necessary contribution to military history, for they serve as the only known account of the Fourth Artillery's 1861 movement from the frontier to the Civil War battlefront.

The Fourth Artillery reached St. Joseph, Missouri, on December 31, 1861, and wagons gave way to rail as the regiment's mode of transportation. This portion of the journey did not pass without incident, however, for just sixty miles east of St. Joseph, Thomas received an alert that fire had broken out in one of the baggage cars. He reached the car within minutes but succeeded in rescuing only a few items before it became engulfed in flames. The fire consumed ammunition, rations, and the personal effects of many soldiers, including Thomas's, and he and Elizabeth lost personal property and cash in excess of one thousand dollars. [7]

Rail lines became a part of the sectional struggle in Missouri, and episodes of vandalism inflicted by jayhawkers and border ruffians alike rendered numerous lengths of track impassable. The origin of the fire that destroyed the property and possessions of the Fourth Artillery remains undetermined, though it is interesting to note that just a few days earlier, on December 28, Elizabeth wrote that the command anticipated difficulty with the upcoming journey since the "rails [were] torn up for seven miles" and the people of the region held strong secessionist ideals.[8]

The United States government held Thomas, as commanding officer of the regiment, personally and financially responsible for its loss. Later, in the spring of 1864, Thomas provided a full report to Congress and requested partial relief of his liability to the government. He asked for no compensation for personal losses, but he did appeal for "charitable action" on behalf of his men who "nobly had . . . remained true to their flag when every one of their officers [Thomas excepted] had barely deserted them." Eben Swift, the regiment's surgeon, corroborated Thomas's account and insisted that Thomas "did all that any Officer could have done to save the property." In 1872 the government requested that Thomas once again explain both the events of the 1861 freight car fire and his outstanding balance with the government. Thomas outlined the steps he had taken to be forgiven the remainder of the debt and reminded the Treasury Department that in order for a military member to be granted a resignation, all indebtedness to the government must be settled. As his resignation had been granted in July 1864, Thomas had considered the matter closed. It was not, however, and the case remained open until June 1887, when the secretary of the treasury finally "accepted an offer to compromise a claim of the government against Thomas R. Tannatt as Acting Quartermaster 4th Artillery, by the payment of $10. and costs, which sums have been deposited."[9] Thomas's dissatisfaction with governmental operations and bureaucracy, which grew substantially after the Battle of Petersburg in June 1864 and contributed to his decision to resign from military service, may well have begun here.

The "War Era" East

Thomas and the Fourth Artillery regrouped, reorganized, and resumed their journey after the fire and arrived in Louisville in early January 1862. Thomas reported with his men to Gen. Don Carlos Buell and received assignment as commander of the artillery installation known as Camp Gilbert, while Elizabeth searched the city for suitable lodgings.[10] Filling her days with useful and productive activities proved challenging in Louisville, and Elizabeth soon discovered that the life she had known as an army wife on the frontier differed a great deal from one in an urban setting in wartime. At Fort Randall she and Thomas had lived together under the same roof, separated only by his short reconnaissance missions or her visits home to Manchester. In Dakota, Elizabeth had obligations and responsibilities as the wife of the commanding officer, she maintained her own home, and the wives and families of the fort's officers and men provided her with company and occupied her time and energy. In Louisville, on the other hand, Elizabeth lived apart from Thomas, in a rooming house where others prepared her meals and laundered her clothing, and where household management was neither expected nor desired from her. She did make the acquaintance of some of the other women who resided in the Croghan House, and visited with them occasionally, but for the most part she passed the days and nights in her room alone, sewing, knitting, and writing letters. The Louisville winter did little to lift her already dampened spirits, and most of her journal entries begin with a weather report and some combination of the words *rainy, gloomy, foggy,* and *unpleasant.*

Elizabeth was bored and unsure of how to rectify the situation, though it is certain that Louisville, perched precariously between the Union and the Confederacy, provided a number of opportunities for those interested in contributing to the war effort. Bordered by three slave states and three free states, Kentucky hoped to remain neutral during the war, and Abraham Lincoln and Jefferson Davis both accepted this stance until the late spring of 1861, when the Louisville and Nashville Railroad accelerated its program of delivering supplies to Confederate depots in Tennessee. Tensions culminated in Kentucky in early September, when Gen. Ulysses S. Grant descended on the town of Columbus and turned back Gen. Leonidas Polk and his Confederate forces, thus keeping Kentucky officially in the Union. To a greater degree here than elsewhere, perhaps, the Civil War pitted family members against one another, as exemplified by the case of statesman Henry Clay, whose four Confederate grandsons stood across the line from three others wearing Union blue.[11]

Elizabeth's journal entry for January 9, 1862, indicates that 160 sick volunteers arrived in Louisville that night and were "left without beds [and] only a little straw to sleep on."[12] Although surviving journals and letters give no firm indication that she engaged in wartime work or volunteered as a nurse, Elizabeth's obituary suggests that at some point she "had been actively engaged in the nursing of the civil war."[13] Her 1863 journal, written while Thomas was stationed at Fort Corcoran, Virginia, includes several mentions of post hospitals, and particularly of wartime casualties. "A man by the name of Waldron died at the hospital at DeKolb this last week of congestive fever," and "Tom Salisbury died before his wife or children arrived," she recorded on October 11, and on Sunday, November 22, she noted that "my visit to the Soldiers Home was very interesting Corpl. Winn died there six months ago."[14] It is likely that letters or journals detailing Elizabeth's war work have not survived and that her name was absent from official rolls, since only thirty-two hundred of the nearly twenty thousand women who engaged in medical support activities during the Civil War were listed as members of the Women Nurses, under the supervision of Dorothea Dix.[15]

Numerous opportunities were available to women who wanted to participate in the war effort, and Elizabeth may have engaged in one or more of these. Dr. Elizabeth Blackwell headed the Woman's Central Relief Association in New York, formed in April 1861, and in June of that year Abraham Lincoln established the United States Sanitary Commission. According to Elizabeth Leonard, however, popular opinion held that "ladies" belonged neither on the battlefield nor in field hospitals, and newspapers perpetuated this disapproval through their reticence to run advertisements recruiting nurses. This not only created delays in delivering adequate numbers of nurses to the battlefront but also generated confusion and uncertainly as to where and when such opportunities actually existed. As a result, many women formed, and participated in, state, local, and other unofficial nursing corps, thus rendering complete and accurate rosters of Civil War female nurses virtually impossible.[16] At the same time, according to Jeanne Marie Christie, issues of class and social standing stood between the women who served as army nurses and the officers' wives who traveled with their husbands from post to post. Christie suggests, for instance, that "many of the officers' wives and daughters chose to avoid the injured soldiers," preferring "the protocol and pleasures of the elite establishment, dining with officers, visiting with one another, hosting parties . . . and dancing in the evening hours while the military bands played for them."[17] Apparently, while they found it acceptable to travel with the army, a number of officers' wives held the opinion that nursing was "unacceptable" for middle-class "ladies." If Elizabeth did engage in nursing during the war, she probably did so early on, before Thomas received the promotions in rank that would cause such activity by his wife to be viewed as unseemly.

Elizabeth's very presence in Kentucky in wartime might seem strange, raising the question of why she did not leave Thomas to the military tasks before him and return to Massachusetts for the duration of the war. The record reveals, however, that in traveling with Thomas to military posts in Kentucky, Virginia, and elsewhere, Elizabeth heeded the example set by the wives of many senior officers who followed their husbands to the battlefront, or at least to a regiment's headquarters. Mary Logan joined her husband, Gen. John A. Logan, at Memphis in the winter of 1862 and returned to her Illinois home only when the regiment broke camp to march on to Vicksburg.[18] Elizabeth Custer followed George Armstrong Custer throughout the war, residing in a number of Virginia locations and in nearby Washington DC during the 1864 Richmond campaign.[19] Julia Dent Grant, perhaps the most famous of these wartime officers' wives, located herself and one or more of her children near General Grant's headquarters on a number of occasions.

In 1864 and 1865, for instance, she and six-year-old Jesse resided in City Point, Virginia, during the Richmond campaign that culminated with Robert E. Lee's surrender at Appomattox. [20] In keeping with the example set by these wives of senior officers, then, Elizabeth accompanied Thomas as his assignments took him from Louisville to Nashville and on to Forts Albany and Corcoran in Virginia.

Boredom and loneliness alone do not account for the feelings of listlessness Elizabeth experienced in Louisville, however, and clues to other explanations are found in her journal. In early 1862, Elizabeth, now twenty-four years of age, referred on numerous occasions to feeling unwell. These comments stand out, since she seldom complained of ill health and had recorded not a single malady during her sojourn on the Dakota frontier. On January 10, after spending the entire day in her room, Elizabeth "at night went down . . . and stopt at an apothecary store and got some Iodine and Wright Pills." She then "came home, had tea & then came up stairs and retired [but] did not sleep well."[21] Women of Elizabeth's class seldom ventured out alone at all, particularly during wartime, and that she did so in the evening hours adds a bit of secrecy and intrigue to her errand. While she might have purchased iodine for any one of a number of reasons, Elizabeth's acquisition of Wright's Indian Vegetable Pills is most interesting. Wright's Pills were touted as a nineteenth-century cure-all, advertised in an 1849 edition of the *Brooklyn Daily Eagle* as "one of the best medicines in the world for the cure of giddiness."[22] Native American images decorated the product's wrappings and were intended to convey to nineteenth- and early-twentieth-century customers that these "natural" remedies would cure anything that ailed them. In fact, William Wright developed his pills in 1837, in Philadelphia, and neither he nor they had any connection to Indians or herbal remedies.

Wright's Pills did not cure Elizabeth's giddiness, at least not immediately, for on Sunday, January 12, she still felt unwell and "did not dare to go out so stayed from church all day"—and Elizabeth seldom missed church services. [23] Not until the following September would journal entries reveal that in January 1862, Elizabeth was in the early weeks of her first pregnancy, and while it is possible that these events were completely unrelated, her feeling unwell for days at a time, purchase of a remedy for "giddiness and dizziness," and a shopping excursion on January 14 to acquire new knitting needles and an additional supply of yarn are likely intertwined and related to her pregnancy. [24]

In late January 1862, Thomas accompanied General Buell to Nashville, where, as assistant inspector of artillery, Thomas had charge of Nashville's Ordnance Depot. [25] As Union forces pushed the Confederate army out of Nashville, Thomas and his men confiscated and collected the iron products and weaponry left behind and sent these materials to Union supply depots for repair, retrofit, and redistribution to Union soldiers.[26] The assignment appealed to Thomas, and he wrote to B. F. Browne in Manchester that "my command gives me perfect satisfaction. . . . [I]n matters of policy they more than surpass my expectations."[27] Elizabeth joined Thomas in Nashville in mid-March and recorded her surprise at the shortages and inflated prices suffered by citizens of the Southern city, a situation created, at least in part, by Union blockades of rivers and rail lines.[28] "They have been deprived of every luxury," she wrote, noting that the price of pork had reached twenty-five cents per pound and flour ten dollars per barrel, while little else remained in the shops, "no vegetables or anything more *hardly*."[29] It has been suggested that, with the possible exception of Virginia, Tennessee suffered more damage and destruction than any other state during the Civil War, and Elizabeth's observations make it clear that wartime shortages and privations adversely affected the Tennessee population as early as 1862.[30]

Thomas's term of duty in Nashville was an abbreviated one, and on July 14, 1862, he received an appointment as colonel of the Sixteenth Massachusetts Volunteers, with orders to assume command of the regiment near Fort Corcoran, Virginia.[31] He and Elizabeth departed Nashville together, but this time, with the arrival of their first child just two months distant, Elizabeth opted to return to Manchester rather than accompany Thomas to Virginia.

The Civil War

Thomas and the Sixteenth Massachusetts served with Gen. George B. Mc-Clellan during the 1862 Peninsula campaign and saw their first significant action from June 25 to July 1 at the Battle of the Seven Days. The emotional and psychological effects of the week-long engagement remained with Thomas throughout his lifetime and help to explain abrupt changes to his thoughts and attitudes on both the army and the war. On August 5, just weeks following the Seven Days, McClellan returned his troops to Malvern Hill from their entrenchments at Harrison Landing on the James River, and Thomas penned a letter to Elizabeth, complete with a labeled sketch of the camp. The tone of this letter differed significantly from any other he had written. Always confident in his ability to carry out orders and lead his men, Thomas also respected those traits in his adversaries, a number of whom had been West Point classmates. This letter, however, exuded a calmness, almost a detachment, about the upcoming events. "Tonight I will be on the alert," he wrote, "and if they want to try my lines let them come on they will find more in numbers than they expect."[32] This pre-engagement overconfidence was common among soldiers of both armies and, according to Allan Nevins, is attributed in part to their relative youth. The average age of Union army enlistees was just twenty-five years, with many of their officers only a few years older.[33] Thomas, for instance, celebrated his twenty-ninth birthday less than two months after the Battle of Malvern Hill.

Other factors contributed to this pre-battle assurance, among them the feeling, as expressed by a Confederate, that in battle a man sought to become a hero and felt "that he is a man and that he is in a man's place."[34] Expanding on this theme, James McPherson suggests that while most Civil War soldiers, regardless of affiliation, seemed to be "spoiling for a fight" and eager for an opportunity to "see the elephant," officers saw their first battlefield experiences as the opportunity to prove their worth as leaders—to their men and to themselves.[35] Thomas probably experienced all of these shifting emotions as he wrote to Elizabeth on August 5, and he was certainly also affected by the horrific realities of war witnessed in the Seven Days' battles just fought.

The last conflict in the Battle of the Seven Days, the Union victory at Malvern Hill on July 1, proved the superiority of Northern artillery more than any other battle of the war, but as Confederate general Daniel H. Hill reported simply, the result of that superiority "was not war—it was murder." The Confederacy sustained casualties of over fifty-five hundred killed and wounded in this battle, more than double the losses suffered by Union forces.[36] In addition to affirming the might of Union artillery, the events of Malvern Hill and the Seven Days succeeded in altering the battle attitudes and opinions of many who fought there, and much of their bombast and bravado was replaced with dread, horror, and the numbing detachment present in Thomas's August 5 letter. This shift is best articulated by a colonel in command of a New York Zouave regiment who remarked, "We had started out in the spring gay, smart, well provided with everything. . . . [W]e were returning before the autumn, sad, weary, covered with mud, with uniforms in rags," and by a Confederate enlisted man who revealed, "I cannot describe the change nor do I know when it took place yet I know that there is a change for I look on the carcass of a man now with pretty much such feeling as I would were it a horse or hog."[37]

Skirmishes took place between Union and Confederate soldiers on August 5 and 6 at Malvern Hill, and although no full-scale battles ensued, injuries were sustained.[38] A letter from Elizabeth's brother Lewis to their cousin Samuel Forster Tappan, stationed on the Colorado frontier, indicates that on August 5, Thomas's horse was shot and his saddle pierced, and his West Point biography suggests that he sustained a shoulder injury as well.[39] Although these circumstances would seem sufficient to explain the ninety-day sick leave that followed—from August 24 to November 28—the medical report that accompanied Thomas's discharge papers two years later reveals that he also suffered from "severe nervous prostration followed by paralysis which unfitted him for duty."[40] In the late nineteenth century the term "nervous prostration" referred to cases of depression or nervous breakdown, where the principal symptom was mental and physical exhaustion, and it is likely that these symptoms resulted directly from Thomas's experience at Malvern Hill.

Thomas's extended sick leave did have a positive component, for it allowed him to be in Manchester with Elizabeth on September 24, 1862, for the birth of Lillie Tappan Tannatt.[41] By the end of November his health had recovered sufficiently to allow him to rejoin his regiment at Falmouth, Virginia. The pace of the war continued to accelerate, and two weeks later, on December 13, Thomas and his regiment took part in the Battle of Fredericksburg. In the aftermath of this battle, Thomas wrote Elizabeth from the headquarters of the Sixteenth Massachusetts Volunteers, and the self-assurance embraced before Malvern Hill, just five months earlier, had evaporated completely. "I am not as manly as in former days," he wrote. "The sight of suffering softens my heart and God grant it may make me a better man."[42] Thomas's flagging enthusiasm for battle mirrored that of his compatriots on the field, for as David Day of Worcester, Massachusetts, declared in June 1863 after participating in his second battle, "Who can compute the woe, anguish and sorrow of his day's work? I cannot get over my horror of a battle."[43]

During a visit to the corps hospital following the Battle of Fredericksburg, Thomas encountered a young corporal whose injury he had witnessed during the battle. "The Corpl . . . was laying down in the ranks in front of me as I was walking along my line urging my men to keep down, [when] a ball came whistling and plunged into *his* neck," Thomas wrote to Elizabeth. "As he was carried by me I said a word to him he replied 'it had better be me than you Colonel,' doubtless it was meant for me. God even guides the unerring bullet and all for some wise ends."[44] Just as Thomas had relied on his faith during the trying days at West Point, he turned to it again as the war raged on. The words of the young corporal seem to have reinforced Thomas's mission and reminded him of his objective: Union victory and the return to homes and families of as many men as possible at war's end.

Late in 1862, Maj. Gen. Joseph Hooker reassigned Thomas to Headquarters, Defenses of Washington, where he took command of the newly named First Massachusetts Heavy Artillery Volunteers.[45] Shortly after his arrival there he became concerned with the quantities of beer consumed by his men, and their resultant behavior. In January 1863 he issued General Order no. 14, which prohibited the sale of lager beer at any post garrisoned by the regiment. The order did not condemn the consumption of alcohol due to the drunkenness it might cause but suggested instead that "the use of this beverage only increases a thirst for stronger drinks, and deprives the family of the Soldier of his earnings." Thomas also felt that the men of the regiment should conduct themselves in such a way as to bring respect and honor to their home state, and since "drinking and profanity are not characteristics of Massachusetts men at home, let it not become the case by an honorable service."[46] The issuance of this order is curious, as Thomas was not a teetotaler at this time and had never made mention of an aversion to alcohol. In February 1864, however, after attending officer gatherings where many in attendance consumed alcohol in excess, he declared a commitment to sobriety, which he appears to have upheld for the remainder of his life.[47]

Many aspects of life during the Civil War era are difficult to rationalize and comprehend, and one that stands out as most curious was the determination of the civilian population, and the Northern middle class in particular, to alter their day-to-day lives as little as possible, despite the fact that war literally raged around them. While a number of the activities undertaken may appear frivolous, the Civil War middle class should, perhaps, be lauded for attempting to maintain a sense of normalcy during an episode in American history that was anything but normal. Elizabeth Tannatt, army officer's wife and member of the middle class, intended to lead a "normal" life, war or no war, and within a month of Thomas's return to active duty following his sick leave she made plans to join him and reunite her family.

By 1863 the army found it necessary to monitor and restrict the movements of both men and women into and out of areas recently occupied by the Confederacy. This need for strengthened surveillance arose at least in part from the activities of the numerous women who acted as spies for both the Union and Confederacy and who, prior to this security crackdown, enjoyed relative freedom of movement between Northern and Southern encampments.[48] As a result, and since respectable women did not travel without escort in the mid-nineteenth century, Elizabeth called upon her brother Lewis to accompany her and five-month-old Lillie as they made the trip from Manchester to Fort Albany in February 1863.[49] Just weeks later, in a letter to her mother, Elizabeth wrote of the sightseeing she had enjoyed in the region held, until recently, by the Confederacy, and informed her she had gone "to rebel Gen. Lee's house, and a few days previous I visited Fort DeKalb."[50] In keeping with the objective of preserving "normalcy," the transplanted Northern military population treated war-torn Virginia almost as a vacation opportunity, and Elizabeth entertained a number of visitors during her stay there. Lewis paid a weekend visit in August, and he and Elizabeth toured the sites in Washington. Spending a full day in the capital, Elizabeth and her brother "drove to the church wh. Washington used to attend, went in and sat in the pew he owned," and later "saw some photographs of views from the battle field of Gettysburg," which Elizabeth found "perfectly horrid to behold. I shall never forget them." Lewis's trip coincided with the end of their cousin Carrie Hooper's six-week stay in Virginia, and she returned to Philadelphia in his company.[51]

During their time in Virginia, the Tannatts slipped easily into the role of a high-ranking military couple, and Elizabeth's journal is crowded with calls made and received and with lunches and teas attended and served. "Mrs. Col. Whistler and family called in the evening," she recorded on August 6, 1863; the next day she traveled to Arlington and "saw Mrs. Carlysle Gen DeRussy & staff"; and on Sunday, August 9, "Mrs. Col. Wright, the Col. Dr. Skinner, Capt. & Mrs. Carlysle, Dr. Dutton" all called at the Tannatt home.[52] This plethora of socialization and the relative safety and calm afforded the military community at Fort Albany had a most unusual, though certainly not unique, affect on some of its members. It appears that a number of the fort's female residents, the wives of its officers in particular, began to view it not as a military installation in wartime but as a civilian community with a democratic style of governance, and they did so to such a degree that they began to criticize, and suggest changes to, army policy. Thomas took his military duties very seriously and knew he must bring an end to this unsolicited interference, but at the same time the tone of his circular, issued in May 1863, indicates that he did find some humor in the situation. "It is with regret that the Col Comd'g learns that certain ladies connected with this Regiment have felt it incumbent upon themselves to express an Official opinion upon matters connected with the administration of regiment duties," the circular began. He assured the women that their presence was welcome and beneficial at Fort Albany, but at the same time he reminded them of their very limited role in a military community. "Whilst the presence of ladies in the camps undoubtedly adds a pleasing feature to the Social hours of a military life, their *efficient* opinions must necessarily remain of little worth until duly commissioned," Thomas's circular concluded.[53] And while it seems unconscionable that women living on a military post during wartime might offer policy suggestions, Thomas was not the first officer who faced such events. In her memoirs, Mary Logan recalled that during her tenure in Memphis, the wife of one of the regiment's colonels, a Mrs. Sloane, proved very disruptive to the efficient and effective operation of the regiment. "She was one of those women who are always interfering," Mary recalled, "and crossing the members of her husband's regiment." Colonel Sloane solved this particular problem by sending his wife away from the post for the duration of the war.[54] At Fort Albany, Thomas judiciously named names neither in the circular nor in surviving letters and journals, thus maintaining the anonymity of any offending party.

On August 11, 1863, suddenly and without indication that Thomas's health had failed, Elizabeth wrote of "much hurrying, packing, putting in order washing drying and ironing," and the Tannatts left their Virginia home in the care of others and departed for Manchester. [55] The medical report accompanying Thomas's resignation papers reveals that in the summer of 1863 he contracted malarious fever, resulting in a sixty-day sick leave. [56] Malaria was one of the most common diseases to sweep through Army of the Potomac camps, and only infectious childhood illnesses, such as measles and chicken pox, arose more often and afflicted more soldiers. Troops from New England and the Great Lakes region seemed particularly susceptible to malaria, and by war's end more than 1.2 million cases of the disease had been reported. Malaria ravaged soldiers in Virginia during the war years in part because of poorly constructed drainage systems that allowed water to puddle, turn stagnant, and become vast breeding grounds for disease-carrying mosquitoes. Although malaria seldom proved fatal, it did cause prolonged periods of illness and incapacitation to those who contracted it. Most frustrating was its "hydra-headed" nature, which allowed soldiers to suffer from several strains of the disease simultaneously and experience relapses of any or all of them, often throughout their lifetime. [57] Thomas suffered episodes of ill health throughout his eighty years, and while it is likely that at least some of these were recurring bouts of malaria, neither he nor Elizabeth mentioned the disease again once he left military service.

The absence of family records for the duration of this 1863 leave suggests that the family took advantage of Thomas's convalescence to enjoy the peacefulness of Manchester and the hospitality of the Tappans. They returned to Virginia in October, Thomas's health sufficiently restored to allow him to resume command of his regiment. By November the Tannatts' lives had returned to "normal," and Thomas and Elizabeth hosted a Thanksgiving dinner for the officers of the regiment. Apparently just one other woman joined them for the holiday meal, and Elizabeth's record of the event confirms that "separate spheres" for men and women were firmly in place and observed in Civil War–era military establishments. "This evening Thos. Had all the officers here of the Regt.," she wrote. "Col. Whistler was here his wife spent the evening up stairs with me." [58] This separation of the sexes was not at all unusual in the nineteenth century, particularly among the upper and middle classes. In the years prior to the Civil War, women's literature lauded the virtues of domesticity, piety, purity, and submissiveness, later referred to by historian Barbara Welter as the "Cult of True Womanhood," and from this grew the concept that the home, which protected women from the evil influences of the business and professional world beyond it, constituted woman's proper and "separate" sphere. Following the evening meal, it was quite common for women to retire to the parlor or kitchen while the men discussed politics, civic issues, and in this case military matters over cigars and refreshments. [59]

It is unclear if Elizabeth engaged household help during her short tenure on the Dakota frontier, but she clearly did so while the family resided in Virginia, though exact terms and accurate counts of household servants remain muddled. In the fall of 1863, "Kate" appears in Elizabeth's journals, probably as a nanny for Lillie, as she seems to be primarily occupied with the child's care during bouts of teething and illness.[60] It is likely that she also performed and assisted in household tasks, particularly if she was Elizabeth's only help. At the same time, "Isaac" is mentioned in Elizabeth's journal on a couple of occasions, and since he most often appeared in connection with outings, he probably served as a groom or stableman.[61] Elizabeth's failure to give details on her household help leaves much to speculation. It would be nice to know, for instance, if Kate and Isaac were former slaves. It is quite possible they were, since the Tannatts engaged their services while stationed in occupied Virginia, but Elizabeth's lack of description and detail makes verification of this point impossible.

It is curious that Elizabeth makes but a few cursory references to slaves in her surviving letters and journals, particularly since she resided in a former Confederate city with a significant African American population and seems to have shared the abolitionist sentiments embraced by members of her family. The absence of a single thought or comment on slavery in particular, and of African Americans in general, in Thomas's surviving papers is made all the more puzzling by a statement from West Point's 1914 reunion publication. "Was appointed Brigadier General of Massachusetts Colored Troops, by Governor Andrews, but declined the command," the publication reported of Thomas, but neither additional information nor documentation on the matter has survived, either in Thomas's personal or official military records.[62]

The Tannatts seem to have suffered more than their share of personal tragedy in these early years of their marriage, and it struck again on New Year's Day 1864 when, in the early evening, fire destroyed their Virginia home.[63] The cause of the house fire remains unknown, but the blaze rendered the house uninhabitable and caused the Tannatts to lodge temporarily at General DeRussy's Arlington headquarters before moving into a log house at nearby Fort Cass, Virginia.[64] This fire also convinced Elizabeth to leave Virginia and army life behind, and she and Lillie returned to Massachusetts to wait out the war in Manchester.

The Battle of Petersburg—June 1864

Thomas commanded the First Massachusetts Heavy Artillery Volunteers from January 1, 1863, until May 1864. At that time he joined forces with Grant at Spotsylvania, with Thomas commanding the brigade in the Richmond campaign during May and June 1864.[65] Thomas saw a great deal of action during this period as his troops participated in the Battles of Ny River, North Anna, Tolopotomy, Cold Harbor, and, finally, Petersburg. On the morning of June 16, 1864, the Army of the Potomac, led by Generals Grant and George G. Meade, approached Petersburg, Virginia. At the same time, twenty-five hundred Confederate troops under the command of Gen. P. G. T. Beauregard established positions from which to defend the city and awaited reinforcements from north of the James River.[66] By day's end the Union forces had pushed Beauregard's lines to the outskirts of the city at a cost of more than two thousand Union casualties, a loss General Meade later deemed as having "not been great" in the light of enormous losses suffered in other battles.[67]

During the Battle of Petersburg, Thomas's brigade and that of Gen. Gershom Mott formed an attacking column, and J. F. Whipple, a member of the First Massachusetts Heavy Artillery, recalled that "it was a magnificent sight to see the long lines advancing with gleaming bayonets, even though to almost certain death."[68] Leverett Bradley, another of Thomas's men, wrote that the First Massachusetts "had not advanced more than a hundred yards when we were met by a terrific fire of musketry from the enemy directly in our front. . . . The fire was returned, and then began a battle royal which lasted until ten o'clock in the evening."[69] When the fighting finally ceased the night of June 16, Thomas's brigade had lost 274 men, with 157 from the First Massachusetts killed or wounded, Col. Thomas R. Tannatt among them.[70] The official record indicates that "in the afternoon a charge was made upon the enemy's works, which resulted in our driving their front line and securing a position near their works. Col. Thomas R. Tannatt, commanding brigade, was wounded." The record also reveals that two days prior to the battle, the Fourth Maine was relieved of duty by special order, as their term had expired. The loss of these men and the transfer of others to the Nineteenth Maine totaled over 450 men and certainly contributed to the number of Union casualties.[71] The casualty list of officers, too, ran particularly high at Petersburg, with Thomas just one among more than thirty killed, wounded, or captured in the fracas.[72]

"Charged enemys [sic] works at 6 p.m.," Thomas wrote in his journal on June 16, "struck in my head delirious for hours."[73] Three days later, while lying in the field hospital, Thomas outlined an account of the incident for B. F. Browne, his Manchester friend and confidant. "I was among my men on foot and had rallied them to jump into a deep revine [sic] directly under the enemys line when I was struck in the head and fell," he wrote. "The ball completely demolished my cap visor and was turned by the X corners on my cap which are upon a thick piece of leather. I did not recover my consciousness until near morning my forehead was indented and the skin just broken. The Surgeons consider my escape wonderful and say the blow would have killed most men."[74] A medical report submitted by J. N. Willard, the surgeon serving with the regiment at the division hospital near Petersburg, confirmed that "Colonel Thomas R. Tannatt, 1st Mass, H.A., received a contusion in the forehead by a minié ball, on June 16th 1864, rendering him unconscious at the time and since causing considerable cerebral disturbance."[75]

It is curious that Thomas wrote first to Browne rather than to Elizabeth, but perhaps he feared that a letter posted from a field hospital would prove too upsetting to her, as she was in the final months of her second pregnancy. He did enclose a separate letter addressed to her and asked that Browne deliver it at the same time he delivered the news of Thomas's injury. Thomas's letter to Elizabeth differed substantially from the one he wrote to Browne, and while it remained relatively free of battle details, Thomas did recount the events both prior to and following his injury, and particularly his disappointment in being denied his request to resume command of his men. "I reported to Gen Birney that I was able to resume command," he wrote. "He said I could not, that after the injury to my head and its effect I was unfitted for any excitement and must remain quiet, much against my will." The remainder of the letter is a tirade against the army and the manner in which it used heavy artillery in battle. "The principle seems to be to slaughter the H.A.," Thomas wrote, blaming these tactics for the exceptionally high number of casualties suffered at Petersburg. "They are put into every possible hole, where Gen's will not put old men. All the HA regiments are reduced one half already and of 7 cols 4 are killed and two have been wounded." He informed Elizabeth that the brigadier generals in the field did not lead men into battle but rather sent them in under the command of colonels while the generals waited safely in the rear, and that "ambitious Gen care little how many valuable lives are lost, if it can be heralded that a line was gained of which they had no loss in distance than a mile in rear." It appears that his displeasure and dissatisfaction did not extend to those at the highest levels of command, however, for Thomas closed with "Gens Grant & Mead as well as Hancock know little of such doings or they would soon be [here]."[76]

This apparent lack of concern by field generals for the men and lower-grade officers engaged in battle was not limited to Petersburg, and it caused ground troops from both armies to lose respect for and confidence in their leaders. "The men were not tired of fighting," James Madison Stone of Worcester, Massachusetts, wrote following the Battle of Bull Run, "but they were tired of being sent to the slaughter by incompetent generals."[77] After Malvern Hill, a private from the Ninth Virginia wrote that Gen. Lewis Armistead "cares nothing at all for the men. He is full enough of saying 'go on boys' but he has never said 'come on' when we are going into a fight."[78]

Unable to continue as commanding officer of his brigade, Thomas requested, and the army granted, a twenty-day disability leave. He returned to Manchester to allow his wounds to heal. The Civil War continued for an additional ten months, ending on April 9, 1865, with Lee's surrender at Appomattox, and Thomas saw no further action. The slow-healing nature of his wound delayed his recovery, extended his disability leave, and intensified his disenchantment with the army. On July 15 and 18, 1865, Pres. Andrew Johnson accepted Thomas's resignations as colonel of volunteers and captain of the Fourth Artillery, respectively.[79] In appreciation for and recognition of his gallant and meritorious service in the field and his command of a brigade for a period of more than three months, Thomas also received honorary promotion to the rank of brevet brigadier general, which entitled him to be referred to as "General" for the remainder of his life.[80]

In later years, as he recalled the events leading to the abandonment of his chosen career, Thomas maintained that he had "resigned from [the] army completely broken in health."[81] He might have added that frustration with the actions of his superiors contributed to this decision, for Thomas's health had certainly not declined to the point where he was unfit for business or service.

Black Hawk, Colorado, and the Mining Experience

As the war continued to the south, Thomas rehabilitated in Manchester, and on September 16, 1864, he, Elizabeth, and Lillie welcomed the arrival of new family member Eben Tappan Tannatt.[1] Just a month later, Thomas and Lewis Tappan departed for the Colorado mining regions where Tappan brothers Lewis, William Henry, and George had been in business for some time and had, in the early 1860s, established Denver's first store catering specifically to the needs and interests of Colorado's gold miners.[2]

The Colorado gold rush began in the summer of 1858 when William Green Russell found gold on Little Dry Creek near present-day Englewood. Rumors of vast gold deposits spread quickly throughout the country, and by the following spring the mining camp had grown to include more than eighty log cabins and tents. Not until John Gregory arrived in the region, however, did mining commence in the high and treacherous mountains, and in April 1859 he discovered gold above the gulch that would soon bear his name and house the Colorado mining communities of Black Hawk, Central City, and Nevadaville.[3]

Elizabeth's brothers offered Thomas an interest in their Colorado business venture, which he refused. Instead, he traveled west strictly for purposes of rehabilitation, hopeful that Colorado's dry climate might slow or even eliminate what he referred to as the "recurring attacks of congestion" he continued to suffer as a result of his war wound.[4]

Elizabeth did not accompany Thomas to Colorado; instead, she passed the fall and early winter in Manchester caring for the children and visiting with family and friends. And while she offered no written objection to Thomas's departure or to being left for an indeterminate period of time with a two-year-old and a newborn, it appears that she felt abandoned by siblings and husband alike when she wrote on Thanksgiving Day 1864, "I am the only one of 8 at home."[5] How odd this holiday must have seemed to Elizabeth, who, as a member of Manchester's large and gregarious Tappan family, had enjoyed so many holidays filled with people, activity, and conversation. This feeling of "abandonment" is reinforced by Elizabeth's "tally" of the Thanksgiving absentees and its inclusion of three older brothers who had been dead for a number of years.[6] "How sad the retrospect of life to an old pilgrim as he sits in a church long familiar to him, and sees not one of his old acquaintances!!"[7] she wrote to Thomas, recounting the events of the day, and informing him that Sally Tappan had attended Thanksgiving services at the old church that morning alone. On that Thanksgiving, Elizabeth's thoughts might have extended beyond her aging parents and the absence of her siblings and husband, and to the changes the recent Civil War and its aftermath had inflicted upon everyday life in the peaceful harbor town of Manchester-by-the-Sea.

By the time Col. Eben Tappan entered the cabinetry trade in the mid-1810s, "the 'store-houses of Charleston, Mobile, and New Orleans' as well as those in New York were stocked full of Manchester furniture." [8] With westward expansion and the outbreak of the Civil War, however, Manchester's primary industry fell upon hard times. Opportunities elsewhere, particularly in a prewar West replete with lumber, waterpower, and other natural resources, beckoned young craftsmen from the eastern seaboard, and in the process, populations of New England towns began to decline and family businesses were abandoned. Three of Eben Tappan's sons—William Henry, Lewis, and George—went west in the prewar years, and while the precise fate of Colonel Tappan's cabinetry business is unrecorded, it is likely that with these departures, and the severe decline in the trade itself, he phased out his cabinetry endeavors and focused instead on the general store. At the same time, the onset of the Civil War and the placement of Union blockades at southern ports caused all trade with the South to come to a halt. Manchester's cabinetry trade nearly disappeared, with just three mills doing business during the war and only one surviving into the twentieth century. [9] Elizabeth watched helplessly as the Manchester of her girlhood slipped away, but the social and economic decline she witnessed was certainly not confined to Manchester or to Massachusetts. Jacqueline Jones has noted that "wartime social conflicts . . . foreshadowed long term trends caused by a changing regional and national economy," which forced artisans throughout New England to "de-skill" and give up their craft for factory employment or seek work elsewhere. Maris Vinovskis has suggested that the war brought a severely negative economic turn to the North as, in a sharp departure from earlier decades, both the rate of industrialization and the growth of individual wealth dropped significantly. [10]

As Elizabeth awaited his return, Thomas augmented his period of rehabilitation with a brief, albeit unofficial, association with the army on the Colorado frontier. The Indian Wars raged on the plains as Confederates and Yankees squared off in the East, and on January 11, 1865, Thomas received a letter from Col. Thomas Moonlight, commanding officer of the Eleventh Kansas Cavalry. Moonlight's letter directed Thomas to proceed to Leavenworth, Kansas, and deliver to Major General Curtis "such dispatches as you may receive from these headquarters." [11] It is clear from the official records that Thomas accomplished his mission, for Moonlight wrote to Maj. C. S. Charlot, "I forwarded to you some time ago, per hands of Colonel Tannatt, a history of affairs in this Territory, and also what I thought should be done in the premises to alleviate the sufferings of this people, and if possible remove the evil . . . [and] I have learned indirectly that Colonel Tannatt delivered the documents."[12]

This flurry of activity followed closely on the heels of the Sand Creek massacre in November 1864, when Col. John M. Chivington and a regiment of Colorado volunteers attacked a Cheyenne and Arapahoe village camped on Sand Creek, near Fort Lyon. Black Kettle, leader of the Southern Cheyenne, had taken particular care to avoid an attack, and he located his camp on a site specifically assigned to him by the commander at Fort Lyon, Maj. Scott J. Anthony. As the troops rushed his camp, Black Kettle lifted an American flag and a white flag of truce, but since Chivington's orders had been to "kill and scalp all," the soldiers paid the flags no heed, and the result was full-blown massacre, with casualties numbering somewhere between 150 and 500, including many women and children. Prior to Sand Creek, many Cheyenne and Arapahoe had given up the fight against the settlers and the army, but this massacre once again united them, and with the single goal of revenge.[13]

The old adage "it's a small world" certain applied to mid-nineteenth-century America, and in 1864, at the time of the Sand Creek massacre, one of Elizabeth's cousins, Lt. Col. Samuel F. Tappan, served with Chivington and was also, perhaps, his greatest antagonist. Sam Tappan wrote with disdain of Chivington's boastfulness following the unprovoked attack at Sand Creek and recounted that Chivington "strided up and down the room, anticipating promotion for his valor . . . he then walked the room saying, 'it don't take me six months to find [I]ndians.'"[14] Chivington did not, however, receive his expected accolades; in fact, court-martial charges were brought against him, but because they were not filed until after he had left the army, they could not be pursued. He did not escape unscathed, however. He was forced to resign from the Colorado militia and was denied any association with Colorado's drive for statehood. Chivington left Colorado and embarked upon his own decades of wanderlust, and he is best remembered, not for heroic acts, but rather for "a cowardly and cold-blooded slaughter, sufficient to cover its perpetrators with indelible infamy, and the face of every American with shame and indignation."[15]

In early 1865, Col. Moonlight encountered great difficulty raising volunteer regiments to deal with the Indian attacks that followed Sand Creek, and not because Coloradans necessarily hesitated in fighting Indians. Rather, it appears that a "factional spirit" existed on the Colorado frontier, as elsewhere, and supporters of the Union and the Confederacy simply could not cooperate with one another. Conflicts among white settlers, the military, and the Indians continued in Colorado into the late nineteenth century, but this isolated instance seems to be Thomas's only direct involvement in these matters.

Thomas returned to Manchester within weeks of delivering Moonlight's dispatches, and on January 30, 1865, Elizabeth wrote in her journal that he had arrived "very unexpectedly."[16] For the next several months the family lived quietly, without the usual plethora of correspondence and journal keeping, though it is now evident that they used this time to prepare for a relocation to Colorado. The tasks of organizing and packing were sadly interrupted on May 7, 1865, when, as Elizabeth confided to her journal, "Lillie died this morning twenty min. past eight."[17] There had been no previous mention of the two-and-a-half-year-old being ill, and it must have been devastating for Thomas and Elizabeth to leave their firstborn buried beneath a small stone simply marked "Lillie" in Manchester's "1661" cemetery. "The loss of a child such as Lillie was must have fallen very heavily upon you," Elizabeth's brother William Henry wrote from Colorado. "Upon the Col. this loss must have been keenly felt for he almost idolized the poor Child."[18] A newspaper article carefully pasted into one of Elizabeth's scrapbooks memorialized Lillie's death and celebrated her short life. "Bright, beautiful and precious," it read, "she was the joy of her parents and the pet of a wide circle of friends."[19] Child mortality was not uncommon in the nineteenth century, even in the "civilized" East, but each occurrence brought deep despair and loss to the families whose seemingly healthy children quickly sickened and died. Lillie's death did not alter the Tannatts' plans, however, and the lure of the wealth, position, and prestige to be gained in Colorado tugged at Thomas as it had thousands of others. In July 1865 he returned to Colorado, this time in the company of Elizabeth and ten-month-old Eben.

The traditional, solitary prospector did not last long in Colorado's mountainous mining regions, as extraction of its ores was difficult, often impossible, without machinery and the capital to finance it. After finding a vein laced with gold, most prospectors sold their claims to eastern corporations that soon controlled the majority of the mines, provided them with state-of-the-art equipment, and staffed them with professionally educated engineers.[20] Thomas became affiliated with one of these New York–based corporate conglomerates prior to his departure from the East, and he traveled to Colorado as resident engineer and general manager in charge of its interests.[21] The Tannatts settled in Black Hawk, in what would become Gilpin County, and Thomas quickly became absorbed with his business affairs.[22]

Black Hawk became the center of milling activity for Gregory Gulch's gold mines, as it possessed the abundant water supply necessary to operate water wheels and sluices. Ore from mines throughout the region traveled by wagon, and later by train, to Black Hawk, where it went through the many processes necessary to extract the maximum amount of gold from quartz rock. As with gold rush towns throughout the West, Black Hawk's population peaked at the height of gold extraction during the 1870s, then declined sharply with only two hundred people remaining in town by the turn of the twentieth century. Miraculously, Black Hawk escaped the fires that destroyed many mining towns, and a number of buildings constructed in the 1860s, including the Presbyterian church, the Gilpin Hotel, and Blake's Livery, still stand.

As had been the case in California after the discovery of gold at Sutter's Mill in 1848, individuals from all occupations and social backgrounds, and for every imaginable reason, flocked to the Colorado gold fields after William Green Russell's initial strike in 1858. Although most traveled west expecting to "get rich quick," prosperity in Colorado was available through a number of avenues, as exemplified by Thomas, the Tappan brothers, and individuals such as Frank Hall, who left New York in 1859 and traveled to Colorado with five other men, one of them a previous visitor to the region. Hall worked as a quartz miner for the Black Hawk Gold Mining Company in 1862 and 1863, but in late 1863 he turned his attention to gentler, and probably more lucrative, pursuits when he went to work for Ovando J. Hollister, publisher of the *Black Hawk Mining Journal*. In 1866, Territorial Governor Alexander Cummings named Hall his territorial secretary, and during Hall's eight years in office, due to the frequent and prolonged absences of Territorial Governors Cummings, A. C. Hunt, Edward M. McCook, and Samuel H. Elbert, he played a principal role in shaping the politics and policies of Colorado Territory. After leaving the political arena, Hall wrote the first comprehensive history of the region, the four-volume *History of Colorado*. Unlike most other gold rush immigrants, Hall remained in Colorado and enjoyed the prosperity and position he had achieved. He died in Denver in 1917.[23]

In his own quest for prosperity and position, Thomas served as agent for a number of mines and mining companies, and while some of these associations were short-lived, it appears his service with the Manhattan Gold Mining Company lasted the duration of his stay in Colorado. The organization, made up of a number of eastern stockholders, owned several mines, the Manhattan and the Great Western among them. Making eastern shareholders understand and appreciate the difficulties involved in establishing and operating successful mining ventures in distant Colorado seems to have been Thomas's most trying task, and in numerous pieces of correspondence he attempted to explain various aspects of doing business on the mining frontier. In August 1865, for instance, he defended a number of his economic decisions to George B. Satterle, secretary of the Manhattan Gold Mining Company. "I am almost of the opinion that 'it costs a mine to work a mine,'" Thomas wrote as he detailed the expenditures associated with a number of essential goods and services. He strongly suggested that "the only rule is *buy nothing here that* can be purchased at wholesale East."[24] Thomas did not exaggerate the severity of this economic situation. Black Hawk's nearest railhead lay six hundred miles distant in St. Joseph, Missouri, which meant that goods and supplies must be collected there and transported via ox wagon to Colorado. This resulted in exorbitant costs for both product and transportation.[25]

It appears that as Thomas explained his actions and accounts over the years, Satterle and the others acquiesced to his suggestions and decisions, one situation at a time, though this certainly did not create a pleasant and cooperative work environment. The business of successful mine management was difficult enough without having to defend every action and decision to the members of a board of directors, none of whom ever visited their Colorado mines. "I sometimes feel that I would give much for ten minutes conversation with the Board of Directors," Thomas wrote to Satterle in November 1865, "knowing that they feel a great desire to do the best and only fail from want of knowledge."[26]

Despite these difficulties with management, Thomas enjoyed the business of gold mining. As a West Point–trained engineer, he understood the workings of the sophisticated machinery needed to extract both the quartz from the mountains and the gold from the quartz. At the same time, the excitement generated by a particularly large strike was not lost on him. In November 1865, Thomas expressed unrestrained excitement when he reported that forty-seven and one-half ounces of refined gold had been extracted from the ores of the Great Western mine. He wrote Satterle that "this return has made me gold hungry and nothing short of steady returns and good profits will make me feel that I am doing my best for the Manhattan. . . . I have worked two nights until midnight," he continued, and unabashedly admitted to feeling "as gay over my sweep as any child with a new toy."[27] Differences in the character and value of ores extracted from a single mineral vein are common, and throughout much of the Gregory Gulch region a discovery that might first appear to be a major "strike" could quickly fizzle to one of nothing more than low-grade ore, or "mill dirt." Most mines in Black Hawk and Central City, however, contained very rich veins known as "free gold" veins, their minerals visible to the naked eye, and the discovery that so excited Thomas was likely one of these.

Enthusiastic over significant gold strikes and seemingly happy with his situation in Colorado, Thomas continued to have difficulty with the mining companies, particularly in the areas of accounting and finances. "Petty cash accounts" apparently did not exist on the mining frontier, and on numerous occasions Thomas was forced to advance personal funds to cover company expenses, a practice that became particularly problematic in the fall of 1867. During the Tannatts' early days in Colorado, as Thomas attempted to impress upon the shareholders the inflated costs involved in living on a frontier, he noted that "for a house I would hardly descend to at home I must pay $700 rent."[28] It seems that Thomas did pay this exorbitant rental fee for a period of time, but by the summer of 1867 he and Elizabeth had made arrangements for the construction of their own home. Cash flow was a problem, however, and that fall he appealed to Satterle for assistance in receiving funds owed him by the companies. "Mrs. Tannatt, very properly insisted that if we were to remain here we must build," he wrote, "as she could not live as she had in a house 3/4 up stairs without help."[29] No correspondence from Satterle or any of the New York shareholders made its way into the Tannatt records, but since Thomas's pleas for reimbursement cease and the Tannatts remained in Colorado for another two years, it appears that the companies eventually settled his accounts and reimbursed the three thousand dollars owed him.

While Thomas dealt with the mines and their owners and boards of directors, Elizabeth undertook the task of establishing a proper home amid the dust, dirt, mine tailings, and variety of personalities and characters present on the mining frontier. It is evident that she engaged domestic help while in Colorado, although, as was the case in many western mining towns, she found it difficult to retain individuals for any length of time. "Kate is to let me know if she comes early next week," she recorded in her journal on January 2, 1867, then on January 10 noted that "Molly Smith came this p.m. to live with me. . . . Have not heard from Kate & so would wait no longer." By March 19, however, "Mollie left" and was not replaced until May 1 when "Hannah Simpson came to live with me yesterday."[30] From the time of the first discoveries of gold in California in the late 1840s, women enjoyed an abundance of business opportunities on the mining frontier. Single women and miners' wives established boardinghouses, saloons, general stores, laundries, and restaurants, while others taught school, engaged in prostitution, or turned to mining themselves. As recent scholarship has shown, working women on the mining frontier could engage in occupations far more pleasing, and more lucrative, than domestic service, and even those who did accept domestic employment often used it as a stepping-stone to other opportunities. As a result, those who wished to engage domestic servants often found the task both difficult and repetitive.[31]

"Really the women did more in the early days than the men," Central City resident Augusta Tabor revealed of Gregory Gulch's nineteenth-century female population. "There was so much for them to do, . . . there were so many men who could not cook and did not like men's cooking and would insist upon boarding where there was a woman."[32] It does not appear that Elizabeth took in boarders, but she did offer a sense of home and family to men living alone on the frontier. When twenty-seven-year-old miner Albert Stettleberg died in January 1867, the Tannatts held his funeral in their home, and the duty of notifying family and friends in the young man's hometown of Baltimore fell to them as well. "I pity the poor widowed mother when she hears the death of her only son," Elizabeth wrote in her journal the evening following the funeral.[33] Ovando Hollister wrote in 1867 of the manner in which mining community populations reacted to the deaths of young miners, and he might have been describing Elizabeth when he wrote that "every woman in the community seems to imagine herself the mother or sister of the deceased. . . . The expense is provided for, no one knows how. In the same way cases of destitution from sickness are relieved."[34] At thirty-three and twenty-nine years of age in early 1867, the Tannatts, as a married couple with children, represented home and stability to Black Hawk's single, male population.

Beyond Thomas's business correspondence, personal papers do not exist for the first eighteen months of the Tannatts' tenure in Colorado. The silence was finally broken by a statement found among Thomas's financial records that indicates a payment of twenty-five dollars to H. B. Tuttle "To Special Attendance for Mrs. T" and announces the birth of the Tannatts' third child, Miriam "Minnie" Hooper Tannatt, on September 13, 1866.[35] Minnie's birth led to a period of social involvement for Elizabeth, and while there was no shortage of activity in the Black Hawk–Central City region, those deemed "respectable" enough for middle-class women had to be carefully considered and selected. Journalist, author, and diplomat Bayard Taylor presented a series of talks in both Central City and Black Hawk in 1866, and this is the type of event Thomas and Elizabeth might have attended together. While the residents of Gregory Gulch no doubt enjoyed his talks, Taylor found few redeeming qualities in Colorado's mining towns. "I am already tired after only a few days of this long, windy, dusty street," he commented the evening before his departure; "[I] shall joyfully say good-bye tomorrow morning."[36] Other distractions and modes of entertainment available to Black Hawk residents included an amateur dramatic troupe, a skating rink, and the performances of traveling stock companies and musicians staged at the Montana Theater in Central City.[37] In addition, church teas, Bible studies, social calls, and regional recreational activities abounded in the mining district, and as its middle-class female residents organized and participated in these they worked as well to bring dignity, morality, and order to their towns.

One of the ways middle-class women achieved the stability and civility they sought in mining communities was through class division and separation. Paula Petrik's discussion of the women of Helena, Montana, and their diligence in creating and maintaining social divisions makes it clear that, as in established cities and towns in the East, social stratification played a key role in societal organization on the frontier.[38] Elizabeth certainly socialized exclusively with other middle-class women, the mothers, wives, daughters, and sisters of mining company engineers, agents, and merchants, as it would have been out of the question, and a breach of middle-class propriety, for her to consort with the "lower" class of women who worked in Black Hawk as laundresses, cooks, and prostitutes. Elizabeth and her cohorts, in replicating middle-class female patterns found in the East, called upon and visited each other often, and it appears that few days passed without some social contact. "Mrs. Conglon & Lathrop called" on January 2, 1867, Elizabeth "called on Mrs Lathrop" on January 4, and the following day she noted the receipt of several invitations to sleigh parties. She declined these in order to stay home and bake, but on January 7 she "went to sleigh ride with Mrs Schram & Ebe" while "Mrs L. took care of baby." The next day, "Mrs Schram spent the afternoon up here," where Elizabeth "showed her about crocheting a hood."[39] Female companionship and the opportunities appropriate to middle-class women for recreation and socialization seem to have been in adequate supply on the Colorado mining frontier in the 1860s.

Life on a mining frontier certainly differed from anything Elizabeth had known before, but by the time the Tannatts reached Colorado she had lived apart from family and friends for some time, and her experiences at Fort Randall in Dakota Territory and in occupied Tennessee and Virginia during the war had prepared her for any location to which Thomas and his business endeavors might take her. At the same time, the Tannatts were not without family on the frontier, for Colorado and other western locales had become home to a number of Tappans, with Elizabeth's brothers Lewis and William Henry and cousins Samuel and James all residing in the general area.[40] This plethora of male relations did nothing to satisfy Elizabeth's desire for the companionship of female family members, however, and she was no doubt delighted when Lewis married Elizabeth "Libbie" Sanford in the fall of 1866 and brought her to Colorado to meet the "western" Tappans. "The memories of that little visit with you are so pleasant," Libbie wrote in October 1867, following a stay at the Tannatt home in Black Hawk, "that I shall be in favor of passing a day with you frequently, this coming winter."[41] Elizabeth enjoyed Libbie's companionship, though the amount of time they spent together was short and their visits were infrequent. By the late 1860s, Lewis spent a good deal of time traveling between his various business interests in Colorado and the East, where he maintained his permanent residence, and until the birth of their first child in 1870, Libbie usually traveled with him. Elizabeth and Libbie maintained a regular correspondence for many years, but their physical association ended in 1879 when the Tannatts relocated to Washington Territory, just months before Lewis's death in 1880.[42]

Elizabeth visited Manchester as often as she could during her parents' lifetimes, and she did not allow distance to alter this pattern during the family's tenure in Colorado. The frequency of these trips is evidence of both the Tannatts' healthy financial situation—though their papers make very few specific comments on the extent of their wealth—and their middle-class status. Travel, and particularly the extensive trips that Elizabeth took quite regularly, was not an option for most women on a mining frontier. In order to relieve her homesickness, for instance, Maggie Brown of Bonanza, Colorado, requested that family members send her "ginger cakes, persimmons, chestnuts . . . any touch of Virginia."[43] Elizabeth, on the other hand, had the means and the leisure to absent herself from home for extended periods of time in order to visit family members across the country. In the spring of 1867 the Tannatts made their way east, stopping first in McMinnville, Tennessee, to visit Elizabeth's sister, Sarah Ames,[44] and possibly Thomas's younger brother John as well.[45] They proceeded on to Manchester, where Elizabeth expressed concern over the state of her mother's health. "Mother very feeble," she confided to her journal.[46] Sally Tappan was seventy-one years of age in 1867. Elizabeth continued to worry over her mother's health, but as her primary duties and obligations rested in Colorado, she and the family returned there later in the summer as planned. A flurry of correspondence from Libbie the following spring and summer probably made Elizabeth wish she had remained in Manchester, however, for though well intentioned in its relay of news and information from Manchester and the Tappans, the close relationship Libbie had fostered with Colonel Tappan, and particularly with Sally, did nothing but intensify Elizabeth's feelings of isolation and loneliness. "I never knew her so well as she is now," Libbie wrote of Elizabeth's mother in July 1868. "It was wonderful to see how active she was in walking out & running about the house."[47] It pleased Elizabeth that her mother's health had improved so dramatically since the previous summer, but the tone of ensuing letters reveals her growing resentment as Libbie assumed a daughterly role to Colonel Tappan and Sally. "I never have been *so* homesick as I have been the last Summer and Fall," Elizabeth wrote her mother in November 1868, and despite the full and active social life she led in Colorado, the letter continued, "it seems as if I could not stay here another week."[48] Elizabeth revealed to Sally that she often imagined herself back in Manchester with her children, visiting family and friends, though it is unclear if these daydreams of a return to her childhood home included Thomas.

Chores and other household tasks delayed completion of this letter, and when Elizabeth picked up her pen four days later she did so with a much brighter outlook. Rather than continue in the downcast tone of the letter's early pages, she filled the later ones with enthusiasm over current events, both national and familial. "Hurrah for Grant & Colfax," she wrote of the presidential election that had taken place in the last few days. "How did Father vote?"[49] It may seem odd that a thirty-one-year-old daughter would inquire as to how her father had cast his ballot in a mid-nineteenth-century presidential election, but Elizabeth had grown up in a household of politicians and acquired an interest in politics at a very early age. Colonel Tappan served on the Massachusetts state legislature when Elizabeth was just a child, as had his father before him, and discussions on local and national issues were commonplace in the Tappan home—and not restricted to the family's male members.[50]

Thomas's growing frustration with the mining companies and Elizabeth's jealousy of Libbie's position among the Manchester Tappans might have been tempered a bit by their children's apparent happiness in their Colorado surroundings, and Elizabeth enjoyed relating their activities and progress to family in the East. In the fall of 1868, Eben was four and Miriam two, and Elizabeth wrote her mother that "Ebbie wheels Minnie out doors and in, in the little wheelbarrow," and "she don't care if she is upset—has no fear or caution and doesn't cry if tumbled out."[51] The robust health of this two-year-old must have been a blessing to Thomas and Elizabeth, who could not help but reflect from time to time on the fact that their eldest child had died at the same age just three years earlier.

In 1869, maintaining that his health had once again declined and that recurring attacks of "congestion of the brain" rendered him unable to perform his duties as general agent and resident engineer, Thomas resigned his positions in Colorado and returned briefly with his family to Massachusetts before once again relocating them, this time to Tennessee.[52] While war-related health issues plagued Thomas throughout his lifetime, it is unlikely that they were the sole motivating factor in his decision to leave Colorado. Over the course of his tenure in the mining industry, Thomas became increasingly frustrated with the lack of leadership exhibited by mine owners and their boards of directors, much as he had with senior army officers during the war just five years earlier. His professed ailments did not prohibit him from seeking gainful employment after leaving Colorado, and it is likely that he used his medical history to allow a graceful departure from the mining industry, with his business connections and associations on good terms and intact.

Introduction to Railroads: The Tennessee Immigration Association

"In 1869 I removed to McMinnville, Tenn. purchased a country residence and land, just outside the city limits and early became interested in railroad interests and development of oil and iron properties,"[53] wrote Thomas to Capt. William C. Rivers in 1902, in response to the latter's request for biographical information on West Point alumni. Thomas certainly did not make this relocation decision without a great deal of thought, and it is likely that through contacts established during the war, as well as family and friends at home in the region, he knew before leaving Colorado of the promising business opportunities surfacing in postwar Tennessee. Tennessee was the first of the southern states to be readmitted to the Union following the Civil War, and its tale of Reconstruction differs substantially from that of the other former Confederate strongholds—differences that allowed the state to rebuild and become both self-sufficient and productive long before the others.

In the fall of 1865, the newly seated Tennessee legislature accepted the Thirteenth Amendment to the U.S. Constitution, abolishing slavery, and elected senators and representatives to serve in the U.S. Congress. The Radical Republican–controlled Congress refused to seat the Tennessee delegation, however, and proposed that seceded states also be required to accept the Fourteenth Amendment, which guaranteed citizenship to all individuals born or naturalized in the United States, prior to the restoration of congressional representation. After discussion, disagreement, and the possible illegal actions of Gov. W. G. Brownlow and the state general assembly, Tennessee ratified the Fourteenth Amendment. [54] On July 23, 1866, Pres. Andrew Johnson signed the resolution restoring Tennessee to the Union, sparing it the military reconstruction experienced by the other Confederate states. [55]

Shortly after his arrival in the state, Thomas affiliated with the Tennessee Immigration Association, which was engaged in the negotiation, purchase, sale, leasing, and exchange of real estate in any part of Tennessee or the Southwest. While the Tennessee Immigration Association was a privately held venture, the Tennessee state legislature sanctioned a number of agencies engaged in similar pursuits, including the Tennessee Colonial and Immigration Company and the Germany Association of the City of Nashville. [56] By 1872, Thomas had risen to the position of manager of the association's McMinnville branch office and immersed himself in the task of encouraging immigration to Tennessee by a "new" class of people. [57]

Although the terrain still carried the scars of war, New South leaders beckoned displaced and disgruntled northerners and midwesterners of European descent with promises of opportunity and wealth. New South leaders, falling largely into the Reconstruction-era categories of "carpetbagger" and "scalawag," found few redeeming qualities in Tennessee's laboring population, black or white, and looked beyond agricultural pursuits, and to industry and manufacturing, to resuscitate the state's ailing economy.

The terms "carpetbagger" and "scalawag" were widely used by southern Democrats throughout the post–Civil War South to refer to white immigrants from the North and southern whites who supported the Republican Party. "Carpetbaggers" were alleged to be lower-class northerners who packed their belongings into a single carpetbag and ventured south after passage of the Reconstruction Act to benefit economically from the misfortunes of former Confederates. While the term remained popular for some time, the definition was largely inaccurate, since most "carpetbaggers" came from middle-class, not lower-class, backgrounds, and were quite well educated. "Carpetbaggers" engaged in professional pursuits, such as law, publishing, and other forms of business, and invested their personal assets in rebuilding the southern states in which they resided. In addition, many "carpetbaggers" were Union army veterans, a number of them officers who had developed a fondness for the region while serving in the South. It is true that many of these individuals became affiliated with Reconstruction governments, but as a rule this was not the motivating factor for relocation. "Scalawags," on the other hand, were southern whites who joined the Republicans and, according to southern Democrats, were "vile, blatant, vindictive, unprincipled." "Scalawags" had little in common with the South's planter class for most hailed from the region's upland counties and had held the plantation regime in disdain for some time. Hardly loyal Confederates, "scalawags" were as likely to fight against the South as for it, and many joined the Republicans due to their promise to remove members of the planter class from their positions of power in the South.[58]

"We are too poor not to go into manufacturing," wrote A. S. Colyar, president of the Sewanee Mining Company, in Nashville's *Republican Banner* in November 1867, referring to the South in general and southern industry in particular. "We each year grow poorer, the railroads, the manufacturer and the jobber have all grown as rich as Jews at our expense."[59] Arthur St. Clair Colyar, a Tennessean by birth and a lawyer by trade, played an important role in the establishment of the New South. Despite opposing secession in 1861, he joined with his fellow Confederates when it became clear that secession and war were inevitable. Colyar served as a member of the Confederate Congress until 1865, and at war's end he became involved in rebuilding and reorganizing Tennessee's coal, railroad, and manufacturing industries through such companies as the Tennessee Immigration Association, of which he held the office of president.[60]

Thomas proved very useful to Colyar's association, and his New England connections allowed him to reach a wide audience through the articles and advertisements he placed in northern newspapers extolling the favorable conditions to be found in Tennessee. "Editor Cabinet Maker," began one of these, perhaps intended for publication in Manchester's *Beetle and Wedge*, "some months since, a gentleman, reared in the manufacturing interest of your state, was visiting Tennessee. . . . [and] urged my writing you upon the subject . . . finding abundant the varieties so much employed in the interest you represent." The article went on to describe the plenitude of Tennessee's timber, easily accessed by rail lines and located amid the state's numerous streams and waterways advertised by promoters as power sources. Thomas emphasized Tennessee's temperate climate and suggested that seasonal slowdowns in production, common in New England, would not necessarily occur in the South, as water sources remained "unchanged by winter cold" and could therefore produce power throughout the year.[61]

Certainly Thomas, a transplanted northerner, anticipated that potential immigrants might question the possibility of establishing safe and secure homes for their families in the South. Concerns over the lingering antagonism southerners held for those from the North, and the violence that groups such as the Ku Klux Klan inflicted upon freedmen and their supporters, had to be addressed, and Thomas did so in his newspaper articles and advertisements. "I can honestly assure my readers that prejudice finds no support in Tennessee to-day," he wrote, "whatever the past may have presented; her people en-masse have turned a cold parting glance upon the corpse shrouded in the past."[62] These assurances may have assuaged the doubts of some would-be immigrants, but the violence and atrocities committed by Klan members continued throughout the 1860s and 1870s. In the summer of 1868, for instance, Klansmen armed with pistols and ropes boarded a southbound train out of Washington DC in search of Tennessee legislator Samuel Mayes Arnell, who had proposed legislation to make Klan membership a crime. Fortunately, Arnell had booked passage on a different train.[63] Six months later, in February 1869, the body of Capt. Seymour Barmore, engaged by Governor Brownlow of Tennessee to work undercover and acquire names and information on those supportive of the Klan, was pulled from the Duck River with a rope around the neck and a bullet through the skull.[64] In response to Klan violence, Congress enacted three separate Enforcement Acts between 1870 and 1871 to both protect freedmen and their supporters and to destroy, or at least break apart, the Ku Klux Klan. The most far-reaching of these, the Ku Klux Klan Act of April 1871, outlawed such activities as the formation of conspiracies, wearing disguises, and resisting officers and intimidating officials. In addition, the 1871 act gave the president the ability to order military intervention and suspend the writ of habeas corpus in order to suppress these "armed combinations."[65] By 1872 the willingness of the federal government to bring Klansmen to justice had broken the spirit of the Klan, and violence diminished greatly across the South.

Despite the best efforts of Thomas, the Tennessee Immigration Association, and similar agencies, however, the West and Midwest simply presented better business opportunities in the late 1860s and 1870s than the South, and Tennessee's hoped-for hordes of immigrants did not materialize. In fact, Tennessee claimed fewer foreign-born residents in 1870 than it had in 1860.[66] Some northern capital did make its way into the region, however, and coupled with in-state investment, it helped to establish Tennessee's four largest cities—Knoxville, Memphis, Chattanooga, and Nashville—as manufacturing centers. As a result, the state's economic recovery began by the mid-1880s.[67]

The Tannatts left few personal papers from their seven years in Tennessee, and were it not for one of Minnie's school compositions that indicated "then I went to Tennessee," it might appear that Thomas had traveled to McMinnville alone.[68] The family moved to Tennessee together, however, and in May 1874 received the disturbing news from William Henry in Colorado that a fire had destroyed his Central City store, its inventory, and most of his personal effects. "I escaped with but one suit of clothes in which I stood," he wrote to Elizabeth. "The loss has been fearful and I am at loss what to do."[69] Fire represented a constant threat in mining towns, and the Tappan brothers had been fortunate to avoid it as long as they had. It appears that Thomas owned an interest in the destroyed property, for the note asked that "Tom write to me to whom I shall deed his percent," though it is unclear what Thomas did with this percentage interest or with the ensuing insurance proceeds.[70]

The move to Tennessee did not slow the stream of bad news that seemed to follow the Tannatts, and in the spring of 1874 word reached them that Colonel Tappan had died in Manchester at the age of eighty-two. "No one in Manchester was more highly respected," his obituary read. "He will be remembered by those who knew him as a most worthy citizen." The long marriage of Eben and Sally Tappan struck those who had observed it as a happy one, and his obituary further stated that "with the wife of his youth he lived fifty-nine years, in a harmony and union beautiful to witness."[71] It is not surprising that, after a marriage as long-lasting and apparently happy as this one, Sally did not long survive her husband, and just fifteen months after his death, in July 1875, she died as a result of rheumatic heart disease. "She was a woman of rare sweetness of disposition and of beautiful character," her obituary in the *Beetle and Wedge* declared, "one of the best wives and mothers, and was greatly blessed in her husband and children."[72] "It was so sudden as to almost paralize [*sic*] everyone: yet it was the 'sudden death' that she always desired," Lewis wrote Elizabeth from Manchester of their mother's last moments. He related that the night before her death, Sally had wished only to "die as easily as Mr. Tappan." In her last hours she had the company and comfort of Lewis's family and other family members and friends. Lewis's letter continued, "I am thankful that I was present during her sickness and particularly at her death, it would have been sad to have had her die without either of her children with her."[73] In fact, Sally had four living children at the time of her death: Elizabeth and Sarah in Tennessee; William Henry, still traveling and attempting to reestablish himself after the devastating fire a year earlier; and Lewis in Manchester. There can be no doubt that the death of her parents weighed heavily on Elizabeth's heart, and with their passing so too did the reason to visit Manchester, though the appeal of her childhood home never paled.

"After a residence of seven years, my health being improved, I returned to Mass," continued Thomas's letter to West Point's Captain Rivers—the lack of stated motivation behind this move making it all the more curious.[74] In 1876 the United States was in the midst of an economic depression that began in September 1873 with the collapse of banking giant Jay Cooke and Company and grew into a panic that swept through banks and brokerage houses, the stock market, and industry.[75] Thomas does not attribute his decision to leave Tennessee to the depression, but since it particularly affected the already-devastated South, and as opportunity in Manchester had further declined after 1873, it is likely that his Tennessee ventures had evaporated, precipitating the family's return to Manchester and habitation of the now-empty Tappan house. While he insisted that ill health caused his departure from Colorado in 1869, Thomas never suggested that it led to his relocation to or from Tennessee. This is not to suggest that Thomas did not continue to suffer the effects of wartime injury and disease, but rather that his health alone did not account for the family's frequent relocations. It is likely that the loss of the military career for which he had planned and prepared, along with the inability to secure employment to satisfactorily fill its void and restore his sense of self and purpose, plagued Thomas much more than his periodic episodes of ill health.

Thomas's frequent uprooting of his family might seem a bit extreme, but repeated relocation, for business as well as personal reasons, was common in the post–Civil War years and during the 1870s. During this time, America's expanding population spread across the continent, redistributing itself in established cities and towns and creating new ones in what Dean L. May has called "the great American diaspora." [76] In his study on Jacksonville, Illinois, Don Harrison Doyle found that between 1850 and 1870, communities retained relatively small percentages of their populations during a given ten-year period, and those numbers fell substantially during the Civil War decade of 1860 to 1870, when Jacksonville's traceable population dropped to a low of 21 percent.[77] Mobility studies have shown that population constancy rates seldom rose above 50 percent in the mid-nineteenth century, and while some individuals, such as Iowan Junius Wright, "found the turmoils of the Civil War 'irksome'" enough to leave his home in Iowa for the "promise of adventure and wealth in the West," countless others traveled to new locations in search of occupational status, community position, and wealth.[78]

Although the specific reasons behind their departure from Tennessee must be left to speculation, in 1876, carrying with them the emotional and psychological baggage of the war and a decade of displacement, the Tannatts returned once more to Manchester and the security and comfort of Elizabeth's childhood home.

4. Henry Villard and Transportation in the Pacific Northwest, 1876–1882

The Interim

As Thomas and Elizabeth relocated yet again, the lingering effects of the war and two unsatisfying business experiences went with them. The Civil War claimed almost six hundred thousand lives in four short years, fourteen times the casualties of all previous American wars combined, and this, coupled with the fact that brothers had literally fought against their brothers in this war, contributed to deep and slow-healing emotional scars. Few studies have examined the war's impact on the post-conflict lives of its participants, but those that do exist indicate that many Civil War veterans encountered difficulty in making the transition from military to civilian lives.[1]

Historian Thomas Bright has suggested that after the war, soldiers were "cast adrift in a country they no longer really knew," one where "friends had grown up and . . . towns had changed" and where, compared to "the grandeur of the war, every human enterprise seemed insignificant and mundane."[2] Bright's study focuses on two Massachusetts veterans, both of whom had trouble adjusting to civilian life following the war. Arthur Carpenter, who served with the First Battalion, Nineteenth Regiment, U.S. Infantry, wrote home in the fall of 1861, "I begin to think that I have found my sphere." He remained in the army after the war, due largely to a lack of otherwise marketable skills.[3] Without battles and enemies to fight, however, and despite a successful postwar military career that, by 1869, advanced him to the rank of captain and provided him a frontier assignment at Fort Union, New Mexico, Carpenter became a social outcast. As Bright explains, "the war had done more than simply intervene in Carpenter's life, it had drastically altered it," rendering him "a patriot without a cause and a soldier with no more battles to fight."[4] As is the case with so many Civil War veterans, the final chapter of Carpenter's story remains unwritten, for in the 1870s the official record loses track of him.

John Wilder dreaded the end of the war as well, but for different reasons, and at war's end he too was "a displaced person with no place to go." Whereas Arthur Carpenter had a rural upbringing, Wilder came from an affluent Boston family, attended Union College and Harvard Law School, and belonged to the Massachusetts Bar. Wilder joined the army in February 1863 almost on a whim, but soon he realized the benefit of being a commissioned officer and became enthusiastic about both the army and the war. After making captain in June 1863, he moved quickly through the ranks and in 1865 received promotion to lieutenant colonel and judge advocate general of the Department of Florida. "I don't relish the idea of going back home as a beggar which I shall almost be," Wilder wrote at war's end in November 1865, for "I doubt if there is any opening at home either in law or business."[5] More specifically, Wilder found postwar Boston quite tame, perhaps dull, and after mustering out of the army in January 1866 he moved west, settled in Kansas City, and bought an interest in a local newspaper. Wilder's struggle with the routine and order of civilian life continued until 1870, when he was shot down on a Kansas City street by an unidentified assassin, and for reasons that remain unclear. As Bright suggests, Carpenter's and Wilder's experiences make it clear that the years of war were the most exciting and memorable in the lives of many veterans, and "afterwards, nothing could ever quite match it."[6]

Jacqueline Jones has studied New Englanders, both male and female, during the postwar era, and her findings are similar to Bright's. Her study tells the story of John Haley, who served for three years with the Seventeenth Maine and encountered difficulty reestablishing himself after the war. "Here we are, some with whole skins, and some not so whole. Others have been left behind," Haley wrote in 1865 upon returning home from the battlefield. "For myself, I can only wonder that there is a bone left in my carcass when I think of the wholesale carnage through which I have passed. *My* bruises are inward."[7] It appears that the inner bruises stayed with Haley and prevented him from finding stability after the war, for he held a number of jobs, working as a night watchman, a telegraph operator, a bookkeeper, and a reporter for the local newspapers before finally, in 1892, after more than a quarter century of wanderlust, securing a position that both suited and satisfied him, as a librarian. Jones suggests that in Haley's situation this job instability was exacerbated by the economic upheaval the war delivered to New England society as declining opportunities continued to push young men out of their hometowns and toward the West.[8]

Eric Dean, in his study on post-traumatic stress, relates the case of Robert Walsh, who traveled through a number of western states after the war. "I was a wanderer in the wild west at That time," Walsh recalled, "roaming over Colorado[,] New Mexico, Arizona, Texas, Indian Territory and Kansas" yet settling nowhere. [9] These studies make it clear that the restlessness, dissatisfaction, and wanderlust Thomas experienced were quite common among Civil War veterans as they sought ventures and opportunities that might replace the excitement and sense of "worth" which years of military service had provided.

On their return to Manchester in 1876, Thomas and Elizabeth established themselves in the Tappan house at 39 Central Street for the purpose of caring for and maintaining Eben Tappan's property. They clearly saw themselves as more than caretakers, however, and began the process of refurbishment and large-scale renovation almost before they had unpacked their bags. "Gen.

Tannatt, the present owner of the late Col. Eben Tappan's estate, is making great improvements about his premises," Manchester's *Beetle and Wedge* reported in July 1876. "The barn has been removed in the rear of the house, the shop has been moved nearly on the spot where stood the old 'Hooper House,' which now stands directly in the rear of the shop and is connected with the same."[10] Eben and Sally Tappan's estates had not been finalized in the summer of 1876, and this reference to Thomas as "owner" of their property is incorrect. As none of the Tappan children who predeceased their parents left issue, upon the death of Sally Tappan the estate was divided in four equal shares and distributed as separate property to William Henry, Sarah, Lewis, and Elizabeth. These distributions were quite significant, as Eben Tappan left a substantial estate, totaling more than forty thousand dollars in real estate, stocks, bonds, and other personal property.[11]

The issue of separate property was particularly significant in the case of Elizabeth's sister, Sarah, since shortly after the distribution of Tappan assets, she and three of her four children succumbed to the yellow fever epidemic that swept through Tennessee in 1878. Although Sarah's husband, Daniel Ames, survived her, Sarah's Tappan inheritance did not flow to him, but instead was held in trust by him for the benefit of their sole surviving child, Alice Ames.[12] It was not unusual for nineteenth-century American daughters to inherit property from their parents, both living and deceased; in fact, court records from the earliest days of colonial settlement detail bequests in wills, and other provisions made in cases of intestacy, for the benefit of children of both sexes.[13] Further, the passage of the Married Women's Property Acts, adopted first in Mississippi in 1839, in Massachusetts in 1854, and in twenty-nine additional states by 1865, gave American women relief from the English custom of coverture, the right to control both the property and inheritances they brought to a marriage and the funds and goods earned and acquired during marriage.[14] It should be noted that the effectiveness of the Married Women's Property Acts depended on the state in which a challenge to enforce them was levied and the attitude of the judge hearing the case. At the same time, the ability to bring violations of these acts to court was in most cases restricted to middle- and upper-class women with adequate means to engage legal counsel. These caveats aside, passage of the acts brought a change in attitude to nineteenth-century women, who, in securing rights to their own property, began firmly to reject the previously held notion that they, themselves, were property.[15] As will become apparent, Elizabeth took full advantage of the tenets of this legislation and held and administered her separate property interests throughout her lifetime with little assistance from, or interference by, Thomas.

Legal ownership of the Tappan property aside, it is likely that Thomas envisioned this return to Manchester and habitation of Elizabeth's family home as symbolic of the social status he worked to maintain throughout his lifetime. "The General intends making a good and commodious building, suitable for two families," the *Beetle and Wedge*'s article continued in its report on the remodeling project, and it is clear that, in 1876, Thomas anticipated remaining in Manchester and building a life for his family there.[16] Elizabeth did not make her thoughts on the return to Manchester known, but she did take full advantage of the opportunities available to women in the established New England town. Now, at thirty-eight, she thought and acted as Elizabeth Tannatt, the individual, as well as Mrs. Tannatt, the General's wife.

Thomas had been in and around Manchester since his youth and had married one of its own, so he was a familiar visitor to the town's residents, and it is clear that Manchesterites warmly embraced the Tannatts upon their return to the harbor town's comfortable confines. In May 1876, Thomas received a letter from John F. Robards, secretary of the committee finalizing arrangements for the planting of a centennial tree, requesting that he "address the gathering with a few remarks."[17] Thomas seldom refused the opportunity to deliver "a few remarks" to an assemblage, and he accepted the invitation. The ceremony took place on May 19 with the planting on the town common of a large weeping elm, donated by Elizabeth's brother Lewis. The *Beetle and Wedge* reported that the "goodly number" of citizens in attendance enjoyed the musical selections offered by the Manchester Cornet Band and listened attentively to the several speeches delivered by town dignitaries. In his remarks, Thomas expressed "his gratitude to the memory of the forefathers for the civil and religious liberty they had bequeathed to their children" and called upon those children to honor and respect the centennial tree as a symbol of America's second century.[18] Thomas no doubt enjoyed the respect afforded him by the Manchester citizenry, and during the summer of 1876 he set out to pursue any feasible business opportunity that would allow the Tannatts to remain in Manchester.

While Thomas approached the family's return to Cape Ann with optimism and enthusiasm, it must have been somewhat bittersweet for Elizabeth. She had returned home frequently in the years since her marriage in 1860, each time to a warm and happy greeting from her parents. This time, however, no such welcome awaited her as Eben and Sally rested at the "1661" graveyard under a single ornate monument near Lillie's small one. The loss of her parents, and with it the end of her obligations as a daughter, was but one of a series of changes Elizabeth experienced during what would be her last years as a Manchester resident. Her children, at ten and twelve, no longer required the time and attention they had as infants and toddlers, and Elizabeth filled her newfound leisure time with pursuits that appealed particularly to her. Surrounded by women she had known all her life and with whom she shared the commonalities of family, custom, and culture,

Elizabeth became a clubwoman and devoted a good deal of her time to the matters of benevolence and reform.

Women who had actively engaged in Civil War causes did so as members of groups, whether local, state, or national, and this club spirit intensified at war's end as women's clubs and organizations experienced rapid development and expansion. The year 1868 witnessed the founding of the first two women's clubs, Sorosis in New York and the New England Woman's Club in Boston. Close proximity to the birthplace of the women's club movement certainly encouraged female residents in Boston's outlying cities and towns to embrace the club spirit, and in many of them, including Manchester, local women established clubs of their own within the decade.[19]

Becoming organizationally involved and publicly assertive in support of the reform issues that deeply concerned them was a learned behavior for middle-class women, since most had been raised to defer to the judgments and decisions of men. A woman who stepped into the public eye could expect condescension from the population at large and patronization from members of the press. An October 1869 article in the *Hartford Courant*, for instance, described the clubwoman as a "lady in middle life with a winning, refined face . . . unaccustomed to speak in rooms larger than a parlor."[20] These attitudes impeded neither the reformers' convictions in general nor Elizabeth's in particular, however, and the October 1876 edition of the *Beetle and Wedge* reported that the members of Manchester's Woman's Union, likely a chapter of the national Woman's Christian Temperance Union (WCTU), had elected Elizabeth as their president.[21]

Temperance had been actively and vigorously sought in Cape Ann towns and villages for some time, and Elizabeth was no doubt aware of the most notorious of the region's demonstrations against alcohol, the 1856 "women's raid on rum" that occurred just a few miles north of Manchester, in Rockport. On July 8, 1856, the women of Rockport, no longer willing to accept the frequent drunkenness of many townsmen or the humility and shame it brought to families forced to endure poverty and hardship, swept through the town with axes and hatchets concealed under skirts and cloaks and destroyed vast quantities of rum and other alcoholic beverages, the locations of which they had previously identified and marked. Although charges were filed against them by shopkeepers whose stock was destroyed, in December 1859 the Massachusetts Superior Court returned a verdict in favor of Rockport's "hatchet gang."[22]

With the successes of their forebears in mind, the Manchester women of the mid-1870s worked diligently to steer the young men of the town toward pursuits more wholesome than those found at the local tavern, and in the fall of 1876, Elizabeth received a letter from fellow clubwoman Annie Fields concerning the "Boys' Evenings" activities implemented at the high school. It is apparent that the WCTU conducted an ongoing fund-raising effort to finance these alternate activities, for Fields's letter suggested that a report on the success of the Boys' Evenings be delivered to the union's general membership in Elizabeth's "own hall well heated," where the members would "be more willing to respond."[23] Fields's letter strengthens the connection between the Manchester women and the WCTU, for in it she includes passages from a letter written to the Manchester membership from noted author and reformer Elizabeth Stuart Phelps. "Remember me to the Manchester woman's Union," the quoted lines of the letter read. "Tell them I shall not forget them nor their good work."[24] Her election as president of the Manchester Woman's Union was Elizabeth's first documented foray into organizational involvement, signaling the beginning of many years dedicated to philanthropic and reform activity.

Manchester did not, however, provide the opportunity for professional distinction and success that Thomas had hoped for, and as renovations to the Tappan property continued and Elizabeth and the children became actively involved in the community, he found himself once more rethinking his life's direction and reexamining his options. Engineering skills he had gained at West Point and honed in Colorado proved unmarketable in Manchester, since the town's noted cabinetry trade did not rebound after the war, and no other industry requiring engineering expertise emerged to take its place. Neither could Thomas utilize the immigration and recruitment techniques he had practiced in Tennessee, for Cape Ann towns and villages lacked any of the enticements necessary to attract newcomers; in fact, they were losing significant numbers of permanent residents.

The fastest-growing and most lucrative "industry" in Manchester after the decline of the cabinetry trade was the "summer resident," and Richard Henry Dana, author of *Two Years before the Mast*, was the first of Manchester's "summer people." In 1845 he purchased thirty acres between the waterline and the county road and built Manchester's first summer house. The plain yet substantial mansion overlooks the sea, and the beach below it, aptly renamed "Dana's Beach," remains a private family refuge. Although Manchester's emergence as a summer retreat for the wealthy of Boston and New York was not planned, and certainly did not provide viable career opportunities for Thomas and others seeking them, the "industry" did help support Manchester at a critical time and, to its credit, "left no factory blight behind."[25]

In his history of the town of Manchester, William Henry Tappan wrote that changes of occupation in the early days amounted to no more than a shift from the sea to the land. With continued technological innovation and establishment of great industrial centers to the West, however, small tradesmen proved unable to compete and were squeezed out of business.

By as early as the mid-1840s, this Market Revolution caused members of the younger generations "to abandon . . . the homes of their ancestors and seek employment among strangers." [26] Industrial booms were not solely responsible for Manchester's decrease in population and industry, however, and in the years prior to the war the lure of gold beckoned a number of Manchester's sons, convincing them to leave families and businesses behind and join "the multitude hurrying westward" in anticipation of the riches awaiting them, first in California and later in Colorado. [27] Well aware of the sag in Manchester's economy, Thomas should not have been surprised by the lack of opportunity, particularly since all of Elizabeth's brothers had abandoned Manchester as they reached maturity: four to travel west and the other two to seek their fortunes in Boston. [28]

Enter Henry Villard

By early 1877, having accepted the fact that he could not secure suitable employment in Manchester, Thomas decided to initiate an employment dialogue with railroad magnate Henry Villard. Villard numbered among those entrepreneurs who rose to prominence in American business and industry in the post–Civil War era, and he counted as his contemporaries such men as Jay Gould, Leland Stanford, and Collis P. Huntington. Born in 1835 to a well-to-do Bavarian family, Villard left home in the early 1850s, arrived in New York in 1853, and by 1854 had made his way to Illinois and the home of relatives. During this time he gladly accepted any job made available to an immigrant with only a fair command of the English language, though his ambitions inclined toward journalism. In 1859 he secured an assignment with Cincinnati's *Daily Commercial* to travel to the Colorado gold fields and report on developments following the Pike's Peak strikes. [29] While in Colorado, Villard acquired an interest in the Golden City Association that amounted to five shares in the city, each containing four city lots. He later sold these to Elizabeth Tannatt's brother Lewis, and this relationship gave Thomas access to Villard. [30] Villard continued his journalistic pursuits after leaving Colorado and became a Civil War correspondent for the *New York Tribune*. He returned to Germany after the war to recover from malaria, and there he became acquainted with a group of investors who held significant interests in Oregon railroad bonds. These associations launched Villard's railroad career.

By the 1870s, supported by the high yields of grain and cattle produced throughout the region, Portland, Oregon, had become the commercial and trade center of the Pacific Northwest. Despite this growth in sophistication and prominence, however, the region remained isolated, since more than six hundred miles of barren deserts and heavily forested mountains separated it from San Francisco, the nearest large city. This isolation created significant problems for Oregon farmers and businessmen, not the least of which was the inability to efficiently and economically transport their surplus products to markets in the populated regions of California, the Midwest, and the East. Quite simply, the cost of shipping Willamette Valley–grown products to California, or eastern Washington wheat to the Pacific Coast via Columbia River steamships, was greater than the value of the product itself. The arrival of Villard and other outsiders allowed for the expansion of the region's steamship and railroad systems, not only providing better means by which to move products but also quickening and improving communications, encouraging immigration, and hastening the development of industrialization in the Pacific Northwest.[31] "It was in large part because of the railroads," suggests Earl Pomeroy, "that the Far West emerged from a colonial to a mature and more balanced economy," since, in addition to shipping products to points west, railroads also delivered goods that were produced in the east to western destinations.[32] Not to be overlooked were the quantities of land made available for sale by the railroad for purposes of agricultural and industrial development.

Villard became president of the Oregon and California Railroad Company and the Oregon Steamship Company in 1876. The eventual merger of these in June 1879, and the addition of the Oregon Steam Navigation Company the same year, resulted in the immediate formation of the Oregon Railway and Navigation Company (ORN). Villard's next step in amassing a transportation empire involved negotiations with Jay Gould and Sidney Dillon of the Union Pacific, wherein Villard offered a one-half interest in his endeavors in exchange for the extension of Union Pacific lines to the Northwest. Collis P. Huntington and the rest of the California "Big Four" voiced strong objection to a liaison between Villard and Union Pacific, since the proposed extension would divert business from their Central Pacific line. Gould and Dillon took the Big Four's threat to divert railroad traffic from the overland route to the new Sunset Route, through El Paso, Texas, seriously enough to withdraw from negotiations with Villard.[33] The failure to establish a partnership with the Union Pacific disappointed Villard, but it did not slow his empire-building efforts. The creation of the ORN gave him the sought-after monopoly on all shipping and railroad traffic in the Columbia River region, but his later—and secretive—purchase of the shares of Northern Pacific Railroad Company (NPRR) stock necessary to secure a controlling interest in that company proved to be his greatest coup d'état.[34]

In 1880 Villard began purchasing shares of NPRR stock. By February 1881, however, he had expended all of his personal resources and turned to friends and acquaintances for assistance in bringing the deal to completion. Known thereafter as the "Blind Pool," these individuals answered Villard's call and contributed nearly eight million dollars to a venture whose details he could not, at the time of their investment, disclose to them. In June 1881, Villard called the members of the Blind Pool together and revealed his plan: the formation of a corporation established to hold controlling interests in both the ORN and the NPRR, to be called the Oregon and Transcontinental Company. By September the transactions were completed, and Villard commenced the task of orchestrating the construction of a twenty-seven-hundred-mile-long transcontinental line.[35]

Thomas learned through Lewis Tappan of Villard's involvement with the NPRR, and on January 12, 1877, he wrote the railroad magnate. "It occurred to me you might now be in position to have some work for me in some capacity," Thomas wrote, his language making it clear that he and Villard had broached the subject of employment at some point in the past, or at least that Lewis had spoken with Villard on Thomas's behalf. Thomas communicated to Villard that it was his ambition to seek opportunity in the West, and particularly with Villard's ventures there, and added that "from correspondence with my friend Genl. Howard, I know I must confess a desire to engage in Oregon for a few years at least."[36] When Villard did not respond with the expected job offer, Thomas took another step and presented a proposal in June 1877 with terms most favorable to Villard. Thomas was convinced that the West held great business and settlement possibilities, and he felt certain that a carefully designed immigration program promoting America's western reaches would particularly appeal to northeasterners still suffering from the economic devastations of both the Civil War and the recent depression. He reminded Villard of his numerous contacts and acquaintances in the East and pledged to call upon them in order to secure their partnership and support in promoting Villard's business interests. "I could easily reach a large class of men who must forsake the crowded East and thus influence an immigration," Thomas wrote, noting, "especially will this be the case in N.Y. N.H. & Mass where I am better known both in civil & military life." Thomas revealed his innovative plan, which guaranteed a good deal of time, service, and expertise on his part and just a small capital outlay from Villard. "I will go to Oregon to learn and work and give my time & expenses to it if you think I can do enough for you to bear the transportation," he proposed, and "this done I will be prepared for the future and can then be of some use to you should you want me here, or elsewhere."[37]

Promotional efforts to draw immigrants to Oregon predated Villard by about a decade. By 1869, Portland had created a Board of Statistics, Immigration and Labor Exchange, and in 1874 the state organized a State Board of Immigration. Neither of these succeeded in establishing significant immigration programs, however, due in large part to the failure of the legislature to appropriate financing.[38] This non-action by the legislature allowed Villard and other entrepreneurs to take the lead in promotion, and population, of the Pacific Northwest.

Villard realized that acceptance of Thomas's proposal would allow him, for the cost of a single round-trip rail ticket from Boston to Oregon, to send a representative to the Pacific Northwest for the purpose of determining the most productive and efficient means of encouraging immigration to Oregon and accelerating the sale of excess railroad land. The decision was not a difficult one for Villard to make, for he agreed with the logic behind Thomas's proposal and had held the opinion, since his first visit to Oregon in 1874, that promoting and facilitating immigration was the most effective means of encouraging growth in the region.[39] As Thomas's proposal presented risk to neither Villard nor his companies, he accepted it, and within a matter of months Thomas embarked upon his first journey to the Pacific Northwest.

In September 1877, Thomas traveled to Oregon for a firsthand look at the region he was to promote and wrote Villard that his "general impressions of Oregon are favorable. The Willamette Valley and lands on West Side are far in advance of my expectations. In general your enterprises here are of greater magnitude than I had measured and if all can be held intact for a few years you will see results that will richly reward you and those you represent."[40] In addition to making a general survey of the land, Thomas acquainted himself with the wealth of products produced by both nature and farmers in Oregon, paying particular attention to the region's coal deposits. Vast quantities of coal to fuel steamships and locomotives were critical to Villard's enterprises, and Thomas inspected a number of deposits that Villard had expressed an interest in purchasing. He employed the skills and knowledge gleaned during his Colorado mining days to evaluate the deposits but was disappointed by the thinness of the coal veins. "I cannot see any encouragement to spend money on thin veins, found in out-lying hills, and dipping deep under valley," he wrote in advising Villard to forgo this particular purchase.[41] As a result, the purchase of coal deposits would be delayed for a time, though it was not abandoned by Villard and his agents.

While still functioning as agent for German bondholders in the mid-1870s, Villard had established a land office in Portland that operated under the management and supervision of land agent Paul Schulze. This preexisting arrangement precluded, at least for a time, Thomas's objective of securing a permanent position in the West. Instead, Villard appointed Thomas agent of the Oregon Steamship Company, located his offices in Boston, and assigned him the task of securing passengers to travel from Portland to points east along the Columbia River aboard the company's SS *Oregon*.[42] Villard was particularly proud of this ship, as it was the first sea- or rivercraft outfitted with electricity and "received the first dynamo ever designed and manufactured by Thomas A. Edison."[43]

Villard selected Boston as eastern headquarters of the Oregon Steamship Company for a number of reasons, among them the city's long-standing prominence as a commercial center and the presence of a large number of potential immigrants deemed as "desirable" additions to the Oregon population.[44] Returning to the East after several weeks in Oregon, Thomas established himself in his offices and enthusiastically went about his task. In November 1877 he wrote encouragingly to Villard that "matters look favorable for a good N.E. crowd on steamer" with "six families from one town, almost sure."[45] It is impossible to gauge the success of Thomas's immigration efforts, since railroad agents did not maintain precise referral records, and regular, detailed reports from Thomas to Villard on the subject have not survived. It appears, however, from the scattered referral records that do remain, that Thomas's efforts resulted in significant immigration numbers. An examination of lists of passengers traveling through Omaha, for instance, confirms that in April 1878 almost eleven hundred Oregon-bound travelers passed through the depot holding Villard-line vouchers, followed by an additional eight hundred in May, two hundred in June, and almost six hundred in September.[46]

Among the duties and tasks assigned to immigration bureau agents was the design and preparation of pamphlets and brochures made available to potential travelers at railroad stations and bureau offices, lauding the attributes of the Pacific Northwest. "Oregon will be the New England of the West," one of these proclaimed in the spring of 1878, and another, from an early 1879 publication, boasted that "Oregon will offer the same advantages as her earlier developed sister states on the western shore."[47] In addition, foreign-language newspapers across the country published similar notices and editorials in order to inform German, Norwegian, and Scandinavian immigrants of the opportunities awaiting them in Oregon.[48] Thomas became involved with the production of these pamphlets and circulars and, in order to reach large numbers of potential immigrants, worked directly with social service organizations such as the New England Association for the Relief of the Unemployed, headquartered in New Haven, Connecticut, and the Union Relief Association of Springfield, Massachusetts. "Have sent 50 pamphlets & circulars to the society at N. Haven also to society at Springfield," Thomas advised George Saxer, Villard's secretary, in November 1877, and he followed up in early December with a letter to Villard suggesting that some form of compensation be made to the directors of these societies in exchange for business referrals.[49] "I propose saying to each of gentlemen named, that, for every steerage passenger we obtain directly or indirectly through them, I will give a commission of $5.00; and 15.00 for each *Cabin* passenger," Thomas suggested.[50] It is likely that Villard agreed to compensate these individuals in some way for their services, since Thomas did not raise the issue again.

Had Villard not responded, or responded adversely, it is quite certain that Thomas would have revisited the subject in subsequent correspondence.

Villard, apparently pleased with the results of Thomas's labors, continued to add to his list of responsibilities, and by April 1878 he bestowed upon him the title of "General Eastern Passenger and Immigration Agent," though Thomas's employment with the company had been neither formalized nor made permanent. In his new role, Thomas encouraged immigration by making reduced-fare vouchers available for travel on Villard-controlled steamship and railroad lines to passengers traveling between San Francisco and Portland and from Portland to points east.[51] Thomas also arranged to have samples of grain and other products grown in Oregon on display at the various transportation agency locations, and he expressed great consternation when his requests for supplies went unanswered. "I regret that Mr. Schulze has not forwarded the grain I selected and sacked," Thomas wrote Villard in December 1877. "It is convincing in itself and many ask to see something of Oregon products."[52]

His eventual relocation to the West would alleviate some of these administrative problems, but until that time Thomas had to depend on Paul Schulze to ship selected samples to the East. It is clear that tension existed between the two men. Schulze's disregard of Thomas's requests for samples not only aggravated Thomas but proved detrimental to Villard's business, since their effectiveness in promoting interest in Oregon was proved by newspaper reports. The November 12, 1879, edition of the *Boston Journal*, for instance, noted that the city's ticket agent for the Central Vermont Railroad had "some of the cereal productions of the State of Oregon" on display and that "the gem of the collection is a stool of wheat comprising fifty-two large and full ears of wheat, the yield of a single wheat kernel."[53]

By June 1878, Thomas, now forty-five years of age, decided he had fulfilled his end of the bargain struck with Villard a year earlier and looked for reciprocation in the form of an offer of permanent employment. "When in your judgment the work of this office warrants its being considered other than experimental, I would suggest that the sale of tickets settlements, etc. East of Omaha be made East," he wrote on June 4, couching his employment desires in railroad business.[54] Villard responded favorably to Thomas's request, and by the middle of August he named him "General Eastern Agent" and relocated his offices to New York City. In addition to providing a title and company prestige more to his liking, this promotion finally formalized Thomas's employment with Villard and placed him on the payroll.

While Thomas served his apprenticeship with Villard, traveled across the country, and ran his business operations out of Boston and New York, Elizabeth and the children remained in Manchester. After nineteen years of marriage, periodic separation was nothing new to Elizabeth, and as in the past, she seems to have taken Thomas's absences in stride. Her journal, kept religiously throughout 1879, sheds light on her day-to-day activities. Thomas returned to Manchester quite regularly from his Boston and New York offices, and on a number of occasions Elizabeth and the children traveled to spend time with him in those cities and take advantage of the multitude of amenities they offered.

The year 1879 did not dawn favorably for Elizabeth, and from New Year's Day until mid-April she was so seriously ill that she did not leave home.[55] In a rare flash of emotion, she lashed out at Thomas during this period, albeit through her journal, for his unwillingness, or inability, to understand the severity of her illness. "He does not or will not realize I am sick," she wrote on January 31 after he requested that she join him in New York for the weekend.[56] A week later her condition had worsened to the point that her physician was summoned, and on February 8 he diagnosed her malady as "threatened congestion of brain."[57] Elizabeth probably suffered from a form of encephalitis, or inflammation of the brain. Encephalitis is usually caused by a viral infection, and its symptoms vary. In its mildest form, which seems to have affected Elizabeth, these include fever, headache, and loss of energy and appetite. Restlessness, drowsiness, and visual impairment can also occur, and Elizabeth suffered from all of these. When encephalitis occurs in healthy individuals it is seldom serious and most fully recover, though rehabilitation may take weeks or even months.[58] The severity of Elizabeth's illness seems to have peaked in February, and in the weeks that followed she began her slow but steady recovery. As her health improved her spirits lifted, and her anger and frustration with Thomas disappeared as the events of his business life once more took center stage in hers. "Joyful news from T. He has truly surmounted obstacles and seen trying times. I hope he will have a peaceful life now," she wrote on March 4, referring to Thomas's professional association with Villard.[59]

By late 1879, Elizabeth's journal makes it clear that she and the children were preparing to vacate the Manchester house, though no reference is made to their destination. "Mrs. Carter . . . will take house from Oct. 1 $80 per mo.," Elizabeth wrote on September 23, and two days later packing commenced in earnest as she "bro't trunks down stairs."[60] By early October the family had reunited in New York, where they remained through the holiday season. "Christmas—quiet and merry," Elizabeth wrote, no doubt appreciative that the year drew to a close more pleasantly than it had begun, "T. & children and together a happy day."[61]

Unfortunately, adversity revisited Elizabeth early in 1880, and on February 25 she confided to her journal the sad news: "Dear Lew is dead in Leadville. Poor Libbie, Sanford Wm. Terrible so hard."[62] Lewis Tappan died on February 25, 1880, at the age of forty-nine, at Leadville, Colorado. He had contracted a severe chest cold while conducting business at his mines, but his condition worsened after he witnessed a friend and business associate fall down a mine shaft to his death. The shock of the accident caused Lewis to fall into a severe depression which is said to have hastened his death.[63] Lewis's death proved to be especially difficult for Elizabeth to bear, for in the space of just five years she had lost both of her parents, her only sister, and the brother to whom she was the closest. In the light of this most recent Tappan family loss, Elizabeth may have viewed her family's upcoming relocation to the West as a welcome distraction, a means by which to put the sadness associated with these losses out of her mind, albeit temporarily.

Relocation to the West

By 1880, Thomas's expanding responsibilities with the Villard companies made it apparent that he should be based in the Pacific Northwest, and on April 1 he resigned his New York position as general eastern agent to accept a similar one in Portland.[64] The reassignment must have pleased Thomas immeasurably, for he had at last achieved his goal of securing a high-level and permanent position with Villard's companies in the West. Interest in the development and commercialization of the American West did not wane during the latter decades of the nineteenth century; in fact, with the war long since concluded and conflicts with Indians all but eliminated, travelers made their way west for every reason imaginable. Included among these were distinguished easterners who journeyed westward to observe for themselves Oregon's natural wealth and abundance. Thomas's business obligations included acting as host to these guests, but since many of them were acquaintances and colleagues from his army days, the sightseeing tours he conducted often became reunions. "Have just returned from a visit to the Bank Coloma with President Hayes," he wrote Elizabeth from Portland in October 1880, adding that "Gnls. Sherman & McCook are with the party." The First Lady traveled with the company as well, and Thomas was quite taken with Lucy Hayes, a woman he described as "a nice matronly woman full of sunshine."[65]

The number of immigrants moving into Oregon and Washington Territory continued to increase in the 1880s, and the documentation makes it quite clear that the Villard companies—their immigration agents in particular—had taken the business of promotion and recruitment to a higher level than was practiced by any other railroad company. "The good fortune of Oregon flows from the source of all good luck—hard indefatigable labor," the *San Francisco Chronicle* reported on November 7, 1881, hastening to add, "it is not the blindness of the immigrants to the natural attractions of California, but the industry of Oregon agents that robs us of the laboring thousands."[66]

Less than a week later, the *Portland Oregonian* reported that a representative of the *San Francisco Post* had conducted interviews with immigrants on a westward-bound train and learned, to his surprise, that most were destined for Oregon and Washington. One passenger explained the lack of immigrants bound for California:

> Your people have few or no agents east to offer inducements to immigrants. You keep your state entirely in the dark. If you have lands here that can be secured by immigrants we do not know it. We have never heard of land in California that could be obtained at reasonable rates and on favorable terms. Common report has it that all your valuable lands are held by capitalists, who offer no inducements whatever to settlers. With Oregon and Washington the case is different. The territory of Washington, I know, is today more thoroughly advertised east by agents, pamphlets, etc., than any other section of the country.[67]

It must be noted that while Villard's agents may have provided immigrants with misleading information on occasion,[68] their goal was to present a clear and accurate picture of the conditions that awaited these newcomers in the Pacific Northwest. The vehicle by which they accomplished that goal was the publication, in 1882, of an eighty-eight-page booklet entitled *The Pacific Northwest.* "Persons beyond the active years of life, and without that adaptability to circumstances belonging to them, will also run considerable risk in emigrating," the booklet warned, advising that "to such, old communities usually afford better opportunities for self-support than new ones." The booklet suggested that those considering the relocation of families "should carefully weigh the possible consequences of emigration, both to themselves and to those whose future will be fashioned by their own." It broached the economic issues involved in relocation and advised that "no one should think of emigrating without sufficient means for self-support for at least a short time after reaching his destination," recommending that "families who contemplate settling on lands will require, after providing for all traveling expenses, above five hundred dollars with which to meet the cost of putting up a house, for live-stock, seed, farming utensils, provisions, etc."[69] In late 1881 or 1882, Thomas and C. H. Prescott, general manager of the Portland offices of the Oregon Improvement Company (OIC), collaborated on the production and publication of their own pamphlet, providing would-be immigrants with information on temperature and rainfall, costs and expenses incurred in crop production, distances and fares to various destinations in the Pacific Northwest from the nation's primary departure points, and letters of endorsement from "intelligent and disinterested observers" on the advantages of immigration to the West.[70]

Warnings and advisories set forth in these pamphlets dissuaded few immigrants, and as they moved into the region in greater numbers the need for infrastructure in the settlement areas became apparent. Villard organized the OIC in 1878 and patterned it after the National Land Company, which had earlier facilitated the colonization of Kansas Pacific Railroad lands.[71] The OIC immediately began to acquire key properties such as the Seattle Coal and Transportation Company, the Seattle and Walla Walla Railroad, and 150,000 acres of prime agricultural land in eastern Washington Territory's Palouse region. Villard finalized purchase of the Seattle and Walla Walla Railroad in October 1880, and Thomas traveled to Seattle to take possession of the company, inspect its real estate and physical assets, and discuss proposed modifications and improvements. At the same time, Villard financed a transcontinental survey, designed to unequivocally determine which lands, under the national land grants, belonged to his recent purchase and to locate any assets on, in, or under those tracts. In particular, the survey looked for coal deposits crucial to operation of Villard-owned steamships and trains. Between 1881 and 1884, survey engineers discovered valuable coal deposits in the Green River area, including the rich McKay vein at the Green River Gorge.[72]

Employees of the OIC cleared, fenced, and platted its newly acquired eastern Washington lands into townships equipped with boardinghouses, blacksmith shops, toolsheds, cottages, and outbuildings. In Endicott, for instance, company crews constructed a store with a large hall attached, to be used for public meetings and worship services. In Prescott they built six houses for railway employees and a lumberyard and depot, and throughout the region these workers performed the grading work that, according to a local newspaper, "save[d] the settlers in that region thousands of dollars."[73] The company then offered the parcels for sale to immigrants the transportation companies brought to the region. Villard located the OIC's regional office in charge of these properties at Walla Walla, appointed Thomas its general agent, and on October 21, 1880, incorporated the company for the purpose "of cooperating with the Oregon Railway & Navigation Company in the material development of the state of Oregon, the territory of Washington, and the North Pacific country generally."[74]

Walla Walla was the largest and most dynamic city in Washington Territory when Thomas arrived there in 1880, surpassing both Seattle and Spokane Falls in population and commerce. In 1881, Frank Parker, editor of the *Walla Walla Statesman*, proclaimed the city the "*entrepot* of the whole surrounding country," which "from a mere block of shanties of a few short years since, has grown in wealth and importance," second only to Portland.[75] Walla Walla grew up around Fort Walla Walla, established by Col. Edward J. Steptoe and constructed in 1856, and by the time the Tannatts arrived there it was touted as the region's major cultural center and boasted several large churches, an opera house, and a symphony orchestra.[76]

The recruitment, relocation, and settlement of German Russian families from a number of Midwest locations to eastern Washington's Palouse was among the largest and most impressive of the OIC's projects, and Thomas played a critical role in the process. The national distinction "German Russian" originated in 1763, when Empress Catherine the Great of Russia, a German by birth, invited indebted German farmers to settle in Russia's largely unsettled Black Sea and Volga regions in order to populate and transform them into profitable agricultural communities. Catherine enticed her fellow Germans by issuing manifestos that allowed them to practice their own religion, provided financial assistance for travel and purchase of land, and offered relief from Russian taxation and the obligation to serve in the Russian military. Tens of thousands of Germans took advantage of this opportunity, and for the next century they flourished in their adopted Russian villages, though always remaining German in culture, language, and custom. In 1871, Czar Nicholas II dissolved the privileges Catherine had granted the German immigrants, instituted a new and vigorous tax structure, and demanded service by German Russian males in the Russian army. By late 1875, with Nicholas's taxes and draft notices in full force and effect, many German Russians began leaving the Black Sea and Volga regions, settling throughout the Western Hemisphere, most in the United States, and particularly in the agricultural states of North Dakota, Kansas, Nebraska, Colorado, and Washington.[77]

As early as 1880, the spokesmen for several German Russian community groups responded to OIC brochures and circulars and expressed a desire to see "the Territory we have heard so much of its great yielding wheat fields and wonderful Fruit Country." The immigration of a large number of individuals seemed guaranteed, and, the letter continued, "I think we can locate 230 families there this fall and winter."[78] To further encourage the immigration of this large group, Thomas promised the men temporary employment as laborers for the Oregon Railway and Navigation Company. The guarantee of an income during the bleak and nonproductive winter months, and until farming could commence the spring following their arrival, alleviated one of Thomas's greatest obstacles in convincing extended families to immigrate to eastern Washington.[79]

"There is to be an exodus from Kansas this fall," Walla Walla's *Weekly Statesman* reported in September 1882 as Thomas's negotiations with Phillip Green, agent for the Kansas colony of German Russians, concluded.[80] By mid-October several German Russian family groups had arrived in Walla Walla, where they purchased building materials and household goods before moving to their homesteads. "This organized method of handling immigrants is doing much for the Palouse Country," the *Weekly Statesman* declared. "The ample capital of the O.I. [Oregon Improvement] Co. and their simple method of dealing promptly with new comers, upon an easily understood plan, is most proper."[81] German Russians represented the largest immigrant group in eastern Washington at the end of the nineteenth century, and by 1920 more than eleven thousand first- and second-generation German Russians resided in Washington, the majority situated on farms purchased from Thomas Tannatt and the OIC near the towns of Endicott, Prescott, and Colfax.[82]

Attracting and settling immigrants was but one of Thomas's many duties as agent of the OIC, and he seems to have thrived under the pressure and responsibility. The company established a number of settlements along its affiliated rail lines, with towns such as Endicott and Pullman named for Villard-company investors and business partners William J. Endicott and George Pullman. The birth of a new township did not always proceed smoothly and without incident on the Palouse, however, and community rivalry and jealousy often ensued. In the early 1880s Thomas established the township of Plainville, located approximately three miles west of Colfax "and at the intersection of county roads from Colfax, Rebel Flat, Almota and Penewawa."[83] Colfax businessmen quietly opposed the development of a new town complete with business district so close to their own, and these feelings intensified when local newspapers declared that Plainville "presents much better advantages for a large place than Colfax" and predicted it would be "a successful rival of that city." Thomas's treatment of this potentially hostile situation both displayed his sensitivity to the issues and served as confirmation that Villard had selected the right man for the job in eastern Washington. In order to soothe the people of Colfax and assure them that neighboring townships could be beneficial, Thomas announced that the OIC would give interested individuals holding both residential and business lots in Colfax corresponding lots in Plainville, though he hoped to entice the majority of Plainville's new merchants and businessmen from Walla Walla and Portland.[84] These efforts seemed to satisfy Colfax's leaders, and the establishment of neighboring townships continued without incident.

The obligations associated with Thomas's position with the OIC proved very demanding. Newcomers and established townspeople alike depended on Thomas to see to the efficient operation of the region's infrastructure, and countless citizens made demands on his personal time. Judging from the documentation that has survived, nothing could have pleased Thomas more. It is clear that he worked diligently to earn the respect and confidence of those with whom he associated, and based on numerous local newspaper articles extolling his virtues, he succeeded in these endeavors. "Wherever else his business as general agent of the Oregon Improvement Company has brought him in contact with our people, he has shown a sterling sense of business integrity and has conducted the affairs of the company with marked skill," read an early 1880s Dayton, Washington, article.[85] In Thomas's adopted hometown of Walla Walla, the *Weekly Statesman* observed that "in the selection of General T. R. Tannatt to represent the interests of the O.I. Company, we believe the managers of that corporation have the right man in the right place. . . . If Walla Walla had a few more like the General, we believe the city would be further advanced in the way of improvement a hundred fold."[86]

Thomas's association with Villard and his permanent relocation to the Pacific Northwest finally filled the void left by his resignation from the army more than fifteen years earlier. In Villard, Thomas found an employer who took an active and hands-on interest in his business and provided his management team with the funds and leverage they needed to successfully accomplish their tasks, qualities he had found sorely lacking in Colorado. At the same time, Thomas began to flourish personally in the Pacific Northwest. Rather than depending on his Tappan connections to provide opportunities and open doors, Thomas parlayed his own accomplishments, capabilities, and community involvement into the role of distinguished citizen and community builder.

Elizabeth, Eben, and Minnie—the children now seventeen and fifteen years of age, respectively—joined Thomas in Walla Walla in 1881. As they settled into their new life in the West, Elizabeth resumed the reform and benevolence endeavors she had begun in Manchester, actively engaging in transplanting cultural and organizational aspects of the East to her adopted western home. For the first time after twenty years of marriage, Thomas and Elizabeth felt at home. In the years to come they would devote themselves wholeheartedly to the development of eastern Washington, the adopted homeland they came to love and cherish.

5. Inland Empire "Pioneers," 1880–1890

Civil War Soldiers in the Pacific Northwest

The decades following the Civil War proved disruptive on a number of fronts to those who had fought its battles. While many were plagued throughout their lifetime by the physical wounds of war, others undertook a seemingly endless quest in search of personal and professional opportunity that might provide the excitement, fulfillment, and sense of worth they had experienced while in uniform. At war's end, Federals and Confederates alike returned to towns and cities suffering the many devastations of war, and as once-prosperous businesses closed and permanently barred their doors, veterans with limited funds found themselves with neither livelihood nor the means necessary to relocate and begin again. Only those with healthy economic resources could abandon the East and South and seek opportunity elsewhere. As Thomas Tannatt made acquaintances in the West he encountered a number of middle-class Union army veterans who shared not only aspects of his upbringing and military experience but also his belief that the frontier of eastern Washington Territory could provide that which they desired: "a town to grow with" and achievement won "through competition, self-expression, and control of their environment."[1]

Born a decade after Thomas in 1843, William Inman spent his youth in Missouri and in December 1861 enlisted to fight for the Union with Col. John S. Phelps's Six-month Infantry Regiment, part of the Missouri Volunteer Infantry.[2] When that unit mustered out in the spring of 1862, Inman re-enlisted with the Eighth Missouri Volunteer Cavalry, making captain in 1863. He participated in a number of significant trans-Mississippi battles, including Pea Ridge, Prairie Grove, and the capture of Little Rock, Arkansas. In October 1864, prior to war's end, Inman resigned his commission, retired from the army, and took up residence in Arkansas. For the next three years he served as that state's superintendent of the Bureau of Refugees, Freedmen, and Abandoned Lands, established by Congress in March 1865 to offer relief to those displaced by the war.[3] During his tenure with the Freedmen's Bureau, Inman read the law and by 1867 held a license to practice in Arkansas. By 1879, however, he had wearied of the South and, abandoning his law practice, traveled west, settling in Colfax, eastern Washington Territory. His specific reasons for relocating are unknown, but in terms of furthering his career as an attorney interested in land law and establishing himself as a community leader, burgeoning eastern Washington Territory and Colfax made perfect sense. In 1879 rail lines were being laid in abundance, and the number of immigrants moving into the region far exceeded those locating along the

Pacific coast. As Inman settled into his new environs, he did so less than one hundred miles north of Walla Walla, and just ten months prior to Thomas's appointment as general agent of the Oregon Improvement Company.[4]

William Farrand Prosser, another of Thomas's contemporaries and just six months his junior, hailed from Lycoming County, Pennsylvania. At twenty, Prosser traveled to the goldfields of northern California and mined there until 1858 when he joined the Trinity Rangers, a local militia group charged with putting down Indian "uprisings." With the eruption of sectional hostilities in 1861, Prosser returned east, enlisted with Pennsylvania's Anderson Cavalry Troop, and saw action at the Battle of Shiloh in the spring of 1862.[5] He became a wartime statistic when Confederate cavalry captured him near Lawrenceburg, Tennessee, in June 1862. He remained a prisoner of war until September, when he was turned over to representatives of the Union army in exchange for Confederate prisoners. Prosser subsequently served with the Fifteenth Pennsylvania Cavalry and the Second Tennessee Cavalry, receiving a commission as major in the spring of 1863. After mustering out of the army in July 1865, Prosser remained in Tennessee and engaged in a number of enterprises, including farming and politics.[6] It is likely that he and Thomas became acquainted in the late 1860s while both resided in Tennessee. Thomas's home in McMinnville lay just seventy miles southeast of Prosser's in Nashville, and Thomas, as a manager of the Tennessee Immigration Association, had cause to meet with both state and local officials.

Prosser served as a member of the Tennessee legislature in 1867 and 1868 and as U.S. congressman from Tennessee in 1869 and 1870. In 1879, however, "owing to continued and increasing ill health, contracted during the war," he divested himself of his southern interests and obligations and finalized plans for a permanent return to the West.[7] Prosser secured a position as special land agent for the federal government's General Land Office, responsible for the exploration and survey of lands held and acquired by the United States and for the distribution of these lands to settlers.[8] He established a homestead in Washington Territory's Yakima Valley in 1882, approximately eighty miles west of Walla Walla, and incorporated it as the town of Prosser in 1890.[9] Prosser did not marry until 1880, after his relocation to the West, and Elizabeth's 1882 journal and correspondence with him confirm that the families did socialize in Walla Walla. Elizabeth noted in May 1882, for instance, that her callers included "Col. Prosser's wife and baby," namely, Flora and the eldest of the couple's three children, William. In December of that year, Prosser responded to Elizabeth's recent correspondence "with kind regards to the General."[10]

Thomas Tannatt, William Inman, William Prosser, and others of the middle class who transplanted themselves into the eastern Washington frontier in the late nineteenth century caused the post–Civil War migration to develop differently from those that had preceded it. Unlike earlier migrations, which had been made up largely of agriculturalists, merchants, and fortune seekers, this one included middle-class families who were eager to re-create in the West the familiar trappings of antebellum commerce and society that they had known in the East. As a result, these pioneers took different issues and circumstances into consideration when selecting their final destinations, for while frontier communities might easily support more than one saloon, dressmaker, or general store, it was unlikely that large numbers of leaders and community builders could amicably and effectively reside within a town's limited confines. As John Fahey has suggested, men such as Tannatt, Inman, Prosser, and others scattered throughout the eastern Washington frontier sought a town "to grow with." Staunch Republicans to a man, they actively engaged in frontier politics and civic organizations during both the territorial period and after Washington attained statehood in 1889. Inman served Colfax as probate judge, city clerk, and director and clerk of the schools. He was Whitman County's prosecuting attorney and held memberships in the Independent Order of Odd Fellows and the Grand Army of the Republic. Prosser acted as auditor for Yakima County and as mayor of the city of Yakima, and he was selected to represent Yakima and Klickitat counties at the Washington's Constitutional Convention in 1889. Prosser also held memberships in a number of fraternal and military organizations, among them the Military Order of the Loyal Legion and the Grand Army of the Republic.[11] Thomas's political and organizational affiliations closely mirrored those of Inman and Prosser and will be discussed below.

Perhaps the most meaningful of the affiliations and experiences these men shared were their memberships in the Grand Army of the Republic (GAR) and the Military Order of the Loyal Legion, organizations created specifically for Union army veterans. The GAR was organized in April 1866 at Decatur, Illinois, largely to call attention to the unmet economic and medical needs of Union army veterans and their families. Chapters soon sprang up across the country, and in addition to the organization's work in benevolence and reform, it provided veterans a means of maintaining and fostering acquaintances made on the battlefield. Membership in the GAR was limited to honorably discharged Union veterans with service dates between April 12, 1861, and April 9, 1865, and by the 1890s membership surpassed four hundred thousand. Among its relief efforts, the GAR founded a number of soldiers' homes and played an active role in the fight for federal pension legislation. In 1868, national commander-in-chief John A. Logan issued General Order no. 11, designating May 30 as a day of remembrance for those lost in battle—a day that continues to be celebrated as Memorial Day in the United States. Indianapolis hosted the final GAR encampment in 1949, and its last surviving member, Albert Woolson, died in 1956, at 109 years of age.[12]

The Military Order of the Loyal Legion was organized shortly after Abraham Lincoln's assassination on April 15, 1865, amid rumors that his death was but the first in a planned series of assassinations of high-ranking government officials and part of a conspiracy to destroy the American government. Union army officers, both active and retired, joined forces in order to deter future threats against the federal government. The first official meeting was held on May 31, 1865, and by 1899 more than eight thousand Civil War veterans—the "Original Companions"—held membership in the Loyal Legion, including Thomas Tannatt and William Prosser.[13]

General Tannatt: Mayor of Walla Walla

"Up to and including 1880 the country had a frontier of settlement, but at present the unsettled area has been so broken into by isolated bodies of settlement that there can hardly be said to be a frontier line," declared the superintendent of the United States Census in 1890. Consequently, "in the discussion of its extent, its westward movement, etc., it can not, therefore, any longer have a place in the census reports."[14] Despite this official "closure" of the frontier, however, the concept of "frontier" as a defining aspect of America, and Americans, has not been so easily dismissed. In his work on the establishment of Jacksonville, Illinois, in the early nineteenth century, Don Harrison Doyle defined "frontier" as "that period when the first generation of town boosters fought to seize a leading place in an open, rapidly developing, and as yet unfixed region."[15] Doyle further suggests that "for every Chicago, St. Louis, or even Springfield, there were hundreds of Jacksonvilles whose ambitions for urban prominence were betrayed by the conspiracies of nature, politics, and fate."[16] Walla Walla was one of these Jacksonvilles.

In August 1860 the discovery of gold at Oro Fino Creek, east of Walla Walla on the Clearwater River, triggered the gold rush that transformed Walla Walla from an obscure frontier outpost into the largest city in Washington Territory, with a population of almost fourteen hundred by 1870. Centrally located at the intersection of the Oregon Trail and the Mullan Road, approximately thirty miles east of the confluence of the Columbia and Snake River waterways that provided access to and from the region prior to the railroads, Walla Walla merchants equipped pack trains en route to the mining camps and provided services and supplies to miners and others enjoying the amenities the burgeoning community had to offer. The temporary decline created by the mining slowdown in the late 1860s was righted in the early 1870s as an influx of farmers descended upon eastern Washington, and Walla Walla acted not only as a trade and supply station for these immigrants but as the central milling station for the crops they produced.[17]

In 1880 Walla Walla was the largest and most dynamic city in Washington Territory, eclipsing both Seattle and Spokane Falls in terms of population and industry. An 1879 publication touted it as "justly considered the garden valley of Eastern Oregon and Washington; embracing, as it does, the beautiful and rolling prairie contained within the boundaries of the Snake river on the north and east, the Blue mountains on the east and south, and the Columbia river on the west."[18] By the mid-1880s, as the Northern Pacific Railroad's trunk lines bypassed Walla Walla, the town's prominence began to diminish and the center of trade shifted north toward Spokane Falls. For a few years, however, before Walla Walla's star faded, it was Thomas Tannatt's Chicago.

The citizens of Walla Walla and environs held Thomas in high regard for his successful management of the Oregon Improvement Company, and they showed their confidence in his capabilities by placing his name on the mayoral ballot in the summer of 1883. Longtime Walla Walla resident James McAuliffe had held the largely honorary office of mayor since 1878, and the *Daily Statesman* lauded both McAuliffe and his years of service as a "credit to himself and the city," despite growing opinion throughout the region that "an infusion of new blood would be advantageous to its [Walla Walla's] welfare."[19] That this paper did not support Thomas's bid for mayor comes as no surprise, for the *Statesman* served as Walla Walla's Democratic paper. It had strongly supported Andrew Johnson during his impeachment hearing, and according to one history of the region, "it is said by some that its [the *Statesman's*] attainment of the place of United States official paper in the territory was due to that support."[20] The *Walla Walla Union*, on the other hand, began publication in 1868, and as "the uncompromising radical republican organ and . . . natural counterpart of the Statesman," it strongly supported Thomas both in his bid for mayor and during his term of office.[21] The *Union's* post-election coverage reported that "there is not the least doubt in our mind that General Tannatt will make a capable, active, painstaking, liberal-minded, public-spirited Mayor; that he will prove an official who will take pride in his position and of whom the citizens will be proud." The paper continued its praise by stating that "under his administration we expect to see Walla Walla become noted for its enterprise and hospitality."[22]

Thomas won the mayoral election, earning 58 percent of the popular vote, and on July 27, 1883, he presented his inaugural message. That he favored progress came as no surprise, since the goals of progress and improvement for Walla Walla numbered among those things that had placed him on the ballot in the first place. "In entering upon my duties as your executive officer, I am not unmindful of the difficulties which surround a new and untried field of labor," he began. "It will be my earnest and conscientious endeavor to discharge those several duties in full compliance with the expressed and implied requirements of my oath of office." He followed with a discussion of what he perceived to be his potential shortcomings and remarked that "a life of action has its tendencies towards unfitting one for that deliberation in thought which should ever precede *executive* decision." Thomas was referring to his military career here, but perhaps also to some of his civilian business enterprises that allowed him to carry out operations quite independently, due to the great distances that separated his field offices from corporate headquarters. He followed this admission with a humble request for the tolerance of the townspeople as he learned the lessons of his office. "May I therefore ask of you gentlemen, fellow laborers for the good of our city; some leniency, if at any time, I seem carried beyond the limited powers of my office, in my great desire to see our city progress and improve."[23] It is likely that with this message Thomas strengthened the resolve of his supporters, and perhaps added to their numbers.

Thomas followed these introductory remarks with a detailed discussion of his plans for the improvement and growth of Walla Walla. Here he paid particular attention to the subject of education, which he found woefully lacking in the town. Burton Bledstein has written on the importance of higher education to members of the nineteenth-century middle class, suggesting that "no institution would . . . be more important, more primary for the success of Mid-Victorian social values," than higher education, as "it leveled the society upward—vertically." Bledstein has further stated that in the nineteenth century "it became the function of the schools in America to legitimize the authority of the middle class."[24] Thomas, in keeping with these middle-class values he hoped to transplant in eastern Washington, viewed higher education as integral to the building of viable and respectable communities. Since his arrival in 1880 he had been disturbed by the paucity of educational institutions to prepare local students for college and university study, and in the spring of 1882 he wrote a letter to the editor of one of the local papers in which he called upon the citizenry to dedicate themselves to improvement of the school system. "Walla Walla with her wealth, business prestige and home culture, is to-day far behind Dayton, Weston and many smaller places in everything that marks the school house of our generation," Thomas wrote. He urged that as "the school house is the great assimulator [*sic*] of nationalities, creeds, and local differences," Walla Walla's citizens, "knowing our city, full of faith in its advantages and true to ourselves and future generations," should "vote liberally for a school building."[25]

The Tannatts were personally interested and invested in the educational opportunities available in Walla Walla, since their children, at fourteen and sixteen in 1880, were moving quickly beyond the curricula offered at any school in the Inland Empire, the region comprising eastern Washington Territory, the panhandle of Idaho Territory, and northeastern Oregon. During the 1881–82 academic year, in fact, Eben attended the Wascow Independent

Academy at The Dalles, Oregon, approximately 150 miles west of Walla Walla on the Columbia River. Elizabeth visited him in January 1882, and it appears both mother and son were unhappy with Eben's living situation. Elizabeth immediately arranged for more appropriate accommodations and noted in her journal, "Let E. change rooms to Mrs. Adams; and take meals at Mr. Cooper's. Mrs. W [Eben's original boardinghouse] is too busy and it is too mixed a boarding house for school boys." [26] By "mixed" Elizabeth likely referred to the variety in occupational and class standing of Mrs. W's boarders. Mrs. Adams, at least where Elizabeth was concerned, attracted and served a more appropriate, middle-class clientele. Daughter Minnie did attend Walla Walla schools in the early 1880s, and Elizabeth's frequent references to the institution in her journal suggest that Minnie attended St. Paul's School, for girls, established in 1872 by Rev. Lemuel H. Wells, an Episcopalian missionary. [27]

The issue of taxation for the benefit of building additional, advanced schools had not been rectified by the time of Thomas's mayoral inauguration, and he used the opportunity of his address to revisit the subject, making education an important part of his agenda. "The brilliant point on the sphere of taxation is the Public School. It stands casting the rays of intelligence to all classes, guiding them from the wrong, into the paths of right that will carry our future citizens apart from our jails, courts, work houses, correction institutions." He finished with a flourish, stating that "the tax paid by both rich and poor in support of our schools is returned one hundred fold." Thomas appealed to the full constituency of Walla Walla here, recognizing that only with the support of voters across all class and economic lines would his educational goals for the town be realized. His plea for support did garner some early success, and just two weeks after publication of his inaugural address the school district adopted an aggressive building plan calling for a tax levy of seventeen thousand dollars to be used for the construction of a large school building. No secondary school would be built in Walla Walla, however, until 1889. [28] As mayor of Walla Walla, however, Thomas had finally "arrived."

Thomas proved himself to be a dedicated and hardworking mayor, though perhaps not as influential with Henry Villard and the railroads as his constituents had hoped. Attempts had been made to bring a railroad to Walla Walla since the early 1860s, when agricultural production began to exceed local consumption. Most of this surplus grain, destined for world markets, had to be hauled from Walla Walla to the Wallula landing on the Columbia River, thirty miles to the west, and then shipped down the Columbia to Portland, where it was reloaded onto ships that delivered it to Liverpool and other European distribution centers. As the yield increased, transportation from Walla Walla to Wallula became costly and time consuming. In 1868, thirty local residents, led by Dr. D. S. Baker, who had earlier donated land for the city's first public school, formed the Walla Walla and Columbia River Railroad (WWCR). Shortages of capital and geographic challenges plagued the WWCR and delayed construction until 1872, but three years later the thirty-mile track to Wallula was completed, and the first Walla Walla–bound train arrived at the town's new depot on October 23, 1875. The WWCR enjoyed great success, until it overburdened the capabilities of the Oregon Steam Navigation Company. Baker envisioned extending the WWCR from Wallula to Portland, bypassing the river and the OSN altogether, and considered spearheading the enterprise himself. He found it more prudent, however, to sell the WWCR to the OSN, retaining one-seventh of the stock and the presidency of the company. Villard acquired Baker's remaining interest in 1879, purchased the OSN, and formed the Oregon Railway and Navigation Company. Villard relaid the main line of the WWCR to standard gauge in the spring of 1881, and the line became an integral part of the ORN's operations south of the Snake River.[29]

The Northern Pacific Railroad achieved transcontinental status in 1883, connecting Seattle with St. Paul, Minnesota, and points east. Its main trunk line moved southeast from Seattle to the confluence of the Columbia and Snake rivers at Wallula but then diverted northeast and established a primary railhead at Spokane Falls, in the process bypassing Walla Walla completely.[30] As had become customary with the other transcontinental railroad lines, the NPRR celebrated its completion with a "golden spike" ceremony, on September 8, 1883, at Gold Creek, Montana. Five trains carried three thousand invited guests to the ceremony, including former president Ulysses S. Grant, members of Pres. Chester Arthur's administration, and numerous foreign dignitaries. After a series of short speeches and remarks, workers from the rival railroad crews engaged in a "race" to lay the final twelve hundred feet of track, a task they accomplished in just thirteen minutes. Finally, and with much pomp and circumstance, Villard drove the gold spike and pronounced the NPRR officially complete.[31]

Following the ceremony, Villard and a number of the assembled dignitaries embarked upon a grand tour of the region served by the railroad, and as a result of the Tannatt-Villard relationship the party scheduled a stop in Walla Walla. The "City Council unanimously invited yourself and party to visit our city," Thomas wired Villard in August 1883, adding that "full warehouses will show the value of your lines to Walla Walla valley." Villard responded favorably with "sincere thanks for your kind offer of hospitality" and informed Thomas that the party would arrive in the city on September 17 upon their return from Portland.[32] The unanimous vote by the city council to appropriate five hundred dollars for Villard's visit should not be interpreted to mean that the citizens of Walla Walla wholeheartedly agreed with the allocation of these assets, for numerous members of the community continued to resent Villard's decision to bypass their city, a sentiment heightened by recent railroad and steamship rate increases that discriminated against Walla Walla shippers.

As the date of the visit neared, the local press urged townspeople to "Wake up! Decorate! Be sociable; for this is the chance to advertise our beautiful city and wonderful country to the entire world." Prominent community members spoke out in order to rally the support of the citizens and make them recognize the benefits of Villard's visit.[33] Among these was Judge N. J. Caton, a staunch supporter of Thomas's, who advised the townspeople that "Walla Walla had a chance to come out now or never" and that "the time had come for the people to get out of their lethargy and do all things possible to make this a thriving city, as they can, if they wish."[34] Elizabeth and a number of other ladies of Walla Walla, including "Mrs. Sewell Truax, Mrs. Lieutenant Miller, Mrs. Colonel Blake and Mrs. D. W. Small," entered into the spirit of the occasion, gathering to fill "small satin sacks with wheat and sewing them up in imitation of sacks of grain." The ladies prepared more than three hundred of these, each inscribed "Souvenir, Walla Walla, 1883" and "intended for presentation to the members of the gold spike party."[35]

The media blitz seems to have been effective, and Villard's visit was declared a success. The party, detained by inclement weather, arrived in town early on the morning of September 18 and included naturalist John Muir and William Lloyd Garrison Jr., son of the noted abolitionist and Villard's brother-in-law.[36] Scheduled activities included a tour of Walla Walla, a visit to depots where "piles of wheat" awaited shipment to points west, and meetings with members of the board of trade and the Oregon Improvement Company. More important than sightseeing and meetings, however, Villard's visit to Walla Walla, far from his newly completed railroad but central to his Inland Empire enterprises, demonstrated the high regard with which he held Thomas and served to validate Thomas's role in Walla Walla as a leader and community builder.

Temperance and Reform in Washington Territory

Thomas's duties as general agent of the Oregon Improvement Company, coupled with his responsibilities as mayor, consumed most of his time and attention and left Elizabeth and the children largely to their own devices after their arrival in Walla Walla in 1881. The young community that greeted them had just begun the maturation process from small town to busy commercial center, and quite unlike the New England home Elizabeth had left behind, the few women's organizations in place in Walla Walla operated informally, without national affiliation. This scarcity of organizational development did not discourage Walla Walla's transplanted middle-class female population, however, which welcomed the opportunity to reconstruct the aspects of eastern life absent from their frontier communities through volunteerism and the establishment of local clubs and societies.[37]

By the late 1870s, with its newfound prominence as a trade and commercial center, Walla Walla boasted several fine hotels, and prior to establishing their permanent residence in the city the Tannatts resided in one of these.[38] Elizabeth seemed satisfied with their accommodations, and in February 1882, while receiving two visitors, Miss Johnson and Mrs. Wingard, she expressed pleasure that the noise from the charity event taking place in the hotel's ballroom was not audible in her suite.[39] During her hotel stay, Elizabeth used time she would have spent managing a household to become acquainted with her new surroundings. She took walks to become familiar with the layout of the town and introduced herself to local shopkeepers as she patronized their establishments. This is not to suggest that Elizabeth particularly enjoyed hotel life, however, for her journal entries make it clear that she had grown weary of the family's constant movement and relocation. "Oh for a quiet pleasant home that I can feel is ours," she wrote in January 1882, "one from which I have not constantly to move from."[40] Elizabeth developed friendships with several of Walla Walla's leading female residents during these early months, and these associations ultimately resulted in the organization of a number of benevolent societies and women's clubs, all of which succeeded in establishing eastern middle-class values, ideals, and mores in the Inland Empire.

Thomas, Elizabeth, and the children moved into their Walla Walla home in the late spring of 1882, and in a flurry of journal entries Elizabeth recounted her trials and tribulations in hiring and retaining suitable domestic help. In a departure from the eastern norm, and due to the paucity of women on the frontier willing to engage in domestic service outside their own homes, Chinese men made up a large part of the domestic applicant pool in late-nineteenth-century Walla Walla. From the earliest days of railroad construction in the West, rail companies recruited tens of thousands of Chinese men to lay the lines. During lulls in construction caused by weather and economic downturns, and at the completion of railroad projects, these Chinese workers made their way to the mining frontier, some to test their mining skills and others to establish businesses in both the camps and the region's burgeoning towns. As had been the case with fortune seekers on the Colorado mining frontier, many Chinese men who traveled to Rocky Mountain mining camps as potential miners soon discovered that a multitude of opportunities awaited them. In his study on the Chinese in Idaho's Boise Basin mining region, Liping Zhu has shown that by 1880 Chinese engaged in twenty-eight separate occupations, only one of which was mining. They adapted their agricultural knowledge to the short growing seasons of the Rocky Mountain region and became gardeners, then sold fresh produce door-to-door in the camps. Many later established stores and competed with white rivals, drawing customers to markets with fully stocked shelves and "China goods" such as rice and firecrackers. In China, as in the United States, women performed most domestic tasks, but on the mining frontiers Chinese men realized that these could reap a far greater profit than laboring in the mines. As a result, many Chinese men owned and operated laundries, once again drawing customers from the competition with their first-rate skills. A number became cooks and were hired after leaving the camps by some of the best hotels and restaurants and most affluent families in the West. [41] By the 1880s, with construction of the major rail lines completed, the mines tapped out, and their towns in decline, Chinese men took their acquired skills, domestic and otherwise, and established themselves throughout eastern Washington Territory.

Single men made up the majority of the nineteenth-century Chinese immigrant population in the West, and most found themselves adversely affected by passage of the 1882 Chinese Exclusion Act. The act prohibited additional Chinese immigration to the United States for a period of ten years and denied American naturalized citizenship to those Chinese already in the States. After the act's passage, many wished to return to China, but few could accumulate the funds necessary for the fare. Most, willingly or otherwise, remained in the United States and, due to a scarcity of Chinese women there, faced the probability of confirmed bachelorhood. [42] A number of these Chinese bachelors called Walla Walla home as early as the 1860s, and Elizabeth made reference to Walla Walla's Chinese population in February 1882, when she noted in her journal that "Chinaman Tom brought nuts [and] confections for me." [43] The idea of engaging Chinese males as household servants does not seem to have concerned Elizabeth in the least; in fact, the employer/employee difficulties that arose were much the same as those that occurred between Elizabeth and the female domestics she had previously employed. "Joke got angry because he had to sweep sidewalk," she recorded on May 8, 1882. "I told him to leave if not satisfied." [44] The next day Elizabeth noted that "Joke washed," but despite the appearance that they had resolved their differences, by the end of the week she had "settled with Joke who goes to Weston." [45] Less than two weeks after Joke's departure, Elizabeth noted that "a chinaman named Jim came this afternoon and I have engaged him to come in morning at 7 dollars a wk." [46] Jim's arrival, at least temporarily, put Elizabeth's domestic travails to rest.

The post–Civil War years, and particularly those following the completion of the various transcontinental railroad lines, witnessed a strengthening of the East-West link as newly transplanted middle-class westerners, the Tannatts among them, enjoyed greater ease in maintaining contact with family and friends. By 1880, Elizabeth's immediate "Tappan" family included just her brother William Henry, Lewis's three children, and Sarah's sole surviving child, Alice Ames, all of whom resided in and around Manchester. Her network reached far beyond this immediate family, however, and included numerous members of the Tappan and Tannatt families as well as friends and acquaintances she and Thomas had made throughout their married life. Elizabeth and Libbie Tappan, widow of her brother Lewis, enjoyed an amicable relationship from the time of Libbie and Lewis's marriage in 1866, and Elizabeth was particularly saddened when her aunt Hooper informed her, in a May 1882 letter, of Libbie's failing health. "She has called on Libbie & thinks she is in quick consumption," Elizabeth confided to her journal, no doubt reflecting on the sorrow wrought by Lewis's death just two years earlier as well as the effect the loss of a second parent would have on her nephews and niece, just twelve, nine, and six years of age. "This will be so hard to have Lewis' children orphaned," she added.[47] Libbie's condition did not improve, and three weeks later Elizabeth "found a letter from Augusta containing the news of the death of Libbie."[48] It appears that the children remained in Manchester after their mother's death, possibly in the care of William Henry and Augusta Wheaton Tappan, who had no children of their own. The sons, Sanford and Lewis, later attended Boston schools and settled in the area. Lewis and Libbie's only daughter, Blanche, died in 1883, at the age of eight, and was buried near her father in the Tappan family plot at the "1661" cemetery.[49]

The values and lessons instilled as a part of her strong New England Congregationalist upbringing helped Elizabeth cope with tragedy and tribulation throughout her life, and she certainly used this inner strength to deal with sadness such as that generated by Libbie's death. Elizabeth became active in the Walla Walla Congregational Church shortly after her arrival in the city and, as she had in Manchester with the establishment of "Boys' Evenings," concentrated her efforts on providing the young male population with wholesome alternatives to the numerous saloons and houses of prostitution lining Walla Walla's frontier streets. One of these was an organized Sunday school, and Elizabeth relished her role as an instructor, making a note or two in her journal each week regarding her "scholars" and their progress, though it appears that the low level of interest in religious instruction held by Walla Walla's citizenry caused her some consternation. "The school is flourishing but will run down if Christians don't rouse themselves," she observed early in 1882.[50]

Middle-class women who traveled to eastern Washington Territory in the late nineteenth century embraced community building and the transplanting of eastern manners and mores with as much enthusiasm as their male counterparts, and soon after her arrival in the West, Elizabeth became involved with the establishment and organization of Walla Walla's chapter of the Woman's Christian Temperance Union. Sandra Haarsager, in her work on women's organizations in the Pacific Northwest, has pointed out that the institution of a sense of community and the implementation of order became particularly important to residents of eastern Washington Territory in the late nineteenth century due to the rapid growth of its cities, its mining and logging regions, and the transient populations these industries attracted. She further suggests that "women, through the wctu and later groups[,] tried to create a sense of community and order by advocating controls on behavior, fostering the benefits of literacy and reading, and seeking political power as part of a moral imperative."[51] The wctu also played a vital role in perpetuating the East-West link, as it endeavored to connect women who held similar interests, concerns, and objectives, whether they resided in eastern cities or on the western frontier.

At the same time, women in these burgeoning frontier towns often found that approaching the issue of temperance—the wctu's primary target—with a modicum of caution gleaned the greatest results, particularly when a community's key businesses engaged in the manufacture and sale of alcoholic beverages, as was the case in Walla Walla. J. H. Stahl, "importer and dealer in wines, liquors and cigars," opened the largest of these establishments on Walla Walla's Main Street in 1873, just a few years prior to the arrival of the middle-class population who would find his enterprises objectionable. "In this house we find the *spirit* of enterprise competing for a foremost position among the liquor industries of our valley," an 1879 booster publication proudly touted.[52] It is clear that, in addition to being an astute businessman, Stahl counted himself among Walla Walla's "community leaders," and he diversified his interests, at least in part, to ingratiate himself with the newly arrived easterners. By 1881 he added Stahl's Opera House, a public place "of amusements, furnishing the different grades of drama," to his enterprises. The Opera House was a respectable establishment, one in which Elizabeth and her friends would feel comfortable, and was not to be confused with numerous others in town that "open and shut alternately" as Walla Walla's law enforcement officers strove to protect "the morality of the city."[53]

Susan English has suggested that in finding ways to promote frontier temperance, women "were partly reacting to the importance of saloons in culture," and Elizabeth, through her earlier experience as president of the Manchester Woman's Union, urged the Walla Walla ladies to proceed slowly with their plan to establish a wctu chapter.[54] "Mrs. Dr. Kellogg is earnest to start a Womans [sic] Christian Association, [but] I advise working among our people first getting them interested in a prayer meeting," Elizabeth wrote in her journal on February 4, 1882.[55] Several months passed before Delia

Kellogg's gathering of women came to fruition, but in October 1882 the wctu's national newspaper, the *Union Signal,* reported that a group of fifteen Walla Walla women gathered for a temperance prayer meeting and to listen to the wctu pledge. Although the Walla Walla ladies decided not to accept the pledge at that time, they did continue to hold their prayer meetings.[56] Elizabeth left no journal entries for September 1882, and the article did not include the names of those who made up the Walla Walla assemblage, but it is likely that she attended the gathering. Less than a year later, she would be instrumental in bringing the wctu to Walla Walla.

The wctu grew directly out of the anti-liquor rallies launched by the "Woman's Crusade" in western New York and several other states in 1873 and 1874. Annie Wittenmyer participated in these, and at a convention held in Cleveland, Ohio, in November 1874 the National Woman's Christian Temperance Union organized, with Wittenmyer as its first president. Serious differences over the direction the organization should take soon developed between Wittenmyer and Frances Willard, the corresponding secretary, who envisioned a more politically based agenda and, in particular, believed that the organization could serve as an effective vehicle in the ongoing fight for woman suffrage. This departure from the wctu's original tenets concerned Wittenmyer, who held that suffrage remained a controversial topic for both men and women and that its endorsement by the wctu could prove detrimental to the credibility of the organization. A number of wctu members sided with Wittenmyer on the subject, and Paula Baker has discussed their reluctance to embrace suffrage, which represented to them "a drastic, unnatural step" because "in a proper social order, women devoted themselves to the home and family, while men took part in the somewhat sordid and corrupt sphere of politics." Baker has further suggested that "attempting to induce men to vote for temperance candidates was one thing, but voting themselves struck many rural as well as urban women as a far-too-complete break with the familiar world of separate spheres."[57] Wittenmyer and Willard battled until 1879, when Willard gained enough national support to unseat Wittenmyer and become the wctu's president, an office she held under her death in 1898.[58]

The difference in goals espoused by these reform-minded women supports much of the current research, which reveals that during the post–Civil War years women embraced a new view of reform and of the political role they would play in bringing about societal change. In her work on women's activism in the late nineteenth century, Lori Ginzberg differentiates between women's antebellum and postwar activities. "The heirs of antebellum benevolence had strikingly different perspectives and agendas than their predecessors—in some cases their actual parents," she suggests, "referring less to a mission of moral regeneration and far more to a responsibility to control the poor and 'vagrant.'"[59]

While the activities of Walla Walla's middle-class female population seem to support Ginzberg's theory that postwar reformers accepted a greater responsibility for "control" of the poor and indigent, they also followed Wittenmyer's example and for some time did not incorporate suffrage into their reform agenda. This may have stemmed, at least in part, from the personal experiences of some with the Pacific Northwest's "radical" suffragist, Abigail Scott Duniway.[60] A longtime Oregon resident and editor of the *New Northwest*, a newspaper dedicated to women's rights, Duniway advocated both temperance and suffrage in the late nineteenth century and found it damaging to the early women's movements that the same women who took to the streets and protested against the evils of alcohol refused to take the action necessary to effect their own franchise. "Women who have turned with timid horror from the possible publicity and vulgarities involved in woman's voting have not deemed it too public to kneel in the open street . . . or too vulgar to enter the vilest liquor den and bandy words with degraded sots," she reported in the *New Northwest* in 1874, revealing the less-than-flattering opinion she held of the middle-class membership base of late-nineteenth-century temperance associations.[61]

Duniway first visited Walla Walla in 1871, accompanying suffrage and temperance advocate Susan B. Anthony on a lecture tour through eastern Oregon and Washington Territory. En route to Walla Walla, in the Columbia River town of Umatilla, Anthony found herself in an awkward situation when the bartender-son of an eastern acquaintance offered her a glass of wine. Rather than embarrass the young man, Anthony accepted the glass and took a very small sip of its contents. Word of her "transgression" traveled quickly throughout the region, and by the time the two women reached Walla Walla, the townspeople made neither churches nor theaters available for Anthony's lectures. Not to be dissuaded, Duniway negotiated with town leaders and merchants who were in favor of woman suffrage, or at least interested in what Anthony might say, and rescheduled the talks in the town's new schoolhouse, the city hall, and the bank exchange hall, the latter ironically located in the rear of a saloon.[62] Each talk drew a larger crowd, to the delight of both Duniway and Anthony, and the former reported in her newspaper that "Miss Anthony made scores of converts and frightened the few old fogies in the city almost out of their wits. . . . [T]he women are unanimously resolved to use their right to vote."[63] This last statement represents a bit of wishful thinking on Duniway's part, for while some women in attendance at Anthony's lectures probably did favor suffrage, the prevailing anti-suffrage view kept the issue at bay in Walla Walla until the Equal Suffrage League was organized in 1889.[64]

The several chapters of the eastern Washington WCTU organized at Cheney in the summer of 1883, and in her August 23 newspaper column Willard introduced the newly elected officers as "ladies of exceptional talent themselves and of unusual influence, owing to the positions occupied by their husbands. Mrs. General Tannatt, the president, is a sister-in-law of the gifted Kate Tannatt Woods, of Boston. Mrs. Judge Wingard, the secretary, is an Episcopalian lady, Mrs. John Allen is wife of the district attorney."[65] Caroline Wingard and M. C. Allen held memberships in numerous women's organizations and benevolent societies in the late-nineteenth- and early-twentieth-century Inland Empire and were among Elizabeth's closest acquaintances in the West. "Mrs. General Tannatt" took an active part in the program and presented "an exceedingly interesting paper" entitled "Initial Work of Women in Washington Territory," which was "intently listened to and highly commended," wherein she detailed the reform and benevolent activities of missionaries Narcissa Whitman and Eliza Spaulding.[66]

These WCTU organizing conferences had several purposes. In addition to instituting local chapters and welcoming new members, they served to acquaint WCTU newcomers with Willard's unique set of leadership and management techniques. Through her "Do Everything" policy, Willard encouraged local chapters to create alliances with the labor and political parties in their regions and to target major reform issues such as health, education, and social purity, also referred to as "Home Protection." She did not, however, dictate the specific issues a chapter must undertake and, of particular interest here, did not insist that the Walla Walla women immediately engage in the suffrage battle, perhaps aware that such an action might jeopardize the greater success of the chapter.[67] By leaving specific reform decisions to individual groups, Willard succeeded in building an organization that drew strength from without as well as from within and depended equally on national direction and local control. The end result of Willard's leadership of the WCTU was "the largest single women's organization of the nineteenth century."[68]

Walla Walla's WCTU chapter and its Ladies Relief Society worked closely together in the 1880s, focusing a good deal of their attention on providing food and shelter to those in need. Shortly after his election as mayor in 1883, Thomas received representatives from these two organizations, who sought the city's assistance in their endeavors. The meeting proved a great success, and "it was agreed that the city should furnish suitable eating and lodging rooms and that the relief and temperance associations would attend to the balance of the work." Representatives from the city and the women's associations also agreed that room and board would not be given away but rather offered at greatly reduced prices. In order to encourage participation in the program from the greater Walla Walla citizenry, the women sold tickets redeemable for food and lodging to businesses, merchants, and individuals who, in turn, distributed them to those in need. "It is expected that our business men and private citizens will invest in these tickets," a local newspaper article read, "so that when asked for something to eat, instead of giving money which may be devoted to unworthy purposes, they can satisfy actual need by the outlay of but a small sum."[69]

The Walla Walla "coffee house" opened in early 1884, and while it enjoyed great success and fed significant numbers of people each day, it did not escape controversy. "We may now expect to have the city overcrowded with men out of money and out of work," one newspaper article read, as it anticipated abuses of the program by the "drunken loafers and tramps now infesting the city."[70] The mayor's office immediately addressed the issue, and in February 1884 Mayor Tannatt published a stern warning in the *Walla Walla Statesman* to those who might consider taking advantage of the relief efforts provided by the town's "Christian ladies." In particular, he cautioned that those who planned to spend time and money in the town's saloons and houses of prostitution and then turn to the charity of the "coffee house" for a warm bed and a hot meal would be "dealt with as *vagrants, not as deserving objects of charity.*"[71]

A temperance advocate himself, Thomas had sworn off alcohol twenty years earlier during the Civil War, but he did not favor a legislative prohibition on alcohol, and in 1884 his name appeared on a petition protesting a proposed ban on the sale of liquor. Walla Walla's businessmen certainly did not endorse widespread drunkenness; in fact, the petition began, "We believe as earnestly in the principles of temperance as do the advocates of prohibition." Rather, their concerns rested with the impracticality of a ban that would result in the loss of livelihood and revenue and in "the repeal of our license system" but would "neither prohibit or curtail the use of spiritous liquors," which would continue to be manufactured, sold, and consumed, albeit clandestinely.[72] The Walla Walla constituency successfully defeated the prohibition measure in 1884, but the issue remained a volatile one in Walla Walla and throughout the Inland Empire. Just two years later it caught the attention of Abigail Scott Duniway.[73]

In the spring of 1886, Duniway traveled again to Walla Walla to make arrangements for upcoming temperance lectures and approached Mrs. Stahl, widow of brewer and Opera House benefactor J. H. Stahl, regarding use of the Opera House for that purpose, to which she agreed. However, Duniway found Stahl so agitated over Walla Walla's proposed prohibition legislation, and the economic and personal ruin it would mean to her family if it passed, that she published Stahl's story in the *New Northwest* that March. "Why don't you teach people to let the beer alone?" Stahl asked Duniway, reminding her that men consumed the brew of their own volition and that she had "never in my life ask[ed] a man to buy beer."[74] Although she had been accused of selling out on more than one occasion, Duniway did not support the liquor industry, nor did she disagree with the prohibition of the sale of alcohol. She did sympathize with Stahl, though, and argued that if the proposed legislation meant depriving individuals of their livelihood, then it must be severely flawed. Like Thomas and the Walla Walla businessmen who signed the town's 1884 anti-prohibition petition, Duniway argued that "it is wrong in principle, and cannot be made to stand in law, that a town, county or precinct which deprives an individual of the means of livelihood shall be exempt from paying damages."[75] Then, as had Thomas and the others in 1884, Duniway cautioned Walla Walla's temperance advocates, and particularly the middle-class women whose actions she found so detrimental to the women's rights movement, against acting on impulse. "Be careful," she warned, "lest in going too fast you cut loose from the great train of practical possibility, and injure the cause so dear to every mother's ear, the cause of peace and soberness."

In March 1884, Elizabeth resigned as president of the WCTU's Walla Walla chapter, a decision to which Thomas's disagreement with the town's prohibition backers likely contributed. "I feel I have been unable to but partially perform the duties wh. have devolved upon me," her resignation began, and "should I attempt to meet those duties I must neglect those of home and family." Elizabeth then relinquished her office to "those with more leisure who can be working zealously" for the causes she continued to deem as "sacred."[76] The resignation did not signal the end of her participation in the WCTU, however, and at the eastern Washington regional meeting later that year she accepted an appointment as department superintendent for "Work among Soldiers."[77] Bringing the social and philanthropic opportunities readily available to women in the East to those in the West was very important to Elizabeth, and in addition to her work with the Walla Walla WCTU she became an active participant in Walla Walla's Ladies' Reform Society. She was numbered among those present on March 3, 1886, at the first meeting of the Walla Walla Women's Club, joined there by her close friends and fellow reformers, Caroline Wingard and M. C. Allen.[78]

The Web of Government Bureaucracy and Thomas's Pension

Elizabeth engaged in a relief effort of a different nature in the late 1880s and early 1890s when she embarked upon her campaign to secure military pension benefits for Thomas. In 1862 the federal government had instituted a pension program to provide for Union army soldiers who suffered perma-nent injury or disability "incurred as a direct consequence of . . . military duty" or "from causes which can be directly traced to injuries received or disease contracted while in military service."[79] The program required that veterans apply for these pensions within one year of discharge in order to receive benefits retroactive to the date of injury or disability. By 1873 the government extended the application period to five years beyond discharge, and in 1879 the implementation of the Arrears Act made those who initiated pension claims prior to July 1, 1880, eligible for benefits from the date of injury or disability. By the mid-1880s, the Grand Army of the Republic had become the most active proponent of veterans' benefits, and as they worked to provide pensions for a greater number of Civil War soldiers they specifically targeted the elimination of application deadlines. In remarks made on the military pension system in 1888, Pres. Benjamin Harrison, Civil War veteran and member of the GAR, argued that the decade of the 1880s was "no time to be weighing the claims of old soldiers with apothecary's scales," and within two years Congress enacted the Dependent Pension Act of 1890.[80] Substantially different in scope from earlier acts, it was designed to provide a pension to every honorably discharged soldier who had served at least ninety days and whose disability prevented him from performing manual labor, regardless of financial standing or conditions under which the disability occurred. The 1890 act received hearty endorsement from the GAR, whose representatives declared it "the most liberal pension measure ever passed by any legislative body in the world."[81]

Thomas first made application for an army pension in 1886.[82] In February 1887 he received notification from the surgeon general's office that while the records did confirm granting of a twenty-day general disability furlough following his injury, the "records of wounded pertaining to the battle of Petersburg Va. June 16–20, 64 furnish no evidence in this case."[83] It appears that here the War Department referred to no further evidence of permanent injury or disability, a prerequisite for receipt of a pension as set forth in all pension acts. The War Department did acknowledge that Thomas had sustained injuries during the Battle of Petersburg, based on the Command Return for June 16, 1864, Second Brigade, Third Division, Army of the Potomac, which reported that "in the afternoon a charge was made upon the enemy's works, . . . Col. Thomas R. Tannatt, commanding brigade was wounded," and on Third Division Hospital Chief Surgeon O. Everts's June 23, 1864, notation to Thomas's file stating that "This officer should be permitted to leave the field immediately on account of injuries received."[84] The department did question, however, the "permanence" of the disability, since no documentation to substantiate such a claim had been provided them.

The War Department's negative response did not cause the Tannatts to abandon hope of securing Thomas's military pension, and Elizabeth initiated a letter-writing campaign in search of individuals who might corroborate Thomas's claim. She received affidavits from Clayton McMichael and R. S.

Littlefield, both of whom had served with Thomas in 1864, and from Frank Daulte, who lived on the same floor of a New York rooming house as Thomas in 1878 and 1879. Littlefield and Thomas were wounded at the same time, and Littlefield recalled that they spent at least two nights together in the division hospital. "We must not let the General lose a battle, or more justly his due as a participant," he wrote Elizabeth.[85] McMichael agreed to provide a second affidavit in 1889, assuring Elizabeth, "I have a very clear recollection of the hurt received by Col. Tannatt, for whom I then had a most pleasant friendship."[86] While these statements from wartime comrades attested to the fact that Thomas had suffered a serious wound, Daulte's affidavit verified the long-term disability he experienced as a result of the wound. "He was subject to frequent ill turns; head trouble, resulting, as he informed me, from a wound in his head; and, at such times, was unable to attend to business," Daulte recalled. He related a particular incident, in July 1879, when Thomas "arose from his bed, during the night, and fell heavily to the floor, in an unconscious state; awaking me. I went to his room, & found him lying upon the floor, bleeding freely from the mouth." A nearby physician, Dr. T. A. Tellkampf, was summoned and "pronounced the case, a severe congestion of the brain, & attributed bleeding to rupture of small blood vessels in the throat, from intense congestion." Daulte noted that Thomas suffered a similar episode on August 13, that "I was with him frequently during his illness," and that later "a nurse employed to attend him Day & night, he being, at intervals, delirious & unconscious."[87] Daulte's statement likely helped to sway the War Department in favor of Thomas's pension, though payments did not begin for a number of years. Elizabeth's last known correspondence to the War Department, complete with affidavits and countless doctors' reports, was dated March 1892, but no evidence of pension payments appears in the records until 1897.[88] At that time, and until his death in 1913, Thomas received quarterly pension payments of thirty dollars, and from 1913 until her death in 1920, Elizabeth received a widow's pension in the amount of twenty-five dollars per quarter.[89]

The diligence with which Elizabeth pursued Thomas's military pension is curious, for the Tannatts did not appear to need the payments for their support and maintenance. It is likely that Elizabeth viewed the pension as a benefit Thomas was owed both for his service to the country and as compensation for the episodes of ill health he suffered throughout his life. Thomas and Elizabeth's finances are but vaguely detailed in their records and consist for the most part of random pages of household accounts with no specific information on income. Thomas drew military pay from the time of his commission as second lieutenant in 1858 until his resignation from the army in 1864, and he earned salaries from the Colorado mining conglomerates, the Tennessee Immigration Association, and eventually from

Henry Villard. Of particular interest, however, are his periods of unemployment and his early pro bono work for Villard. Since these intervals without wages or salary appeared problematic to neither Thomas nor Elizabeth, they clearly had other funds available to them. During Thomas's intermittent periods of unemployment, and the family's terms of residence in Manchester, the Tannatts enjoyed the hospitality of the Tappans, not an uncommon occurrence in the nineteenth century. And as Eben and Sally Tappan had accumulated some wealth over the course of their lifetimes, they would not have asked room and board of their daughter and her family. Elizabeth did receive inheritances from the estates of her parents and her brothers Lewis and William Henry, and these may have been substantial. Thomas and Elizabeth also held interests in several income-generating properties in Colorado, collecting dividends on them until their sale in the 1870s and 1880s. The records also reveal that Thomas's mother, Mary Gilmour Tannatt, gifted significant sums to several of her grandchildren, and it is likely that she made similar gifts to Thomas's children, and perhaps to Thomas and Elizabeth as well. All speculation as to the source of their funds aside, the Tannatts achieved and maintained middle-class status throughout their married life and clearly had adequate funds at their disposal to support their chosen standard of living.[90]

Tannatt's Farmington Vision: Commercial Center on the Palouse

Thomas resigned as mayor of Walla Walla in 1884, owing to increased responsibilities with the Oregon Improvement Company brought about by the continued growth and expansion of transportation and its related interests in the Pacific Northwest. Prior to the completion of his transcontinental link at Spokane Falls, Villard had plans in place for construction of a railroad link to connect Colfax and Pullman, proceed north through Farmington, and on to the Coeur d'Alene mines. The link organized as the Columbia and Palouse Railroad, though its financing from the Oregon and Transcontinental Company, engineering from the ORN, and design intended specifically for Northern Pacific trains identified it as a Villard enterprise. Construction of the Columbia and Palouse began at Palouse Junction in the spring of 1882, and by November 1883 trains ran between Colfax and Palouse Junction, though Villard's forced forfeiture of control of his railroad interests in late 1883 and early 1884 delayed the entry of a railroad into Farmington until 1886.[91]

Villard's personal downfall began several months before the NPRR's 1883 golden spike ceremony, when it became apparent that actual construction costs had greatly exceeded the estimates. As the railroad was largely financed through the purchase of bonds, Villard was concerned that a second mortgage and another tier of bond sales would reduce the value of the original preferred stock and cause bondholders to sell. His foreboding was realized, and in December 1883, after news of the overruns had been made public and the value of Villard stock fell to a low that made survival of his companies seem unlikely, Villard resigned the presidencies of both the Oregon and Transcontinental Company and the ORN. On January 4, 1884, he resigned from the NPRR as well, and within weeks of his resignations officers from the various companies struck deals with eastern-based syndicates to provide the backing necessary to pay off remaining debt and provide temporary operating capital.[92] With the needed funds in place, the companies dispatched crews and the business of railroad building re-commenced in earnest.

In February 1885 the Eastern Washington Railway, a subsidiary of the NPRR, reincorporated as the Spokane and Palouse Railway for the purpose of constructing a rail line south of the NPRR's main line to "some eligible or practical point in the Territory of Washington on or near the Snake River."[93] The southern terminus of the Spokane and Palouse's first phase of construction lay at Belmont, Washington, roughly fifty railroad miles south of Spokane Falls and a site considered by the NPRR as having the potential to become "the most important agricultural and commercial center of the famous Palouse country."[94] Within a matter of months, the railroad platted a town site, offered residential and commercial lots for sale, and introduced its plans for the construction of all necessary railroad-related buildings, though the residents of Farmington, less than ten miles to the east of the Belmont site, were not pleased with the NPRR's decision to bypass their town, already established as a center of trade and commerce, in favor of the undeveloped and unpopulated Belmont.

The ORN had not sat idly by while the NPRR formalized plans to extend their operations into the Palouse, and survey crews were dispatched between Colfax and Farmington armed with the task of ascertaining the most efficient route for construction of a rail line. By November 1885, C. H. Prescott, general land manager of the ORN, in association with a group of local landowners led by George Truax, one of Farmington's first settlers, secured all necessary lands for construction of the proposed line, issued construction contracts, and witnessed the rapid grading and laying of the twenty-seven miles of track. On the last Sunday in September 1886, the Farmington extension began moving passengers and freight. In a show of good faith and commitment to the region, the ORN relocated its eastern Washington offices from Walla Walla to Farmington at the beginning of this construction phase and named Thomas its general manager. In this capacity, he "laid out and incorporated [the] Railroad Addition to the town," developing in the process a fondness for the region that would cause him, within the space of just a few years, to make Farmington his permanent home.[95]

With his transfer from the Oregon Improvement Company to the Oregon Railway and Navigation Company, Thomas became more involved with the placement of rail lines in the region, and his duties included negotiating with the Coeur d'Alene and other local Indians as well as dealing with the federal government's Office of Indian Affairs when the railroad sought to lay track across reservation lands. "Am in camp at Spring just above the mouth of Saint Joseph, on railroad right-of-way," he wrote to Chief Saltees of the Coeur d'Alene in July 1886 while on an inspection tour of the Coeur d'Alene mining region. The party had observed a posted notice against trespassing, and Thomas, out of respect and eager to maintain amicable relations, immediately sent word via courier informing Chief Saltees of his location and his purpose for being there. "I am connected with railroad company," the letter continued, "my party consists of an Assistant, wife and two young ladies. . . . My party will not destroy game, fish or timber. . . . Please send me a permit that will protect myself and party from any annoyance."[96] Within a short time Thomas received a reply that gave "Gen'l. T.R. Tannatt of Oregon Railway & Navigation Co. and Party . . . permission to camp at different points on Coeur d'Alene Indian Reservation until Sept. 10, 1886."[97]

The cordial relationship Thomas enjoyed with the Coeur d'Alene did not extend to many of the railroad men in the region, ORN associates among them, so eager to construct their lines that they did so without regard for the legality of that placement. In the spring of 1888, Sen. John H. Mitchell forwarded a dispatch he had received from Thomas to the secretary of the interior advising that "Elijah Smith is acting in bad faith" and that the "Indians have virtually withdrawn consent for railroad to cross."[98] Research conducted by the Office of Indian Affairs concluded that the railroad in question was either the Spokane and Palouse or the Washington and Idaho, both of which had been granted only preliminary survey permits, not construction permits. Although petitions by these railroad companies to lay lines across the Coeur d'Alene reservation had received favor in both houses of Congress, bills approving such construction had not been passed by the spring of 1888.[99]

Thomas retired from the ORN late in 1888, before resolution had been reached on the railroad/reservation issue. Now fifty-four and fifty-one years of age, respectively, he and Elizabeth moved to Farmington, where they had purchased several city lots and significant acreage upon which Thomas intended to plant fruit trees. The coming of the railroad expanded an already-growing Farmington and launched the town into its most prosperous period. A number of new industries moved into the community, among them a flour mill, brick factory, planing mill, creamery, and brewery, and by the late 1880s the population of the city limits had boomed to more than twelve hundred, with at least as many residing on nearby farms and ranches. Three hotels, several stores, bakery, laundry, livery, and three daily passenger trains served this burgeoning population where land value had increased five hundred-fold since George Truax purchased his first lots less than twenty years earlier. Several individuals in the Farmington area experimented with the planting of apple and pear trees during the 1880s, and their success led to the establishment of two apple-packing plants in the area. These successes also convinced Thomas that orchardist would be the next occupation listed on his résumé.[100]

A number of circumstances lead to Thomas's retirement from the ORN. Villard's departure and the promotion by new railroad company executives of those whom Thomas held in low esteem certainly contributed to his decision. It is also possible that recurrences of ill health played a role, for although neither Thomas nor Elizabeth refers to specific episodes of debilitation in surviving journals, an 1887 letter received from Elizabeth's aunt Augusta reveals they did exist. "We are greatly distressed at the condition of your husband's health," Augusta wrote, and "hope he will soon be permanently better."[101]

Their relocation to Farmington allowed Thomas and Elizabeth to become involved with new opportunities and challenges. Firmly established as Inland Empire community builders, still in their early fifties, and with child raising and professional obligations behind them, during the last decade of the nineteenth century they turned their attention more fully to those things that interested them most: matters of civic and community importance and commemoration.

6. Retirement and Reflections on the Past, 1890–1920

Inland Empire Entrepreneurs—The Tannatts as Business Partners

As the nineteenth century waned, Thomas and Elizabeth Tannatt entered into retirement, and for the first time in thirty years their choice of domicile was dictated by neither business nor the military but by personal preference. For the Tannatts, that preference pointed to Farmington, Washington. In Farmington, Thomas saw potential similar to that which he had enjoyed in Walla Walla a decade earlier, and in selecting it as his retirement home he may have hoped to engage once more in the process of community building and leadership. By his own account, Thomas retired from the Oregon Railway and Navigation Company "owing to continued impaired health," and he relocated to Farmington in order to live quietly and engage "in orchard work and care of my landed interests."[1] When he wrote these words in 1902, Thomas had substantially lightened his business commitments, though this is not to suggest that he led a quiet and inactive retirement. In the late 1880s and 1890s Thomas remained active in a number of business enterprises and fraternal and military organizations, and he served as a member of the board of regents of the newly established Washington Agricultural College and School of Science, located in Pullman.

Thomas's ventures in early retirement included the establishment of the Poplar Crest Commercial Orchard in Farmington, specializing in apples and pears; and T. R. Tannatt, Dealer in Hardware, Iron, Steel, Doors, Sash, Paints, Oils, Etc., in Palouse City, specializing, apparently, in nothing in particular but stocking everything customers might require. The Tannatts' relocation to Farmington coincided with eastern Washington's population boom, and Spokane replaced Walla Walla as the region's largest city,[2] growing from a small town of just 350 at the beginning of the period to an established western city with more than one hundred thousand residents by 1910.[3] In response to this northerly population shift away from Walla Walla, Thomas established, and reestablished, his enterprises in order to be accessible to the consuming public. His hardware business, for instance, began as a small store in Farmington. By 1890, however, the extension of the railroad to Spokane and the founding of several communities along its line caused Farmington's "hinterland" to shrink from a diameter of approximately thirty miles to just a few, and businesses began to decline as consumers now purchased retail goods in stores closer to their homes. In 1890 the town's population stood at twelve hundred, but just ten years later that number had dropped to five hundred, and business and industry that had moved into Farmington during the 1870s and 1880s abandoned the town as well. The Farmington in which Thomas had seen such promise in the 1880s did not recover, and as was so often the case, it became just another small agricultural community among many.[4] By 1891 Thomas had relocated his store to Palouse City, and this move generated a good deal of business as the town served as a major railroad junction. Palouse City lay approximately twenty-five miles south of Farmington, and while Elizabeth maintained the family's primary residence there, Thomas, once again, spent a substantial amount of time away from home. Now, however, his absences also separated him from his Farmington-based business interests, and these circumstances caused him to depend more often on Elizabeth's business sense.

In December 1891, Thomas wrote Elizabeth from Palouse City and re-quested that she deal with the bank in the collection of note payments owed him. Clearly unhappy with the bank, or perhaps its banker, Thomas asked Elizabeth to "call and get my book and see if he will give matter attention through you." He also advised her that "I send Mr Quarles a bill of $10.07 with request that he remit or pay amt to you."[5] In addition to these financial matters, Elizabeth assumed responsibility for the orchards during Thomas's frequent absences. After the particularly long and harsh winter and spring of 1893, which produced significant Inland Empire snowfalls into late April, she expressed concern for the potential of the season's crop. "On account of wet ground plowing retarded," she wrote on May 6, and of even greater concern, "apple & pear trees still in bud."[6] Elizabeth's ability to oversee the Farmington operations relieved Thomas of a great burden, and it is clear that he depended on her assistance in performing the day-to-day tasks and obligations associated with his many interests.

Although Thomas and Elizabeth spent significant amounts of time apart during the fifty-three years of their married life, they obviously felt deep love and devotion for one another. In the early 1890s, Thomas composed a quick letter to Elizabeth, detailing the events of his day, inquiring of hers, and revealing "Lonesome tonight and I feel blue." Then, as he did with each and every letter he wrote her, he closed with "Lovingly, T."[7] The subject of Thomas's ill health reappears after 1890 in the Tannatts' letters and journals, though Thomas worked diligently to keep these episodes of debilitation from interfering with the rest of his life. "The walk in was cooling to my head which for two weeks have given me much trouble," he wrote Elizabeth in December 1891 from Palouse City, after returning to his boardinghouse from a dinner engagement.[8] And on February 14, 1892, in a letter to Elizabeth and Minnie, Thomas revealed that "from supper Thursday until dinner Saturday not a spoonful of food passed my lips," a condition he attributed to "neuroglia in head face swollen and return of my old bowel trouble."[9] In Thomas's later years, the lasting effects of his wartime injuries and illnesses, specifically his head wound, seem to have brought on, or at least contributed to, nervous disorders that rendered him incapacitated for days at a time. Undue stress apparently brought on these nervous attacks, and in the early 1890s Thomas wrote Elizabeth that while the Palouse City store was proving to be a great success, on that particular "Friday & Saty had a heavy trade which fell too much on me." He would not let his fatigue hinder his schedule, however, and assured her that "to night I will take more medicine and break up these chills and flushes of fever as I must go to Colfax Tuesday."[10]

Another side of Thomas is revealed in letters from his later years, and one from late 1891 in particular portrays him as a kind and lovable gentleman. While in Palouse City, he kept rooms in a local boardinghouse, and on the evening of December 8 he wrote Elizabeth that "Mrs Martin and Katie came in at 4 to make my bed" and "Katie sat in my lap and chatted. She is a bright thoughtful child very well mannered."[11] The Tannatts' first grandchild, Hazel, Eben's daughter, was born in the early 1890s, and this "gentler" Thomas may have been the result of his new role as a grandfather.

Elizabeth's involvement in and propensity for business affairs extended beyond the family enterprises, and throughout her married life she dealt with the property received as gifts and inheritances from her family without apparent assistance or interference from Thomas. In 1880, upon the death of her brother Lewis, Elizabeth inherited an interest in a parcel of property in Central City, Colorado. She retained this interest until 1891, when a lengthy correspondence ensued with U.S. senator N. P. Hill, longtime family friend and her acting agent in Colorado, over the sale of the property. Hill informed Elizabeth that a local merchant had offered five hundred dollars for her interest, though Hill was quite certain she would not accept the offer, despite the fact that five hundred dollars was a significant amount of money at the time.[12] Hill was correct, and in a letter dated July 27, Elizabeth asked him to try and secure a higher bid, and "if you can make a sale for $650 [to Miller] or any one else please do so."[13] Unfortunately, the property did not bring the desired price, and when Elizabeth finally sold her interest in the spring of 1892 she was fortunate that C. C. Miller still desired to purchase the property for his original offer of five hundred dollars.[14]

The East-West Link

Elizabeth's dealings with N. P. Hill are representative of the bond she and Thomas maintained with friends and family in the East from whom they had been physically separated for many years. Late-nineteenth- and early-twentieth-century technological advances allowed post–Civil War immigrants to the West, and particularly those belonging to the middle class, to sustain their East-West links. Telegraph and telephone lines provided efficient and effective means of communication, and as early as 1884, during

Thomas's tenure as mayor, Walla Walla residents enjoyed limited telephone service.[15] At the same time, expanded railroad routes carried both passengers and the mail, making visits and reunions with friends and loved ones realistic and attainable.[16]

Family remained very important to Elizabeth throughout her life, and the East-West link allowed her to maintain regular and time-efficient contact with her Massachusetts relations. The well-being of the children of her deceased brother and sister weighed heavily on Elizabeth's mind, and she utilized improved methods of communication to remain available to them despite their physical separation. Alice Ames, daughter of Elizabeth's sister, Sarah, moved to Massachusetts after the death of her mother in 1878 and lived with Hooper relations there until she married. By the 1890s Alice's letters resembled medical reports as she kept Elizabeth informed of the various maladies striking aging family members. In particular, Alice informed Elizabeth in 1892 that William Henry "& his wife had had the Grippe. . . . It is a wonder that he got over it as well as he did, being so old." William Henry was seventy-one in 1892. "It is too bad that Uncle Tom has had to give up his business on account of his health," Alice's letter continued, probably referring to Thomas's retirement from the Oregon Railway and Navigation Company, and at the same time confirming that the East-West link operated in both directions.[17] In 1899, now married and with a young son, Alice responded with enthusiasm to her receipt of Elizabeth's gift of Washington apples. "We all had a taste," she wrote, and Harlan, Alice's young son, "said he wished that he lived next door to Aunt Lizzie."[18]

Elizabeth's relationship with her sole surviving brother remained strong into the new century, and in 1900, at almost eighty years of age, William Henry enjoyed good health, despite a bout or two with the grippe, and spent a great deal of time traveling throughout New England. "We have just returned from a visit of 2½ weeks at Lewises near Providence," he wrote, referring here to the younger son of their deceased brother Lewis. "Found them all well and delightful[,] situated about 5 miles from the City, on an electric line & also on the New York & New Haven R.R. . . . L is a barber Fletcher & Tappan an[d] appear to be doing a nice business." William Henry's letter continued, "They have i.e. L & wife a beautiful little girl called Elizabeth, who is extremely interesting and as bright as babys ever become."[19]

It is not surprising that the close-knit Tappan family worked diligently to maintain their East-West link, for they had done so since Elizabeth's brothers first ventured westward in the 1850s. The Tannatts, however, remained largely absent during Thomas's and Elizabeth's married life, so the unexpected appearance of several letters from Tannatt family members in the 1890s serves as an even greater testament to the ease and effectiveness of the East-West link. In May 1893, Thomas and Elizabeth received a letter from John

G. Tannatt of North Greenfield, Wisconsin, the son of Thomas's younger brother Henry, and through this letter they learned of the death of Arthur Tannatt Woods, son of Thomas's sister, Kate. John Tannatt's letter also makes reference to an inheritance of twenty-five hundred dollars received from his grandmother Mary Gilmour Tannatt, the origin of which is rather curious since this was a great deal of money in 1893 and since during Thomas's youth his mother did not appear to have cash in such large quantities.[20]

The Tannatt East-West link expanded in 1901 with the receipt of a letter from T. C. (Tennie) Tannatt, widow of Thomas's brother John, who still resided in McMinnville, Tennessee. Her inquiry into the condition of Thomas's health makes it clear that the family had maintained some correspondence over the years. "It would be very nice for me if I lived close enough so any of you could run down & give me the light of your presence once in a while," Tennie wrote, "how it would help me along over some of the rough ways," for although "I have a great many friends in McMinnville, . . . I feel there is a stronger tie binds me to my husbands [sic] relatives."[21] For the Tappans and the Tannatts, the East-West link bridged the separation created by distance, allowing aunts, uncles, cousins, and grandparents in such diverse locations as Massachusetts, Tennessee, Washington, and Wisconsin the opportunity to build and maintain close familial ties.

The Washington Agricultural College and School of Science

The establishment and success of his businesses brought Thomas a great deal of satisfaction, but these could not match the honor and pride he felt in 1893 when Washington's governor, John McGraw, appointed him to the board of regents of the state's new land-grant college, the Washington Agricultural College and School of Science, located in Pullman, approximately forty miles south of Farmington. Through the provisions of the Morrill Act of 1862, land-grant colleges received land and other federal support in exchange for offering military training to male students and structuring their curricula to focus on "practical" studies such as agriculture, home economics, and engineering. Further funding, made available by the Hatch Act of 1887 and the Smith-Lever Act of 1914, supported agricultural research in each state and established agricultural extension stations within the land-grant colleges, intended to deliver newly developed scientific methods directly to the region's farmers.[22]

Pullman claimed just 350 residents in 1892 and seemed an unlikely choice as the location of the state's new land-grant college. Despite a colorful description of the time, which suggested that "through the principal village street . . . filed the prospector's train of pack horses or burros with their tinkling bells or, in single file, on parti-colored cayuses, a long line of Indian bucks followed by their squaws and papooses," and notwithstanding "the cowboy with chaps and sombrero and clinking spurs [who] clanked along the streets or lounged about the doors of the saloon," the college admitted its first students in January 1892.[23]

The establishment of institutions of higher education numbered among the first tasks undertaken by the Washington State legislature after the territory attained statehood in 1889, and the federal support accompanying land-grant colleges created a competitive atmosphere among Washington's counties, each eager to locate the institution within its boundaries. Since the University of Washington was established in Seattle in 1861, on land given to the territory by Congress for support of higher education, the legislature decided to locate the new college in either the central or eastern reaches of the state.[24] By 1891 the legislature had narrowed its selection pool to Whitman County in the east and Yakima County in central Washington, with acting governor Charles E. Laughton favoring Whitman County, and perhaps even Pullman. Paul Schultze of the Northern Pacific Railroad, Thomas's nemesis during his tenure with Henry Villard, favored Yakima County and vigorously lobbied to have the college located there, but to no avail. In April 1891 the legislature decided on Pullman.[25]

The Washington Agricultural College witnessed episodes of blatant dishonesty and fiscal mismanagement during its first years, and while these resulted in the dismissal of the original regents, they also brought Thomas to Pullman, and to the college. "The agricultural college is now without a board of regents," the *Pullman Herald* reported in March 1893. "The old board was not confirmed, and it now rests with Gov. McGraw to appoint a new board."[26] By the end of the month, the governor selected and appointed five men to serve as members of the college's new board of regents, and in April, when one of them declined, Thomas received the appointment. "Mr. Tannatt is highly spoken of by all who know him, and will doubtless make a first-class regent," a *Herald* article noted. The paper suggested that the new board anticipated making significant changes to the institution when they convened, but it assured readers that the changes "will be for the good of the institution, as the regents are all fair-minded, conscientious men, who will labor for the upbuilding of the college, and thus for the interest of the state."[27]

On December 13, 1892, less than a year after the new college opened its doors, the then-sitting board of regents dismissed the college's first president, George W. Lilley, for a number of infractions, including "poor accounting practices" and "overcrowded dormitories," and appointed John W. Heston as his successor. In his history of the university, George A. Frykman has suggested that Heston was doomed to failure from the start. Just thirty-nine at the time, Heston apparently looked even younger, and this contributed to his inability to gain either the respect or the attention of a faculty that had dissolved into opposing factions. When the new board of regents convened in May 1893 and set about restoring some semblance of order to the young academic institution, they dismissed all but seven members of the faculty and, determined not to retain a president appointed by a discharged board, called for Heston's resignation as well. [28] Two months later, on July 22, the board selected Enoch A. Bryan, formerly of Vincennes University in Indiana, as the college's new president. Bryan's longevity speaks volumes for his success: he served as president of the college from 1893 until 1916.

The regents worked diligently over the next several years to expand and modernize the college, and in March 1895 they achieved great success in convincing the state legislature to appropriate funds in excess of those already allocated for the period. "Practically all that was asked for was allowed," the college newspaper, the *Evergreen*, reported in March 1895. "Twenty thousand dollars was secured for the erection of a girls' dormitory; $3,000 to establish a school of dairying; $4,000 to purchase additional campus lands; $1,000 to build a piggery and granary; $1,500 for sugar beet experiments; $2,500 to establish an experimental station at Puyallup, and $7,500 to build a steam-heat and light plant at the foot of College hill." [29] It is apparent that in submitting their allocation requests, President Bryan and the regents had taken every aspect of the college into consideration and had requested funds that would benefit all of the college's students in some way.

The regents enjoyed a surprisingly wide range of influence in the 1890s, extending to such domains as the redesign of cadet uniforms. Although Thomas did not receive direct credit for this endeavor, he likely played a role in outfitting the college's cadets for military drills and exercises. "The new uniforms are modeled after the West Point fatigue uniforms, which are considered to be the neatest in use in military schools," the *Evergreen* reported in December 1896. "They are of a handsome cadet blue, trimmed in wide black braid," the article continued, "[and] it must be said that the students and Board of Regents showed good taste and an appreciation of appearance when they effected this pleasing change the latter part of last year." [30]

Thomas served as both president and vice president of the board of regents during his tenure from 1893 to 1899, and he sat on a number of important and influential committees: the Experiment Stations Committee, the Building and Purchasing Committee, and the Auditing and Finance Committee, among others. His greatest accomplishment as a regent came in 1895, when, utilizing his engineering skills, he presented a resolution for the preparation of plans, specifications, and estimates for "a well standpipe, pump & permanent cover for reservoir[,] based on consumption 15 times greater than present requirement." Anticipation of the college's continued growth, along with the added strain to an infrastructure already showing signs of obsolescence, prompted these actions. The resolution passed, and under Thomas's watchful supervision, construction of the new well system commenced late in the summer of 1895.[31]

Thomas found his association with the board of regents revitalizing, and his willingness to respond immediately to the needs of the college— even when that attention led to neglect of his personal interests—makes clear the importance he placed on both the institution and his role as its regent. Since members of the board hailed from cities and towns across Washington, meeting locations rotated in order to ease the burden of travel, and in anticipation of the work the regents would do once finally convened, a spirited feistiness returned to Thomas's letters as he detailed for Elizabeth his plans and itinerary. "Mr. Stearns will arrive via OR&N [and] Mr. Blandford cannot come neither Ingraham," he advised her from Pullman in November 1893, referring to board members H. S. Blandford of Walla Walla, J. W. Stearns of Tekoa, and E. S. Ingraham of Seattle.[32] "We will no doubt have to leave for Walla Walla in morning as Prndt Bryan and Blandford suggests as important matters call for action by a quorum," and the college's curriculum was likely the topic under discussion at this meeting of the board of regents.[33] Accusations had arisen both in and away from Pullman that Bryan and the regents felt that administering an "agricultural college" was beneath them and an embarrassment and that they hoped to redefine the school as an academic "university." In later years, as he wrote his history of the college, Bryan clarified his interpretation of the Morrill Act of 1862 and the goals and objectives he and the board had established for the institution, all in keeping with Congress's statutes and requirements for land-grant colleges. "It was our belief that it was useless to put the farm boy to labor at tasks with which he was already familiar," Bryan wrote; instead, he and the regents set out to establish a curriculum "aimed at the development of those [agricultural] sciences and at the development of trained leadership in industry."[34]

The 1891 state charter required that, in addition to its main experiment station in Pullman, the college establish at least one such station on Washington's west side, and as a tract of land offered by the town of Sumner had proved unsatisfactory, Bryan and the regents resumed their search in early 1895. "Presdt Bryan and myself leave here Friday morning," Thomas wrote Elizabeth from Pullman on January 30; "will meet Major Ingraham at Puyallup Saty. go out examine land and if possible reach Olympia Saty night at least Sunday." The Puyallup tract proved satisfactory to all, and it ultimately became the permanent home of the Western Washington Experiment Station. Bryan and the regents clearly had additional business in the state capital during this trip, for as Thomas's letter continued, "Will be in Olympia Monday & Tuesday, return to Pullman for meeting Thursday evening and will reach home Friday or Saty most likely Saty as we cannot do all in one evening."[35]

In addition to making regular trips across the state on college business, Thomas spent a significant amount of time in Pullman. The events taking place there made him particularly proud and brought him a great deal of pleasure. He was most impressed with the number of farmers taking advantage of a program called "Winter School," or "School for Farmers," implemented in 1895. "76 Farmers at school to day, more coming," he reported to Elizabeth in January 1895, "all are highly pleased. . . . Farmers here from all parts of State[:] W.W. [Walla Walla,] Waitsburg, Dayton, Endicott, . . . 9 different counties in all."[36] The accelerated program, which lasted just three weeks, provided farmers with the latest information on stock, crops, methods, and machinery and was held during the winter, when they faced the fewest demands. Bryan noted that "much enthusiasm for agricultural education throughout the state had been created by this special school."[37]

While the Washington Agricultural College and School of Science, Enoch Bryan, and the board of regents focused their collective attention on promoting the new institution and attracting more students, the 1890s witnessed the rise of a strong and viable movement for a third political party in the United States. Members of the Farmers' Alliance joined forces with the Knights of Labor and supporters of free silver and sought, according to Ignatius Donnelly's "Omaha Platform" of 1892, "to restore the Government of the Republic to the hands of the 'plain people.' "[38] The Populists, as they became known, held that during the post–Civil War years the welfare of the many had been severely compromised by the greed of the few, and they intended to right these wrongs through reform legislation. Specifically, the Populists argued for governmental ownership of railroad, telegraph, and telephone lines; return to the public domain of unsold railroad land in order to expand the homestead program; a graduated income tax on the rich; an eight-hour workday; and the free and unlimited coinage of silver by the national treasury. The Depression of 1893, which set in just months after Populist candidates gained seats in Kansas, Colorado, and Nevada, convinced many of the country's agriculturalists and working men and women of the soundness of the Populist platform, and the movement gathered momentum and spread quickly throughout the West and Midwest.[39]

By 1896 the Populist Party had risen to a position of prominence in the state of Washington, and as Populist John R. Rogers ascended to the governor's office, he did so with the support of a Populist-dominated legislature. The new administration intended to slash any state expenditure deemed extravagant, and the college at Pullman did not escape unscathed. In the fall of 1897, Rogers demanded that faculty salaries be cut, and the Washington Agricultural College faculty responded in solidarity by agreeing to such cuts for a two-year period. Despite Rogers's threat to close the college when funds were depleted, the combination of a particularly mild winter and President Bryan's ingenuity in manipulating funds—transferring expenditures to the federally funded Hatch and Morrill Acts accounts whenever possible—kept the college operational.[40]

In addition to creating a general state of havoc at the college and among the faculty, Rogers's actions created a rift between members of the board of regents. Most enjoyed backgrounds similar to Thomas's, and as educated, professional, economically "comfortable" men and staunch Republicans they did not agree with the tenets of Populism and found the severity of the Rogers's budget cuts unwarranted. A few, however, agreed with the governor's budget package. The implementation of faculty pay decreases, coupled with an alignment of Regent Stearns with Governor Rogers, proved more than Regent Blandford could bear, and he tendered his resignation.[41] In a long and detailed letter, Thomas attempted to dissuade Blandford by reminding him that their cause was just and that President Bryan, the college, its faculty, and its students deserved their efforts. "Your resignation came upon me like a thunderbolt," Thomas's letter to his friend and fellow board member began, but Thomas hastened to remind him, "this is not the first time, Blandford, that we have had to bear more than either you or I would bear in the transaction of our own business, and all for the good of this institution and in loyal support of President Bryan and the members of the faculty who have made it what it is." Thomas hoped to convince Blandford to return to the board, if only for a short duration, so that together, as regents, they could fulfill their obligation to the man they had placed in the president's office in 1893.

> Now Blandford, we are old, old friends. . . . With you back on the board we are again in full possession and control and never again will the Governor dare to attack your position. . . . I will not bow my neck to any man from a personal standpoint, but for the sake of this college and this grand faculty and the youth of this state I shall go on with the work and carry this burden with me. My integrity, judgment, and conscientious discharge of duty have been called seriously in question; so have yours. All will be right in the end. . . . I ask you to act upon your good judgment and the true nobility of your character.[42]

Despite Thomas's effort to convince Blandford to remain, the governor accepted his resignation and he returned to Walla Walla and his position there as county prosecuting attorney. After Blandford's unpleasant departure, Thomas's position on the board of regents seems to have lost some of its luster, and in 1899, in the midst of his second term, he resigned his appointment. It does not appear that any particular ill will led to this decision, and Bryan's reference to the departure simply states, "General T. R. Tannatt, who from the date of the reorganization in '93 had been a very active and deeply interested member of the board, resigned in the mid-summer of 1899."[43] Thomas's letter to Bryan, dated at Farmington on June 22, however, sets forth the reasons for his early departure. "When Regent Blandford resigned, I determined within myself, that nothing save removal, should sever my connection with the College, until time enabled me to introduce a motion to right a wrong, and restore the salaries of yourself and faithful associates," the letter began. "This has been done, and my resignation is by even[ing] mail forwarded to Gov Rogers." Thomas's letter then became personal, and he assured Bryan, "My friendship and regard for you and the gentlemen of the faculty will with me be life long. I love the College and its grand mission and in all matters touching its interests my loyalty shall never swerve."[44] Thomas clearly saw vindication for Blandford's resignation in the salary restorations, though Frkyman's history of the college suggests that restoration of faculty salaries in 1899 had much more to do with economic recovery than the administrative skill and steadfastness of Bryan and the regents.[45]

The Daughters of the American Revolution and Civic Commemoration

Following his resignation from the board of regents, Thomas returned to Elizabeth and the family home she had maintained throughout their married life. It appears that Thomas closed his hardware store sometime in the early 1890s, but the orchards continued to thrive and he turned his full attention to them and to the promotion of horticulture throughout the region, serving as president of both the Inland Empire Horticulture Association and the Whitman County Horticultural Association.[46] He maintained a close friendship with Enoch Bryan after leaving the board of regents, and in 1902 he issued an invitation to the college's horticulture students to the Horticulture Association's convention. "The work of the convention . . . will, by its very nature, be instructive and profitable to all enlisted for Horticulture work," he advised Bryan, and went on to inform him that both rail rates and lodgings would be arranged for students who wished to attend.[47]

The partnership Thomas and Elizabeth developed early in their marriage seems only to have grown stronger in their later years, and as she acted as his partner and confidante in business, so too did they work together in commemorating the American past and promoting patriotism in the young Inland Empire. At the turn of the twentieth century, Americans, and particularly those of the middle class, began to idealize the memory of the Civil War, now thirty-five years distant, and elevate the status of its representative soldier to that of heroic icon, to be both respected and revered. The Civil War "gave us the American soldier," Thomas Chambers Richmond reminded a Memorial Day audience in 1902, "the highest type of fighting man the world has yet produced—hopeful in adversity, patient in privation, undaunted in temporary defeat, brave in the hour of battle and magnanimous in the hour of triumph."[48] From this adoration—and the sense of nationalism it produced—grew a widespread movement of commemoration as cities and towns across the country took on the task of erecting statues and monuments in honor of their heroes. The young Inland Empire had no Civil War battle sites to memorialize, but it had witnessed struggles between the army and regional Indian tribes, and it was to these that Thomas turned his nationalistic fervor. "My home is within fifteen miles of the spot where Capt. Taylor and Lieut. Gaston fell and Steptoe Butte is ever in view to remind me of Gaston of Class 56," Thomas wrote to Capt. William Rivers in 1902 of Lt. William Gaston, killed in 1858 during an early battle between the army and members of the local Indian population.[49] Although it is unlikely that Thomas and Gaston exchanged more than passing greetings at West Point, since Gaston preceded Thomas by two years, memories of him, of West Point, and of his military service motivated Thomas, and he and Elizabeth embarked upon a campaign for the acquisition and placement of a commemorative monument at the Steptoe battlefield.[50]

Departure from Walla Walla did not slow Elizabeth's interest in philanthropy and organizational involvement, nor had the dawning of the new century lessened the resolve of the West's transplanted middle-class easterners to bring aspects of eastern culture to their adopted cities and towns. Women played a key role in commemorating and memorializing the events of the nation's young past, many through membership in the newly established Daughters of the American Revolution (DAR). The DAR was organized in 1890, largely in response to women being denied membership in the Sons of the American Revolution, established fifteen years earlier. At the DAR founding meeting, held October 11, 1890, in Washington DC, eighteen women produced a constitution detailing the organization's objectives—historical, patriotic, and educational endeavors—and invited the First Lady of the United States, Caroline Scott Harrison, to serve as its first president general, which office she accepted. In 1895 the DAR incorporated, and on May 5, 1896, they received a charter from the U.S. Congress. DAR membership was, and is, open to any woman eighteen years of age or over, proving descent from a man or woman who fought for American independence or rendered aid to someone who fought.[51] DAR chapters organized quickly in the Inland Empire, and just ten years after the founding of the first chapter, Elizabeth was one of "a circle of enthusiastic patriotic women" who gathered on June 14, 1900, to establish Spokane's Esther Reed Chapter.[52] Two years later, just days after Thomas wrote to Captain Rivers, the Esther Reed Chapter held its annual meeting, and Elizabeth, as chapter historian, inspired the patriotic fervor of the membership with her report, which focused on the importance of local historic preservation. "The city of Spokane and surroundings is historic ground rich in incidents that should not be allowed to escape the pen of some historian," she noted, then carried Thomas's message to the gathering, reminding them that "we are within 40 miles of the spot where Captain Taylor and Lieutenant Gaston, U.S.A., fell in May, 1858, in the first serious conflict in eastern Washington between the Indians and the troops of our government."[53]

The publication of Elizabeth's report in a Spokane newspaper generated community interest not only in the Steptoe battle but in the historic preservation and commemoration of all aspects of Inland Empire history. In addition to undertaking the task of memorializing Steptoe, the DAR issued a call for memorabilia and reminiscences of the region's earliest days for eventual placement in (as yet unconstructed) museums. For the next several years, members of the chapter devoted their attention to this latter task of collection, and their slow but steady progress prompted Elizabeth, in her capacity as state vice-regent, to convey to Washington's state regent that the "action aroused considerable interest and called forth favorable editorials from leading newspapers." Further, "early residents have been requested to write descriptive papers—thus preserving information of incalculable value which in a few years will be unattainable." Elizabeth then made a most interesting comment, stating that "research work is adapted to women, they are quick to perceive, persevering, eager to do justice, have the natural 'historical sense' and are active in educational work."[54] At the turn of the century, Elizabeth embraced and endorsed the role of women as civilizers and as preservers of local and national heritage.[55] While the collection project continued, Thomas and Elizabeth turned their attention, and their energy, to the Steptoe Monument.

The battle to be memorialized took place in the spring of 1858 and pitted U.S. Army troops, under the command of Col. Edward J. Steptoe, against a confederation of local Indians, members of the Palouse, Spokane, and Coeur d'Alene among them. As the command marched north on May 16 toward the Colville mining region to investigate the murders of two miners, attributed to the local Indians, they encountered an armed and mounted assemblage of them as it neared present-day Rosalia. Published estimates of the number of Indians gathered that day have ranged from six hundred to fifteen hundred, though a firsthand account by one of Steptoe's men suggests only six hundred.[56] Not anticipating the battle that ensued, Steptoe had ordered that the 150 troops in his command carry only light arms. He conveyed to the leaders of the assembled Indians that his troops intended no harm, but the Indians would not permit the soldiers to proceed. Aware of his numerical disadvantage, Steptoe agreed to reverse his course and march south the following day, in the direction of the troop's home post at Fort Walla Walla.

The following morning, Steptoe and his men had begun their southward march when they were fired upon by a large group of Indians who had not dispersed the night before. Fighting continued throughout the day, and both sides suffered casualties, Steptoe's forces particularly weakened by the loss of two officers (Captain Taylor and Lieutenant Gaston), five enlisted men, and three Nez Perce serving the army as scouts. The number of Indian casualties during this battle is unknown, though a firsthand account reported personal knowledge of fourteen dead and forty wounded.[57] As night fell the soldiers retreated to a small hilltop where they were soon surrounded by their pursuers. Steptoe realized that in order to survive they would have to utilize the cover of darkness and make their way to the Snake River, more than seventy miles distant. According to Thomas J. Beall, one of the longest-surviving members of the battle, credit for the escape rested with "Timothy," the Nez Perce who served as Steptoe's guide. Beall recalled that when the situation seemed the bleakest, Timothy "volunteered to go out and see if there might not be some gap in the ring which the Indians had drawn around us."[58] He succeeded in locating such a gap and led the troop off the hilltop and to the river, where other Nez Perce assisted them in making the crossing. Within a matter of days, the bedraggled troop reached the safe confines of Fort Walla Walla.[59]

On May 17, 1907, Thomas, Elizabeth, and several members of the Esther Reed Chapter traveled to Rosalia to meet with three survivors of the Inland Empire Indian campaign and to determine, or at least agree upon, the location of the battle for appropriate placement of a monument.[60] Two of the three men, Thomas Beall and Michael J. Kenny, had served with Steptoe during the battle, while the third, J. J. Rohn, served with the troop detached the following September by Col. George Wright to recover the remains of those who fell. In a letter written in 1902, Rohn recalled "the graves were open and bones scatered [sic] we brought all we could find to Walla Walla w[h]ere they were buried with great honor."[61] Beall, Kenny, and Rohn each walked the battlefield that May day, and together they agreed on the best location for placement of a monument.[62]

With the battle site identified, plans for procurement and placement of the monument began with acquisition of the site as the first order of business. Eager to assist in the project, the citizens of Rosalia raised the funds necessary to purchase the three-acre plot and presented it to the Esther Reed Chapter, the deed to be held in perpetuity by the Whitman County commissioners.[63] The Rosalians were so efficient and effective in their fund-raising that they collected seven hundred dollars, twice the amount needed to purchase the land, and contributed the excess to the monument fund.[64] According to the original plan, the monument would stand forty-five feet tall and cost ten thousand dollars to construct and place. The organizing committee fully expected to receive this sum, in equal parts, from the state and federal governments, and at the Esther Reed Chapter's sixth annual session, held on June 4, 1907, Elizabeth presented a lengthy paper on the battle and justification for these monetary requests. "During all these years, since the members of the Steptoe Expedition were delivered from peril and fed by the Nez Perces of Alpoma no recompense has ever been made by the War Department or any other Bureau of the Government," the report read, and to add credence to the project at hand, Elizabeth placed the onus of memorialization squarely on the shoulders of those assembled, reminding them that "these matters, often referred to in our daily newspapers, will be lost to History unless some Association assumes the work of record."[65]

In anticipation of the erection and solemnization of the monument a year distant, and on the fiftieth anniversary of the battle, the organizing committee hosted an official dedication ceremony on June 14, 1907. "Nearly 60 visitors from Spokane and many citizens of Rosalia took part in the festivities," the *Spokesman Review* reported, and Elizabeth paid particular attention to her journal entry that day, taking care to write the words "Flag Day" above the printed date and to record the day's events in some detail.[66] "Left for Rosalia on Inland R.R. car decorated with flag," she began, "people in Rosalia took us to view battle-ground guided by the 3 survivors of Steptoe Expedition." Beall, Kenny, and Rohn attended this gathering and, as the battle's sole survivors, became important links to the past as the organizing committee went forward with its task. Thomas concluded the June program with a few remarks, and while his text has not survived, it is likely that it paid tribute to both his fallen West Point comrade and to those intent on commemorating Gaston's last battle in the uniform of his country.[67]

During the first session of the Sixtieth Congress of the United States, held between December 2, 1907, and May 30, 1908, Washington State representative Wesley J. Jones introduced H.R. 21340, the purpose of which was "to appropriate the sum of $5,000 as a part contribution toward the erection of a monument on Steptoe Battlefield, Whitman County, Washington." The bill was referred to the Committee on the Library, where it died without consideration.[68] This failure by the federal government to allocate funds for the project prompted the organizing committee to reevaluate the size and scope of the memorial, and they found that by reducing the height from forty-five to twenty-five feet they would reduce the cost by 50 percent. At the same time, an allocation by the state legislature had become essential, and Thomas played a significant role in attempting to garner support from members of that body, many of whom he had done business with while serving on the board of regents. "'Flag Day' as date of dedication," his letter to legislators and potential benefactors began, "the monument in its accepted design will cost $5000." The letter continued with the assurance that the Esther Reed Chapter assumed responsibility for all expenses and labor connected with road work, parking facilities, and fencing, estimated at one thousand dollars.[69] Despite Thomas's efforts, however, the state legislature followed the example of the federal government and failed, on three separate occasions, to allocate funds for construction and placement of the Steptoe Monument.

Thomas extended his project involvement beyond the state legislature, and in January 1909, while in Spokane on business, he wrote to Elizabeth, "I think I will stop off at Rosalia over one train on Friday. My object is to meet the Rosalia Committee, report what is decided upon, and have them follow it up with legislation."[70] On February 12 he wrote Elizabeth again and advised her that he had "sent out 25 of the DAR folders to surviving members of Col Steptoes class (7) and to those of Taylor and Gastons classes."[71] The failure of the state and federal governments to assist in funding this project did not dampen the resolve of the Tannatts and the others to see it to completion. The Esther Reed Chapter assumed the fund-raising responsibility and held numerous teas, luncheons, and musical programs, contributing all proceeds to the monument fund.[72]

The interment location of those who fell on the Steptoe battlefield, and particularly of Taylor and Gaston, concerned Thomas and Elizabeth as the monument process continued. In his official report, Steptoe noted that once he reached the decision to retreat, he "concluded to abandon everything that might impede our march," including disabled animals, the troop's two howitzers, and the bodies of the deceased, the latter of which were not recovered until September when Rohn's expedition returned to the battlefield and began the process of recovery.[73] "We came upon the bones of many of our men that had lain bleaching on the prairie hills for four months," read the recovery report, most likely filed by Bvt. Maj. W. N. Grier, commander of the detail, noting that bones were "scattered and dragged, in every direction by the bands of wolves that had infested the place." The soldiers' remains were easily located, for as the troop passed the slope of a hill they "came upon a small ravine in which lay the graves of four men—Captain Taylor, a half-breed and two of the dragoons. Silently and mournfully we disinterred their remains," the report continued, "and securely packing them bore them from the field to our camp, in order to transport them to Walla Walla, there to give them proper burial with military honors."[74]

The record indicating the soldiers' re-interment at Fort Walla Walla troubled Thomas and Elizabeth, since later reports suggested that Taylor and Gaston had been removed to the cemetery at West Point. Thomas became obsessed with discovering the truth about the final resting place of his West Point comrade, and in 1909 he and Elizabeth traveled to West Point to conduct their own search for the graves. Despite the relative proximity to Manchester, the death of Elizabeth's sole surviving sibling, William Henry, in 1907 at the age of eighty-five, and the Tannatts' ages, now seventy-five and seventy-two respectively, Thomas and Elizabeth decided to forego a visit to her childhood home.[75] Elizabeth kept a detailed record of their search of the West Point cemetery and noted that as they walked among the headstones Thomas called out to her, "I have found Capt. Taylor's and Gaston's graves." The stone to which Thomas referred was "a modest but pretty monument bearing Lt. Gaston's name," and Albert Rhodes, superintendent of the West Point cemetery, dispelled Thomas's doubt that it was but a memorial, confirming that Gaston's remains lay beneath it.[76] The interment mystery solved, Thomas and Elizabeth returned home to Washington.

Shortly after their return, however, Thomas's health experienced a rapid declined, and this forced the couple to retire from active participation in the monument project, though they closely followed it to completion. In May 1914, Elizabeth wrote Captain Braden at West Point that "the meeting is now in session to arrange for the moving of the Memorial Monument this week, to be erected on the battle-field of to-hots-nim-me, near Rosalia, by our Chapter. This we have worked to accomplish since 1902."[77] The dedication ceremony took place on June 15, 1914, and while the assemblage included Gov. Ernest Lister, the three battle survivors, four hundred uniformed soldiers from Fort George Wright, and an estimated crowd of five thousand spectators, neither Thomas nor Elizabeth was in attendance.[78] Thomas died just six months prior to the dedication, and Elizabeth declined all invitations, not wanting to attend the ceremony without him. Their dedication to the project had not been forgotten, however, and speaking on behalf of the DAR, Netta Phelps recognized that through "having its first suggestion from the loyal heart of a patriot who has recently been called to the higher life, and by his wife, the chapter's much loved historian, . . . has this work come."[79]

The placement of this monument meant much more to Thomas and Elizabeth than the commemoration of an 1858 battle or the loss of a West Point colleague. To the Tannatts, the Steptoe Monument stood as a symbol of their loyalty to, and sense of citizenship in, their adopted western homeland and their dedication to their roles as community builders and as trusted keepers of the region's past.

Final Years and Reflections on the Past

Thomas's health had declined noticeably during the first decade of the new century, and in 1905 he and Elizabeth relocated to Spokane to be closer to their daughter Minnie. In 1906 Minnie married physician Cyrus K.

Merriam, and as Thomas and Elizabeth reached their seventies it is likely that age influenced their relocation decision. [80] The Steptoe Monument project proved to be Thomas's last community endeavor, and it is fitting that it combined the aspects of life he held most dear: the U.S. Army, civic commemoration, community organization and involvement, and settlement and community building in the West. Gen. Thomas Redding Tannatt died at the home of his daughter and son-in-law on December 20, 1913, at the age of eighty, after more than thirty years in the West he had grown to love. "Lincoln Adviser in War Dies Here," his obituary in Spokane's *Spokesman-Review* read, and this headline alone would have pleased Thomas immeasurably. In accordance with his wishes, Thomas's coffin was draped with an American flag, and members of the Fourteenth Infantry stationed at Spokane's Fort George Wright served as pallbearers while "hundreds of friends" followed the hearse carrying his body from the Merriam house to its final resting place at Spokane's Fairmount Cemetery. [81] The *Spokesman-Review* memorialized Thomas as "a man of high sense of honor and integrity," and the Military Order of the Loyal Legion remembered him as "a worthy companion whose memory will be held in grateful remembrance by those who survive him."[82] Thomas had been an active participant in the many communities he called home during the eighty years of his life, and despite the episodes of ill health that continued to plague him, he seems at last to have found happiness, fulfillment, and satisfaction in eastern Washington.

Thomas and Elizabeth celebrated their fifty-fourth wedding anniversary the spring before he died, and the loss of the man with whom she had shared her life for more than half a century affected Elizabeth tremendously. "The memory of him is a consolation in my sorrow," Elizabeth wrote Capt. Lewis G. Holt, who had served with Thomas during the Civil War in the First Massachusetts Heavy Artillery.[83] Holt responded with his own reminiscences of Thomas. "He was a commander to be proud of, and . . . he was always proud of the 1st Mass. H.A.," Holt wrote. "I remember that he said to those of us who were left after the fight at Spotsalvania [sic], (which was our first battle) boys you have today covered the Regiment all over with glory. Well we all remember that with pride for both our Col. and our Regt."[84] From the date of their marriage in 1860, and perhaps before, Elizabeth had proudly promoted Thomas's character and the measure of his accomplishments. More than fifty years later, on the occasion of his passing, it certainly pleased her to learn that General Tannatt continued to be held in high regard by those who had known him.

The Tannatts had not only enjoyed a long and happy marriage; they had also been successful business partners, loyal confidants and correspondents, and, it appears, very good friends. After Thomas died, Elizabeth's participation in her various clubs and organizations diminished considerably, though she continued to walk to church on Sundays, weather permitting, enjoyed calling on friends, and doted on her granddaughter and namesake, Minnie's daughter, Elizabeth. She also reflected on the past, on the long road she and Thomas had traveled together, and on her youth in Manchester. After more than thirty years, Elizabeth was clearly at home in the West, but a fondness for the Manchester of her youth never wavered. "My love for the dear old State increases with age," she wrote her cousin Annie Tappan, a lifelong Manchester resident, in the summer of 1913. "It would be a great cross to revisit the scenes of my childhood."[85]

Sadly, she did not have the opportunity to revisit those scenes, and on February 22, 1920, Elizabeth Forster Tappan Tannatt died at the age of eighty-two. Although the pomp and pageantry that accompanied Thomas's funeral were absent from hers, the obituary that appeared in the *Spokesman-Review* celebrated Elizabeth's life and paid tribute to her many philanthropic and organizational endeavors. In particular, the paper noted that "before the world war started Mrs. Tannatt had begun a series of memoirs of the civil war, but on the outbreak of hostilities with Germany dropped that work and took up active Red Cross work."[86] As had been typical throughout her life, Elizabeth made no mention of her Red Cross activities in her journals and letters, and while her family and many friends mourned her loss, the greater loss to history is the absence of the Civil War memoir she had intended to write.

"He has always been remarkable for personal dignity and modesty," wrote Charles Upham, former representative from Massachusetts, of Thomas Tannatt in 1865, when queried by New York entrepreneurs of the character of the man engaged to manage their Colorado mining interests. "His address is pleasing, and his moral character has been such, from the earliest youth, as to command the highest confidence and respect." [1] Dignity, modesty, and high moral character are the qualities that guided Thomas and allowed him, despite the Civil War–induced maladies that plagued him throughout his lifetime, to contribute to the development of the American West in general, and to eastern Washington's Inland Empire in particular, through his involvement in transportation, settlement and development, and higher education. Dignity, modesty, and high moral character are also the attributes that, to Thomas and Elizabeth Tannatt and others like them, set middle-class, post–Civil War immigrants apart from the mass of the great middle class. [2]

In a reversal of Frederick Jackson Turner's 1893 frontier thesis, which suggested that the frontier itself defined Americans and allowed them to cast off the mantles of cultures inherited from Europe and the eastern United States, historian Dean May has insisted that "the frontier did not greatly alter the people who went there, but rather made it possible for them to realize the deepest aspirations of the cultures from which they came," and that "they built in the West what they would have built in the East had it been possible." [3] These assertions certainly apply to the Tannatts and other members of the nineteenth-century middle class who, due to the adverse conditions inflicted upon the East by the war, sought to distinguish themselves in the West as leaders and community builders and to transplant the aspects of eastern culture they held most dear in their adopted homes.

May has further suggested that on the frontier, "for a generation or more the founding majority dominated not only the minority co-founders, but also most of those who came later." [4] In the case of eastern Washington, this "founding majority" is defined not necessarily as the greatest number but as those who wielded the greatest influence, and Thomas, through his affiliation with the region's most important enterprise, the railroads, certainly belonged to this group. In his management capacity, perched on a middle tier of Alfred Chandler's organizational model, Thomas established himself as an essential cog in the corporate wheel and as a loyal and dedicated member of the community: first as manager of the Oregon Improvement Company's Inland Empire operations, later as the mayor of Walla Walla, and finally as a member of the Washington Agricultural College Board of Regents.

The role Thomas played in the relocation of a substantial population of German Russians from agricultural regions in the Midwest to eastern Washington is probably his greatest legacy, since their agricultural expertise transformed the Inland Empire into one of the world's premier wheat-producing regions, a distinction that continues to the present day. It is a mistake, however, to suggest that Thomas and other middle-class Inland Empire citizens regarded members of this immigrant group as their social equals; in fact, they worked diligently to maintain a level of class separation. Newspaper articles reporting the arrival of the German Russians contributed to this class differentiation by referring to them only collectively, and then simply as "an exodus from Kansas" or "new comers," never as individuals.[5] Thomas, on the other hand, received great personal praise for the role he played in the migration endeavor. Members of the middle class drew clear and concise lines of class differentiation on the Washington Palouse, and despite the common "middle class" moniker, community leaders and the area's immigrant farmers simply did not occupy the same rung on the social ladder.[6]

Don Harrison Doyle, in his community study on Jacksonville, Illinois, has suggested that "the community-builders of the nineteenth century placed far more responsibility on human institutions and ideas to mold the moral environment" than did those who had come before them. Through his temperance, benevolent, and reform policies dating to his years in the military, Thomas certainly fits this model.[7] Doyle relates the story of Charles Eames, son of a successful Jacksonville merchant, editor-owner of a local newspaper, and distinguished member of Jacksonville's upper middle class. Eames's story parallels Thomas's in a number of ways, for Eames's efforts at promoting his Midwestern hometown are reminiscent of Thomas's endeavors in both Tennessee and eastern Washington. Eames published a history of Jacksonville and environs in the late nineteenth century in order to "invest pride and satisfaction in a community that had tried desperately hard to be something more than it was."[8] Thomas might be found guilty of making similar attempts, particularly during the waning days of Inland Empire growth and expansion and his inability to turn Farmington into a major transportation and supply center. The failed Farmington experiment notwithstanding, Thomas did belong to that group of early promoters of eastern Washington who, during the 1880s and 1890s, witnessed and contributed to enormous increases in both population and development, and he took a great deal of pride in statistics that verified his successes. The population of Walla Walla County, for instance, grew from just fourteen hundred in 1870, a number that seemed substantial at the time, to more than thirty thousand by the first decade of the twentieth century.[9] Such statistics certainly helped soothe the lingering sting of the Farmington situation and Thomas's disappointment in the Tennessee Immigration Association.

The concept of molding a moral western environment extended throughout the middle-class population of community leaders and builders, and for women the opportunity to play decisive roles lay in the organizations and associations they modeled after those to which they had belonged in the East. This idea of volunteerism proved to be extremely important in the shaping and establishing of new communities, and Doyle has further suggested that "at the heart of the new community was the idea of voluntary commitment to that community and its institutions."[10] Through her involvement with women's organizations in the East, and harkening back to the reform-mindedness of her father's nephews Lewis and Arthur Tappan, Elizabeth Tannatt knew that the rough-edged cities and towns of the West would not become civilized without the active participation of organizations and individuals dedicated to benevolence and reform. Aware of the benefits to local groups of affiliation with national organizations, and acting in concert with other middle-class women, Elizabeth played an instrumental role in bringing the Woman's Christian Temperance Union and its esteemed leader, Frances Willard, to Walla Walla in 1883 and the Daughters of the American Revolution to Spokane in 1900. At the same time, Elizabeth and her contemporaries, longtime friends Caroline Wingard and M. C. Allen among them, used these associations to lift themselves socially above those they considered socially inferior. Doyle has further implied that an individual's decision to engage in community involvement and volunteerism went far deeper than his or her intention to act charitably, and for most middle-class community leaders and builders "one's commitment to the voluntary community is determined more by carefully calculated personal goals, such as social mobility."[11] As eager as the men to leave their imprint on the West, Elizabeth and other middle-class women became involved in the newly popular activity of commemoration and historic preservation.[12] The most visible reminder of Elizabeth's organizational involvement in eastern Washington is the Rosalia monument, which not only commemorates the 1858 Steptoe Battle but also recognizes the efforts undertaken by members of the Daughters of the American Revolution to bring placement of the monument to fruition.

The vast amount of attention paid by scholars and others to the West's early pioneers and their Oregon Trail journeys in the 1840s and 1850s accentuates the indifference, or disinterest, many have shown toward the late-nineteenth-century middle class and the contributions they made to the development of the region. Melanie Archer and Judith Blau have credited the emerging nineteenth-century middle class with the proliferation of such social institutions as schools, newspapers, and the family, noting that these "helped to shape—and were shaped by—codes of etiquette, public behavior, manners, and distinctive middle-class values," the importance of which, they insist, "should not be underestimated." [13] The difficulty in defining "the" middle class continues to exist, however, as most middle-class studies, this one included, are regional and focus on short periods of time. The goal, of course, is that at some point in the not too distant future some brave scholar will take on the task of producing a synthesis on the American middle class. Until that time, however, local and community studies dedicated to this important yet largely unacknowledged segment of the American population will continue to enlarge and expand a general understanding of, and appreciation for, the nineteenth-century American middle class.

Stuart Blumin has suggested that the nineteenth-century American middle class "represented a specific set of experiences, a specific style of living, and a specific society identity—a social world . . . that was distinct from others above and below it in the tangible hierarchy that was society." [14] Nineteenth-century middle-class individuals knew precisely where they belonged in Blumin's "tangible hierarchy," worked diligently to maintain that status once achieved, and were proud to number themselves among this uniquely American social classification. Ralph Waldo Emerson set forth perhaps the best description of the nineteenth-century middle class in 1860 when he wrote that "all great men come out of the middle classes. 'Tis better for the head; 'tis better for the heart. . . . Plant him down among farmers, firemen, Indians, and emigrants. . . . [S]end him to Kansas, to Pike's Peak, to Oregon: and, if he have true faculty, this may be the element he wants, and he will come out of it with broader wisdom." [15] Emerson's words certainly describe the trials, tribulations, and hard-won successes of Thomas and Elizabeth Tannatt and their middle-class eastern Washington contemporaries, and they would have pleased them enormously.

Tannatt-Tappan Genealogy

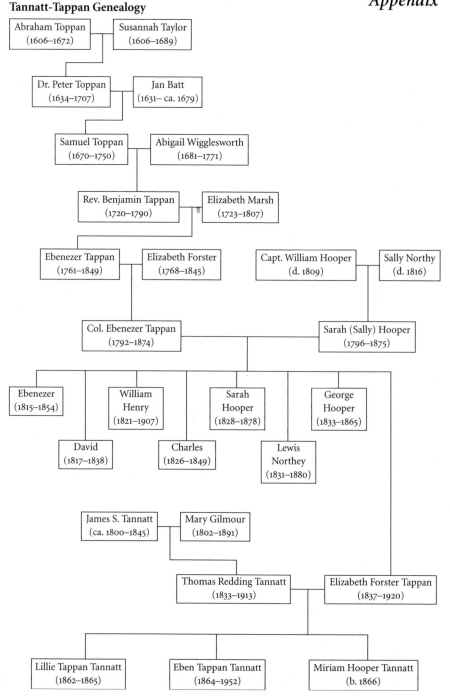

Notes

Abbreviations

ETT   Elizabeth T. Tannatt

TRT   Thomas R. Tannatt

MAC   Northwest Museum of Arts and Culture, Spokane WA

MASC   Manuscripts, Archives and Special Collections, Washington State University Libraries, Pullman WA

MHS   Manchester Historical Society, Manchester-by-the-Sea MA

NARA   National Archives and Records Administration, Washington DC

ORNP   Oregon Railway and Navigation Company Papers, 1876–1882, Cage 4545, MASC

SFTP   Samuel F. Tappan Papers, C. P. Weaver Private Collection, Manchester-by-the-Sea MA

USMA   United States Military Academy Archives, West Point NY

Prologue

1. Sellers, *Market Revolution*, 238.
2. Archer and Blau, "Class Formation in Nineteenth-Century America," 31.
3. Watson, *Liberty and Power*, 31–32.
4. See Wilentz, *Chants Democratic*; Stansell, *City of Women*.
5. Bledstein, *Culture of Professionalism*, 27–33.
6. Archer and Blau, "Class Formation in Nineteenth-Century America," 19.
7. Blumin, *Emergence of the Middle Class*, 16.
8. Blumin, *Emergence of the Middle Class*, 14–15.
9. Wilentz, *Chants Democratic*, 11–12.
10. Beckert, *Monied Metropolis*, 6.
11. Vinovskis, "Stalking the Elusive Middle Class," 586.
12. Beckert, "Propertied of a Different Kind," 286–87. See also Bledstein and Johnson, *Middling Sorts*, 296–98.
13. Bledstein and Johnson, *Middling Sorts*, 25.
14. Bledstein, *Culture of Professionalism*, 4.
15. Bledstein and Johnson, *Middling Sorts*, 8–9.
16. See Jones, "Men and Women in Northern New England"; Vinovskis, "Have Social Historians Lost the Civil War?"; True, "Middle Class Women and Civic Improvement."
17. *Manchester-by-the-Sea, 1645–1970*, 16–17.
18. Vinovskis, "Have Social Historians Lost the Civil War?" 34.
19. Chandler, *Visible Hand*, 77–78.
20. Chandler, *Visible Hand*, 77–80. Chandler's description and discussion of the advent of America's corporate structure suggests that organizational systems were effectively and efficiently put in place with little ensuing confusion, displacement, or turmoil. Other historians have challenged these assertions,

however, and Alan Trachtenberg presents a much bleaker picture of this transition period, suggesting that "economic incorporation wrenched American society from the moorings of familiar values" and that "the process proceeded by contradiction and conflict." Trachtenberg, *Incorporation of America*, 7.

21. Dawley, *Struggles for Justice*, 69–70; see also Wiebe, *Search for Order*.

22. Doyle, *Social Order of a Frontier Community*, 194.

23. Blumin, *Emergence of the Middle Class*, 298.

24. Doyle, *Social Order of a Frontier Community*, 3.

25. Archer and Blau, "Class Formation in Nineteenth-Century America," 33.

1. The Early Years, 1833–1861

1. Lamson, *History of the Town of Manchester*, 331.

2. Lamson, *History of the Town of Manchester*, 291.

3. Tappan Family Tree, n.d., Tappan Family Papers, MHS.

4. Coffin, *Toppans of Toppan's Lane*, 10–11; D. L. Tappan, *Tappan-Toppan Genealogy*, 5; Good, *Family Records of James and Nancy Dunham Tappan*. There is some discrepancy in the name of the ship on which the family traveled; Coffin identifies it as the *Rose of Yarmouth*.

5. D. L. Tappan, *Tappan-Toppan Genealogy*, 5–6.

6. D. L. Tappan, *Tappan-Toppan Genealogy*, 6.

7. Miscellaneous documents, n.d., Tappan Family Papers, MHS.

8. V. Anderson, "Religion, the Common Thread of Motivation," 149. See also Cressy, *Coming Over*; Games, *Migration*; V. Anderson, *New England's Generation*.

9. D. L. Tappan, *Tappan-Toppan Genealogy*, 7.

10. Miscellaneous documents, Tappan Family Papers, MHS; D. L. Tappan, *Tappan-Toppan Genealogy*, 22, 24. According to Daniel Langdon Tappan, the spelling of the family name became quite controversial. Benjamin, the eldest son of Reverend Tappan, began to use the spelling "Tappen," as did many of the New York branch of the family. At this time, Reverend Tappan still spelled it "Toppan." He and another of his sons, David, compromised with young Benjamin and agreed to spell the first syllable "Tap" if he would spell the second syllable "pan." The compromise worked, and "Tappan" became the accepted spelling of the family name by the Manchester branch.

11. W. H. Tappan, "Manchester," 1282–85.

12. D. L. Tappan, *Tappan-Toppan Genealogy*, 23; W. H. Tappan, "Manchester," 1286. The Congregational Church was the sole house of worship in Manchester until 1842, when Elder Elam Burnham of Essex, Massachusetts, began holding Baptist meetings in the town. W. H. Tappan, "Manchester," 1288–89.

13. W. H. Tappan, "Manchester," 1253.

14. Kenny, *Cape Ann: Cape America*, 19.

15. W. H. Tappan, "Manchester," 1263.

16. W. H. Tappan, "Manchester," 1259.

17. Lamson, *History of the Town of Manchester*, 350.
18. D. L. Tappan, *Tappan-Toppan Genealogy*, 23; miscellaneous documents, n.d., Tappan Family Papers, MHS.
19. Lamson, *History of the Town of Manchester*, 290–91.
20. W. H. Tappan, "Manchester," 1286.
21. W. H. Tappan, "Manchester," 1265–66; Countryman, *American Revolution*, 156–59.
22. Kenney, *Cape Ann: Cape America*, 22.
23. *Manchester-by-the-Sea, 1645–1970*, 15.
24. *Manchester-by-the-Sea, 1645–1970*, 16.
25. W. H. Tappan, "Manchester," 1292–93; *Manchester-by-the-Sea, 1645–1970*, 15–17.
26. Watson, *Liberty and Power*, 28–31. See also Sellers, *Market Revolution*; Wilentz, *Chants Democratic*; Dawley, *Class and Community*. For a discussion on the effects of the Market Revolution on craftswomen, see Stansell, *City of Women*.
27. Prior to the invention of the turning lathe, cabinetmakers used a device known as a "spring pole lathe" to turn pieces of wood. The turning lathe was much more time efficient and caused fewer pieces to be ruined due to improper turning. I. Bradley, *History of Machine Tools*.
28. *Manchester-by-the-Sea, 1645–1970*, 15–17; W. H. Tappan, "Manchester," 1292–94.
29. C. P. Weaver, "Tappans of Manchester," n.d., Tappan Family Papers, MHS.
30. D. L. Tappan, *Tappan-Toppan Genealogy*, 48; W. H. Tappan, "Manchester," 1273.
31. D. L. Tappan, *Tappan-Toppan Genealogy*, 51; W. H. Tappan, "Manchester," 1273.
32. Lamson, *History of the Town of Manchester*, 291.
33. *Manchester-by-the-Sea, 1645–1970*, 16.
34. Lamson, *History of the Town of Manchester*, 311. Colonel Tappan's "Torrent" served the town until its retirement in 1885. It has since been preserved and is on display at The Old Police Station in Manchester.
35. Town Records, April 1, 1844, Town Hall, Manchester-by-the-Sea MA.
36. Miscellaneous documents, n.d., Tappan Family Papers, MHS.
37. Lamson, *History of the Town of Manchester*, 206.
38. *Catalogue of the Teachers & Pupils, Chapel School, Manchester, Mass.*, 7.
39. *Catalogue of the Teachers & Pupils, Chapel School, Manchester, Mass.*, 3–6.
40. M. B. Norton, *Liberty's Daughters*, 273.
41. Kerber, *Women of the Republic*, 200.
42. Cott, *Bonds of Womanhood*, 112.
43. For extended discussions on women and education in the late eighteenth and early nineteenth centuries, see Kerber, *Women of the Republic*; M. B. Norton, *Liberty's Daughters*; Cott, *Bonds of Womanhood*; Kaufman, *Women Teachers on the Frontier*; Kerber, *Intellectual History of Women*.
44. *Order of Exercises of the Charlestown Female Seminary*.
45. *Order of Exercises of the Charlestown Female Seminary*, notes written on program by Elizabeth F. Tappan and an unidentified friend.

46. *Highlander* 39, no. 3 (2001): 66; MacLean, *Highlanders*, 264. Craigmillar Castle, a well-preserved Scottish ruin, stands on a hill just south of Edinburgh. Craigmillar is first mentioned in the twelfth century as a site deeded by David I to the Dunfermline Abbey. The Preston family acquired it in about 1374 and commenced construction of a new castle on the site of the old stronghold. Sir John Gilmour purchased the castle from the Preston family in 1660 and expanded and modernized it significantly. In 1946 the Gilmour family gave the castle to Historic Scotland, to be held and protected as a national landmark. See Johnson, *National Trust Book of British Castles*, 202–3; "Craigmillar Castle"; "Castles & Towers of Scotland, Craigmillar Castle."

47. Association of Graduates of the U.S. Military Academy, *Annual Reunion, 1914*, 105–6; Durham, *History of the City of Spokane*, 180.

48. "Common Welsh Surnames."

49. Willard and Livermore, *A Woman of the Century*, 79; miscellaneous newspaper clippings, n.d., Tannatt Family Papers, MASC.

50. Federation of American Scientists, "New York Naval Shipyard."

51. Chauncey Mitchell Depew was born in Peekskill in 1834, attended the Peekskill Academy, and graduated from Yale College in 1856. He served on the New York State Legislature in 1862 and 1863, and as New York's secretary of state in 1864 and 1865. In 1898 he was elected United States senator from New York, a capacity in which he served for twelve years. Depew was involved with railroads for most of his life, and in 1866 Commodore Vanderbilt engaged him as attorney for the New York Central and Hudson River Railroad. He was appointed general counsel and director of the "Vanderbilt System" in 1876, made second vice president of the New York Central and Hudson River Railroad in 1882, and served as president of the same from 1885 to 1898. From then until his death in 1928, Depew served as chairman of the board of directors of the New York Central Railroad Company. Yeager, *Chauncey Mitchell Depew*, v–vi. Although Chauncey Depew and Thomas Tannatt both grew up in Peekskill, attended the same schools until age twelve, and were involved with railroads and transportation throughout their lives, no correspondence between the two, if it ever existed, seems to have survived.

52. Durham, *History of the City of Spokane*, 180; Association of Graduates of the U.S. Military Academy, *Annual Reunion, 1914*, 106; *Hudson River (NY) Chronicle*, September 2, 1845, 3.

53. U.S. Census Bureau, *Sixth Census of Population, Westchester County, New York, 1840*.

54. Willard and Livermore, *A Woman of the Century*, 797–99.

55. TRT, n.d., "Map of Peekskill 33 yrs ago. By One of the Boys," Tannatt Family Papers, MAC.

56. Barber and Howe, *Historical Collections of the State of New York*, 585–87.

57. Fox, *Story of Early Peekskill*, 163–64.

58. Depew, *My Memories of Eighty Years*, 4.

59. Willard and Livermore, *A Woman of the Century*, 797–99.

60. U.S. Census Bureau, *Seventh Census of Population, Essex County, Massachusetts, 1850*; U.S. Census Bureau, *Sixth Census of Population, Westchester County, New York, 1840.*

61. Lamson, *History of the Town of Manchester,* 218; *Manchester-by-the-Sea, 1645–1970,* 32; miscellaneous documents, n.d., Tappan Family Papers, MHS. A further discussion on Eben III and his career as a lithographer is found in B. A. Norton, "Tappan and Bradford."

62. Durham, *History of the City of Spokane,* 180; Association of Graduates of the U.S. Military Academy, *Annual Reunion, 1914,* 100.

63. Charles W. Upham to Jefferson Davis, March 11, 1956, Tannatt Papers, USMA.

64. U.S. Military Academy Cadet Application Papers, 1805–1866, Tannatt Papers, USMA; Cullum, *Biographical Register,* 2:82.

65. Boynton, *History of West Point,* 244–45; Godson, *History of West Point,* 14.

66. Boynton, *History of West Point,* 175–80; Godson, *History of West Point,* 1, 12–13.

67. Boynton, *History of West Point,* 48–68; Godson, *History of West Point,* 11.

68. Boynton, *History of West Point,* 205–7.

69. Boynton, *History of West Point,* 217–18; Godson, *History of West Point,* 13–14.

70. Reynolds, "Education of Engineers in America," 463.

71. Boynton, *History of West Point,* 249, 262–63; Godson, *History of West Point,* 23.

72. Boynton, *History of West Point,* 225, 245, 249.

73. "Official Register of the Officers and Cadets of the U.S. Military Academy, West Point, New York," June 1855–1858, 7, 9, 11, 12, 17, Tannatt Papers, USMA.

74. TRT to Elizabeth Tappan, n.d., Tannatt Family Papers, MASC.

75. TRT to Elizabeth Tappan, n.d., Tannatt Family Papers, MASC.

76. M. H. Knight to TRT, August 30, 1858, Tannatt Family Papers, MAC.

77. TRT to Elizabeth Tappan, March 19, 1858, Tannatt Family Papers, MASC.

78. TRT to Elizabeth Tappan, n.d., Tannatt Family Papers, MASC.

79. TRT to Elizabeth Tappan, n.d., Tannatt Family Papers, MASC.

80. J. L. Colby, MD, July 13, 1864, Medical Certificate, Tannatt Family Papers, MAC; Bernard and Bennett, "Vasospastic Amaurosis Fugax."

81. TRT to Maj. Gen. George W. Cullum, September 28, 1867, Tannatt Papers, USMA; Cullum, *Biographical Register,* 701.

82. ETT to Sally H. Tappan, May 25, 1860, Tannatt Family Papers MASC.

83. See McFarling, *Exploring the Northern Plains,* 220, 234; Athearn, *Forts of the Upper Missouri,* 33–34; Clodfelter, *Dakota War,* 19.

84. Athearn, *Forts of the Upper Missouri,* 33–34.

85. U.S. Adjutant General's Office, *Fort Randall Post Returns, 1856–1892,* June 1856.

86. Wilson, "Old Fort Pierre and Its Neighbors," 292.

87. Wilson, "Old Fort Pierre and Its Neighbors," 292. There seems to be some conflict on this point, as Circular no. 4, issued by the War Department Surgeon General's Office for 1870, suggests that the post was named for Surgeon B. Randall USA.

88. Wilson, "Old Fort Pierre and Its Neighbors," 286–87; Schell, *History of South Dakota,* 68.

89. *Weekly Dakotian* (Yankton, Dakota Territory), June 27, 1861, 2.

90. Wilson, "Old Fort Pierre and Its Neighbors," 291–92.

91. F. Roe, *Army Letters from an Officer's Wife*, 28.

92. F. Roe, *Army Letters from an Officer's Wife*, 82. See also Leckie, *Colonel's Lady on the Western Frontier*; Custer, *"Boots and Saddles"*; Sibbald, "Army Women of the West."

93. Sibbald, "Army Women of the West," 67.

94. U.S. Adjutant General's Office, *Fort Randall Post Returns, 1856–1892*, December 1861.

95. U.S. Adjutant General's Office, *Fort Randall Post Returns, 1856–1892*, January 1858.

96. U.S. Adjutant General's Office, *Fort Randall Post Returns, 1856–1892*, September 1861.

97. Wilson, "Old Fort Pierre and Its Neighbors," 293–94.

98. Wilson, "Old Fort Pierre and Its Neighbors," 294.

99. U.S. Adjutant General's Office, *Fort Randall Post Returns, 1856–1892*, October, November, and December 1861.

100. *Dakotian*, June 6, 1861, 3.

101. TRT to ETT, October 6, 1861, Tannatt Family Papers, MASC.

102. *Dakotian*, June 6, 1861, 3.

103. John Pattee, "Reminiscences of John Pattee," *South Dakota Historical Collections* 5 (1910): 276.

104. ETT Journal, November 30, 1861, Tannatt Family Papers, MASC.

105. ETT Journal, December 6, 1861, Tannatt Family Papers, MASC.

106. ETT Journal, December 7, 1861, Tannatt Family Papers, MASC.

2. The Civil War, 1861–1864

1. ETT Journal, December 27, 1861, Tannatt Family Papers, MASC.

2. ETT to Anna Tappan, June 15, 1913, SFTP, Tannatt Family Papers, MASC.

3. ETT Journal, December 16, 1861, Tannatt Family Papers, MASC.

4. McPherson, *Ordeal by Fire*, 154, Tannatt Family Papers, MASC.

5. ETT Journal, December 23, 1861, Tannatt Family Papers, MASC.

6. ETT Journal, December 7, 12, 20, 1861, Tannatt Family Papers, MASC.

7. ETT Journal, December 31, 1861, Tannatt Family Papers, MASC.

8. ETT Journal, December 28, 1861, Tannatt Family Papers, MASC.

9. TRT to the Honorable Senators of the 38th Congress, n.d., Tannatt Family Papers, MAC; Eben Swift, Sworn Affidavit, March 18, 1864, Tannatt Family Papers, MAC; TRT to the U.S. Treasury Department, August 23, 1872, Tannatt Family Papers, MAC; A. McCue, Solicitor, Department of the Treasury, to the Department of Justice, June 11, 1887, Tannatt Family Papers, MASC.

10. TRT to Maj. Gen. George W. Cullum, September 28, 1867, Tannatt Papers, USMA.

11. McPherson, *Ordeal by Fire*, 153–54; McPherson, *Battle Cry of Freedom*, 293–97.

12. ETT Journal, January 9, 1862, Tannatt Family Papers, MASC.
13. "Mrs. E. F. Tannatt 82, Succumbs," Spokane WA Spokesman-Review, 23 February 1920, 6.
14. ETT Journal, October 11, November 22, 1863, Tannatt Family Papers, MASC.
15. Leonard, Yankee Women, xix–xx; Oates, Woman of Valor, 8–10; Christie, "Performing My Plain Duty," 217.
16. See Leonard, Yankee Women, 3–49; Ross, "Arranging a Doll's House."
17. Christie, "Performing My Plain Duty," 214, 222–23.
18. Logan, Reminiscences of a Soldier's Wife, 128, 130, 136.
19. Leckie, Elizabeth Bacon Custer, 40–51.
20. Simon, Personal Memoirs of Julia Dent Grant, 135–38.
21. ETT Journal, January 10, 1862, Tannatt Family Papers, MASC.
22. 1849 Advertisements and Announcements; "Wright's Indian Vegetable Pills 1901–1933."
23. ETT Journal, January 12, 1862, Tannatt Family Papers, MASC.
24. ETT Journal, January 14, 1862, Tannatt Family Papers, MASC.
25. TRT to Maj. Gen. George W. Cullum, September 28, 1867, Tannatt Papers, USMA; Cullum, Biographical Register, 701.
26. McPherson, Ordeal by Fire, 161–62; Stanley Matthews, Colonel and Provost Marshal, to TRT, April 7, 1862, Tannatt Family Papers, MAC; TRT to Colonel Ripley, Chief of Ordnance, May 6, 1862, Tannatt Family Papers, MAC.
27. TRT to Mr. B. F. Browne, January 6, 1862, Tannatt Family Papers, MASC.
28. TRT to Mrs. L. [Elizabeth] Tannatt, telegram, March 10, 1862, Tannatt Family Papers, MASC.
29. ETT Journal, March 24, 1862, Tannatt Family Papers, MASC.
30. Belissary, "Rise of Industry in Tennessee," 196.
31. The Sixteenth Massachusetts Volunteers organized at Camp Cameron in Cambridge on June 29, 1861. During its three-year duration (it mustered out of service on July 27, 1864, with veterans and recruits transferred to the Eleventh Massachusetts Infantry) the Sixteenth took part in many significant Civil War battles, including Fredericksburg, Chancellorsville, Gettysburg, and the Battles of the Wilderness, losing a total of 245 men. See Keniston, "Regimental History."
32. TRT to ETT, August 4, 1862, Tannatt Family Papers, MAC.
33. Nevins, War for the Union, 2:130.
34. Mitchell, Civil War Soldiers, 18.
35. McPherson, For Cause and Comrades, 30–31. For further discussions of pre-engagement enthusiasm see Link, "Potomac Fever"; Cummings, "Worcester County Soldiers."
36. McPherson, Battle Cry of Freedom, 470.
37. McPherson, Ordeal by Fire, 270, 271.
38. Eckenrode and Conrad, James Longstreet, 88–91.
39. Lewis N. Tappan to Samuel Forster Tappan, n.d., SFTP; Association of Graduates of the U.S. Military Academy, Annual Reunion, 1914, 108.

40. J. L. Colby, MD, July 13, 1864, Medical Certificate, Tannatt Family Papers, MAC; Lenzen, *Diseases of the Ancestors*.

41. Miscellaneous documents, n.d., Tannatt Family Papers, MASC.

42. TRT to ETT, December 31, 1862, Tannatt Family Papers, MASC.

43. Cummings, "Worcester County Soldiers," 49.

44. TRT to ETT, December 31, 1862, Tannatt Family Papers, MASC.

45. Special Order no. 39, December 28, 1862, Tannatt Family Papers, MAC.

46. General Order no. 14, January 30, 1863, Tannatt Family Papers, MAC.

47. TRT Journal, February 22, 1864, Tannatt Family Papers, MASC.

48. For detailed discussions on women's Civil War activities see Leonard, *All the Daring of the Soldier*; Clinton, *Civil War Stories*; Sizer, "Acting Her Part."

49. Lewis N. Tappan to Samuel F. Tappan, February 13, 1863, SFTP.

50. ETT to Sally H. Tappan, February 22, 1863, Tannatt Family Papers, MASC.

51. ETT Journal, August 3, 1863, Tannatt Family Papers, MASC.

52. ETT Journal, August 6, 7, 9, November 22, 1863, Tannatt Family Papers, MASC.

53. Circular, May 26, 1863, Tannatt Family Papers, MAC.

54. Logan, *Reminiscences of a Soldier's Wife*, 135.

55. ETT Journal, August 11, 1863, Tannatt Family Papers, MASC.

56. J. L. Colby, MD, July 13, 1864, Medical Report, Tannatt Family Papers, MAC.

57. Link, "Potomac Fever," 75–77, 82; Vinovskis, "Have Social Historians Lost the Civil War?" 41.

58. ETT Journal, November 25, 1863, Tannatt Family Papers, MASC.

59. See Welter, "Cult of True Womanhood."

60. ETT Journal, November 1, 15, 1863, Tannatt Family Papers, MASC.

61. ETT Journal, October 3, 1863, Tannatt Family Papers, MASC.

62. Association of Graduates of the U.S. Military Academy, *Annual Reunion, 1914*, 108; TRT Military Records, NARA.

63. ETT Journal, January 3, 1864, Tannatt Family Papers, MASC.

64. ETT Journal, January 17, 1864, Tannatt Family Papers, MASC.

65. In August 1863, Thomas received an additional promotion to captain of the Fourth Artillery. Edwin M. Stanton, Secretary of War, to TRT, September 2, 1863, Tannatt Family Papers, MAC.

66. McPherson, *Battle Cry of Freedom*, 740–41; McPherson, *Ordeal by Fire*, 424–25; Bowman, *Civil War Almanac*, 211.

67. Howe, *The Petersburg Campaign*, 57.

68. A. S. Roe and Nutt, *History of the First Regiment*, 179.

69. L. Bradley, *A Soldier-Boys Letters*, 41.

70. Howe, *The Petersburg Campaign*, 53–55. See also Brian Holden Reid, "Another Look at Grant's Crossing"; Temple, "Signal Officer with Grant."

71. U.S. War Department, *War of the Rebellion*, 1st ser., 40, pt. 1:184.

72. U.S. War Department, *War of the Rebellion*, 1st ser., 40, pt. 1:57.

73. TRT Journal, June 16, 1864, Tannatt Family Papers, MASC.

74. TRT to B. F. Browne, June 19, 1864, Tannatt Family Papers, MASC.

75. J. N. Willard, June 24, 1864, Medical report, Tannatt Family Papers, MASC.

76. TRT to ETT, June 18, 1864, Tannatt Family Papers, MASC.
77. Cummings, "Worcester County Soldiers," 35.
78. McPherson, *For Cause and Comrades*, 59–60.
79. TRT to Maj. Gen. George W. Cullum, September 28, 1867, Tannatt Papers, USMA; Cullum, *Biographical Register*, 701.
80. Association of Graduates of the U.S. Military Academy, *Annual Reunion, 1914*, 109.
81. TRT to Maj. Gen. George W. Cullum, September 28, 1867, Tannatt Papers, USMA.

3. The Aftermath of War, 1864–1876

1. ETT Journal, September 16, 1864, Tannatt Family Papers, MASC.
2. ETT Journal, October 20, 1864, Tannatt Family Papers, MASC; Miscellaneous documents, Tappan Family Papers, MHS; *1866 Denver/Auraria City Directory*.
3. Bancroft, *Gulch of Gold*, 11–12, 14–32. For a detailed study on William Green Russell see Spencer, *Green Russell and Gold*.
4. TRT to Maj. Gen. George W. Cullum, September 28, 1867, Tannatt Papers, USMA.
5. ETT Journal, November 24, 1864, Tannatt Family Papers, MASC.
6. Eben III died in 1854 at the age of thirty-eight, David died in 1838 at the age of twenty-one (Elizabeth was just a year old when he died), and Charles died in 1848 at the age of twenty-two. Tappan Family Bible, Tappan Family Papers, MHS.
7. ETT to TRT, November 24, 1864, Tannatt Family Papers, MASC.
8. *Manchester-by-the-Sea, 1645–1970*, 15–16; unidentified newspaper clipping, Tannatt Family Papers, MASC.
9. *Manchester-by-the-Sea, 1645–1970*, 17.
10. Jones, "Men and Women in Northern New England," 82–83; Vinovskis, "Have Social Historians Lost the Civil War?" 43.
11. Thomas Moonlight to TRT, January 11, 1865, Tannatt Family Papers, MAC.
12. U.S. War Department, *War of the Rebellion*, 1st ser., 48, pt. 1:726.
13. See Andrist, *The Long Death*, 88–92; Brown, *Bury My Heart at Wounded Knee*, 86–92; Welch, *Killing Custer*, 143–44.
14. Enochs, "Clash of Ambition."
15. "Chivington, John M.," *New Perspectives on the West*.
16. ETT Journal, January 30, 1865, Tannatt Family Papers, MASC.
17. ETT Journal, May 7, 1865, Tannatt Family Papers, MASC.
18. William Henry Tappan to ETT, May 26, 1865, Tannatt Family Papers, MASC.
19. Unidentified newspaper clipping, Tannatt Family Papers, MASC.
20. See Bancroft, *Gulch of Gold*, 156–58; Smith, *Rocky Mountain West*, 191–92.
21. TRT to Maj. Gen. George W. Cullum, September 28, 1867, Tannatt Papers, USMA; Hollister, *Mines of Colorado*, 145–76.
22. See Hollenback, *Central City and Black Hawk, Colorado*; Smith, *Rocky Moun-

tain West, 37–38; Blevins and Jensen, "Gambling as a Community Development Quick Fix"; City of Black Hawk, *Black Hawk History*.

23. Turner, "Frank Hall," 328–29, 335–38, 343, 351.
24. TRT to George B. Satterle, Esq., August 3, 1865, Tannatt Family Papers, MASC.
25. McNeill, *Gathering Gold*, 53, 55; see also Smith, *Rocky Mountain Mining Camps*, 197–99.
26. TRT to George B. Satterle, Esq., November 1865, Tannatt Family Papers, MASC.
27. TRT to George B. Satterle, November 5, 1865, Tannatt Family Papers, MASC; McNeill, *Gathering Gold*, 51, 53.
28. TRT to George B. Satterle, August 3, 1865, Tannatt Family Papers, MASC. The seven hundred dollars to which Thomas refers most likely represented rent for a period of one year.
29. TRT to George B. Satterle, Esq., 1867, Tannatt Family Papers, MASC.
30. ETT Journal, January 2, 10, March 19, May 1, 1867, Tannatt Family Papers, MASC.
31. See Petrik, *No Step Backward*; Jameson, *All That Glitters*; Levy, *They Saw the Elephant*.
32. Smith, *Rocky Mountain Mining Camps*, 188.
33. ETT Journal, January 17, 18, 1867, and miscellaneous newspaper article, both in Tannatt Family Papers, MASC.
34. Hollister, *Mines of Colorado*, 449.
35. H. B. Tuttle, Receipt, September 22, 1866, Tannatt Family Papers, MASC.
36. Bancroft, *Gulch of Gold*, 191–94; Athearn, *Coloradans*, 70; "Bayard Taylor"; Bancroft, *Gulch of Gold*, 194.
37. Wolle, *Ghost Cities of Colorado*.
38. Petrik, *No Step Backward*, 62–63.
39. ETT Journal, January 4, 5, 1867, Tannatt Family Papers, MASC.
40. Elizabeth's brother George Tappan had been in Colorado in the early 1860s as well but died in 1865, prior to her arrival there, of undisclosed causes. ETT Journal, May 11, 1865, Tannatt Family Papers, MASC.
41. Elizabeth S. Tappan to ETT, October 25, 1867, Tannatt Family Papers, MASC.
42. "Lewis Tappan," *Rocky Mountain News*, February 26, 1880; "Death of Mr. Lewis N. Tappan," *Leadville* (CO) *Chronicle*, February 25, 1880.
43. Gibbens, "Virginia Family," 43.
44. When she married in 1856, Sarah Tappan chose neither a Manchesterite nor a New Englander but Tennessean Daniel Ames. A letter from Lewis to Sam Tappan wherein he referred to Ames as "Rebel boy" makes it clear that he thought little of his sister's choice. Lewis N. Tappan to Samuel F. Tappan, March 26, 1862, SFTP.
45. ETT Journal, May 25, 1867, Tannatt Family Papers, MASC. Capt. John G. Tannatt died of consumption in McMinnville, Tennessee, on October 13, 1884, at the home of his father-in-law, Capt. James Clift. His obituary described him as "formerly a citizen of this county and well known in this community," and "a large concourse of friends" accompanied his remains to their resting place. *McMinnville Southern Standard*, 18 October 1884.

46. ETT Journal, May 25, 1867, Tannatt Family Papers, MASC.
47. Elizabeth S. Tappan to ETT, July 9, 1868, Tannatt Family Papers, MASC.
48. ETT to Sally H. Tappan, November 4, 1868, Tannatt Family Papers, MASC.
49. ETT to Sally H. Tappan, November 4, 1868.
50. Elizabeth's brothers Lewis and William Henry also served on the state legislature, and William Henry served as a Massachusetts state senator in 1885 and 1886. Lamson, *History of the Town of Manchester*, 379.
51. ETT to Sally H. Tappan, November 4, 1868, Tannatt Family Papers, MASC.
52. TRT to Capt. William C. Rivers, June 1, 1902, Tannatt Papers, USMA.
53. TRT to Capt. William C. Rivers, June 1, 1902.
54. When Brownlow called the general assembly into session to ratify the Fourteenth Amendment, the Conservative members left the hall in order to block the amendment's passage. The Speaker of the House issued warrants for the arrests of these legislative members and the general assembly ordered the arrest of two of them, considered them thereafter apprehended and "present" for the vote, and ratified the amendment. Zebley, "Samuel Mayes Arnell," 253.
55. Folmsbee, Corlew, and Mitchell, *Tennessee*, 355–57. See also Patton, *Unionism and Reconstruction in Tennessee*; Alexander, *Political Reconstruction in Tennessee*; Cooper, "Tennessee Returns to Congress"; Zebley, "Samuel Mayes Arnell," 246–59. For discussions on Reconstruction throughout the South see Foner, *Reconstruction*.
56. Belissary, "Rise of Industry in Tennessee," 207.
57. Tennessee Immigration Association letterhead, Tannatt Family Papers, MASC.
58. See McPherson, *Ordeal by Fire*, 557–58; Foner, *Reconstruction*, 294–95.
59. Belissary, "Rise of Industry in Tennessee," 198.
60. *Arthur St. Clair Colyar*; Folmsbee, Corlew, and Mitchell, *Tennessee*, 385.
61. Unidentified newspaper article, Tannatt Family Papers, MASC.
62. Unidentified newspaper article, Tannatt Family Papers, MASC.
63. Zebley, "Samuel Mayes Arnell," 254.
64. Folmsbee, Corlew, and Mitchell, *Tennessee*, 363.
65. Foner, *Reconstruction*, 454–59.
66. Belissary, "Rise of Industry in Tennessee," 208–9; Folmsbee, Corlew, and Mitchell, *Tennessee*, 389–90.
67. Belissary, "Rise of Industry in Tennessee," 213–14; Folmsbee, Corlew, and Mitchell, *Tennessee*, 390. For a detailed account of the post-Reconstruction South see Ayers, *Promise of the New South*.
68. Miriam "Minnie" Tannatt, Composition Book, n.d., Tannatt Family Papers, MASC.
69. William H. Tappan to ETT, May 1874, Tannatt Family Papers, MASC.
70. William H. Tappan to ETT, May 1874.
71. Unidentified newspaper article, Tannatt Family Papers, MASC.
72. *Manchester Beetle and Wedge*, August 1875, 3.
73. Lewis N. Tappan to ETT, July 18, 1875, Tannatt Family Papers, MASC.
74. TRT to Capt. William C. Rivers, June 1, 1902, Tannatt Papers, USMA.

75. See Foner, *Reconstruction*, 512–13; Wiebe, *Search for Order*, 1–3.
76. May, *Three Frontiers*, 89.
77. Doyle, *Social Order of a Frontier Community*, 93–95.
78. May, *Three Frontiers*, 89.

4. Henry Villard and Transportation in the Pacific Northwest, 1876–1882

1. Vinovskis, "Have Social Historians Lost the Civil War?" 34, 57–58. Vinovskis suggests that "almost nothing is available on the postwar life course of Civil War veterans" (34) and that "very little attention has been paid to the terrible costs of the conflicts to those who lived through them" (57).
2. Bright, "Yankees in Arms," 209.
3. Bright, "Yankees in Arms," 199.
4. Bright, "Yankees in Arms," 209.
5. Bright, "Yankees in Arms," 209.
6. Bright, "Yankees in Arms," 218.
7. Jones, "Men and Women in Northern New England," 70.
8. Jones, "Men and Women in Northern New England," 84–85.
9. Dean, *Shook Over Hell*, 169.
10. *Manchester Beetle and Wedge*, July 1876, 2.
11. Miscellaneous documents, Tannatt Family Papers, MASC; ETT Journal, October 8, 1875, Tannatt Family Papers, MASC; Lewis N. Tappan to TRT, April 15, 1876, Tannatt Family Papers, MASC.
12. *Salem Register*, September 26, 1878; miscellaneous documents, Tannatt Family Papers, MASC.
13. M. B. Norton, *Founding Mothers and Fathers*, 111–15.
14. See Weatherford, *American Suffragist Movement*.
15. See Woloch, *Women and the American Experience*, 1:194–95; S. Evans, *Born for Liberty*, 76–77; Kerber and DeHart, *Women's America*, 570–71.
16. *Manchester Beetle and Wedge*, June 1876, 2.
17. John F. Robards to TRT, May 17, 1876, Tannatt Family Papers, MASC.
18. *Manchester Beetle and Wedge*, June 1876, 2.
19. See Blair, *The Clubwoman as Feminist*, 15–38.
20. Donnelly, *American Victorian Woman*, 131; see also Mintz, *Prison of Expectations*; Ginzberg, *Women and the Work of Benevolence*.
21. *Manchester Beetle and Wedge*, October 1876, 2. Boston native Mary Ashton Rice Livermore served as president of the Massachusetts WCTU from 1875 to 1885 and attended and taught at the same Charlestown Female Academy that Elizabeth attended in the 1850s. Livermore's presidency of the state organization certainly motivated the establishment of local chapters throughout Massachusetts. See Willard, *Woman and Temperance*, 418–33; Humphrey, *Women in American History*; Livermore, *The Story of My Life*.
22. Parsons, *Hannah and the Hatchet Gang*; Kenny, *Cape Ann: Cape America*, 75–76; Marshall, "Rockport."

23. Annie Fields to ETT, October 7, 1876, Tannatt Family Papers, MASC.

24. Annie Fields to ETT, October 7, 1876; Willard, *Woman and Temperance*, 432–34.

25. Bicentennial Committee for the Town of Manchester, *Part of Manchester's Heritage*, 8. See also Lamson, *History of the Town of Manchester*, 192; Kenny, *Cape Ann*, suggests that the arrival of Manchester's summer residents transformed it into "a feudal barony of absentee landlords" (22).

26. W. H. Tappan, "Manchester," 1278.

27. W. H. Tappan, "Manchester," 1279; Lamson, *History of the Town of Manchester*, 350.

28. William Henry Tappan went west in 1848 and was involved with the establishment of military posts in Oregon, Washington, Montana, and Idaho territories and with other territorial matters. In 1856 he moved to Colorado Springs and established hardware stores in Colorado Springs and Central City. Charles Tappan also left Manchester for the West in the late 1840s, perhaps in search of gold. He died at sea in November 1849 en route to the Sandwich Islands from San Francisco. Lewis N. Tappan traveled to Kansas after leaving Manchester and was elected secretary of the Senate under the controversial Topeka Constitution. In 1859 he moved to Colorado, where he established the first supply store in Denver dedicated to the needs of miners and became well known in both Denver and the Gregory Gulch mining region. His younger brother, George Tappan, joined him there in the early 1860s. Eben Tappan III, the eldest of Eben and Sally Tappan's children, became a lithographer and established the Boston firm of Tappan and Bradford, probably in the mid-1830s. David Tappan was serving an apprenticeship of some sort in Boston when he died in 1838 at twenty-one years of age. See *Manchester Cricket*, January 26, 1907, 1; *Boston Transcript*, February 27, 1880; unidentified newspaper clippings and Tappan Family Bible, Tappan Family Papers, MHS.

29. Villard, *Pike's Peak Gold Regions*, vii–xi; Lewty, *To the Columbia Gateway*, 29.

30. Smalley, *History of the Northern Pacific Railroad*, 248; Villard, *Pike's Peak Gold Regions*, 135.

31. Pomeroy, *The Pacific Slope*, 93, 98.

32. Pomeroy, *The Pacific Slope*, 102.

33. See Lewty, *To the Columbia Gateway*, 31–32; Villard, *Memoirs*, 2:284–89.

34. Hedges, *Henry Villard*; Smalley, *History of the Northern Pacific Railroad*, 253–64; Villard, *Memoirs*, 2:271–78.

35. Lewty, *To the Columbia Gateway*, 65–71. See also Fahey, *Inland Empire*, 28–30. It is interesting to note that Villard gathered his several companies together under the control and protection of a holding company at the same time American business and government began to monitor and legislate against monopolistic corporate activities. See Wiebe, *Businessmen and Reform*.

36. TRT to Henry Villard, January 12, 1877, ORNP. Gen. Oliver O. Howard was in the West serving as a member of the board of commissioners appointed by the secretary of the interior, with the duty of relocating the Nez Perce and Palouse tribes. See Trafzer and Scheuerman, *Renegade Tribe*, 105–9.

37. TRT to Henry Villard, June 4, 1877, ORNP.

38. Hedges, "Promotion of Immigration," 183.

39. Villard, *Transportation in Oregon*, 47.

40. TRT to Henry Villard, September 4, 1877, ORNP.

41. TRT to Henry Villard, September 12, 1877, ORNP.

42. Hedges, "Promotion of Immigration," 190.

43. Villard, *Transportation in Oregon*, 78.

44. Hedges, *Henry Villard*, 114.

45. TRT to Henry Villard, November 7, 1877, ORNP.

46. Hedges, *Henry Villard*, 120–21.

47. Unidentified clippings, Tannatt Family Papers, MASC.

48. Hedges, *Henry Villard*, 114; Dahlie, "Old World Paths in the New."

49. TRT to George Saxer, November 28, 1877, ORNP.

50. TRT to Henry Villard, December 5, 1877, ORNP.

51. Hedges, *Henry Villard*, 119.

52. TRT to Henry Villard, December 5, 1877, ORNP.

53. *Boston Journal*, November 12, 1879.

54. TRT to Henry Villard, June 4, 1878, ORNP.

55. ETT Journal, April 22, 1879, Tannatt Family Papers, MASC.

56. ETT Journal, January 31, 1879, Tannatt Family Papers, MASC.

57. ETT Journal, February 8, 1879, Tannatt Family Papers, MASC.

58. Kunz, *Family Medical Guide*, 274–75.

59. ETT Journal, March 4, 1879, Tannatt Family Papers, MASC.

60. ETT Journal, September 23, 25, 1879, Tannatt Family Papers, MASC.

61. ETT Journal, December 25, 1879, Tannatt Family Papers, MASC.

62. ETT Journal, February 25, 1880, Tannatt Family Papers, MASC.

63. "Lewis Tappan," *Rocky Mountain News*, February 26, 1880; "Death of Mr. Lewis N. Tappan," *Leadville* (CO) *Chronicle*, February 25, 1880.

64. Unidentified newspaper article, Tannatt Family Papers, MASC.

65. TRT to ETT, October 8, 1880, Tannatt Family Papers, MASC. By "Bank Coloma" Thomas refers to the Kalama River, which drains southwest from Mount St. Helens and empties into the Columbia River approximately twenty-five miles north of Portland. U.S. Geological Survey, *Major Hydrologic Features in the Mount St. Helens Region*. The "Gnls." are William Tecumseh Sherman and his aide-de-camp, Alexander McCook.

66. *San Francisco Chronicle*, November 7, 1881.

67. *Portland Oregonian*, November 12, 1877.

68. To the chagrin of the governor of Washington Territory, Edward S. Salomon, who complained in 1871 that "numerous reports have been written and published on the resources of this Territory, [and] people . . . have come here with great expectations and found themselves sadly disappointed," a number of railroad companies and others did participate in the publication and distribution of misleading promotional materials. And despite Salomon's claims that the territory offered "inducements enough to settlers, and it is en-

tirely unnecessary to state anything but the truth," historian Carlos Schwantes has suggested that this boosterism was essential in convincing settlers to choose Pacific Northwest destinations over California. Gates, *Messages of the Governors*, 167; Schwantes, *The Pacific Northwest*, 288–95.

69. Hedges, "Promotion of Immigration," 201–2.

70. Land Department of the Oregon Improvement Co., *Eastern Washington Territory and Oregon*.

71. Hedges, "Promotion of Immigration," 197.

72. Unidentified newspaper article, Tannatt Papers, masc; Hanscom, "Coal Company Town," 13–14.

73. Miscellaneous newspaper articles, n.d., Tannatt Family Papers, masc; Hedges, "Promotion of Immigration," 126; Scheuerman and Trafzer, *Volga Germans*, 141–42.

74. Villard, *Transportation in Oregon*, 85.

75. Parker, *Washington Territory*, 4.

76. Edwards, "Walla Walla," 43.

77. For more complete discussions on German Russians see Scheuerman, "Germans from Russia"; Scheuerman and Trafzer, *Volga Germans*; Koch, *Volga Germans*; Walters, *Wir Wollen Deutsche Bleiben*; Williams, *The Czar's Germans*.

78. Scheuerman and Trafzer, *Volga Germans*, 134.

79. Scheuerman, *Pilgrims on the Earth*, 77.

80. *Walla Walla Weekly Statesman*, September 30, 1882.

81. *Walla Walla Weekly Statesman*, October 21, 1882.

82. Scheuerman, *Pilgrims on the Earth*, 101.

83. In 1870 James Perkins arrived in the eastern Washington region he later named Colfax, in honor of Vice President Schuyler Colfax. Perkins built the first sawmill in the area, claimed land, and became a banker and merchant in the town. Fahey, *Inland Empire*, 5.

84. Unidentified newspaper articles, Tannatt Family Papers, masc.

85. Unidentified newspaper article, Tannatt Family Papers, masc.

86. *Walla Walla Weekly Statesman*, n.d., Tannatt Family Papers, masc.

5. Inland Empire "Pioneers," 1880–1890

1. Fahey, *The Inland Empire*, 5.

2. See McPherson, *Ordeal by Fire*, 229; Bowman, *Civil War Almanac*, 88–89; U.S. Army, *Missouri Infantry Regiment, Phelps's Account Book, 1862—Information Sheet*.

3. The bureau distributed food, clothing, and other necessities to those in need and participated in the establishment and operation of schools for freedmen, theretofore prohibited from obtaining an education. McPherson, *Ordeal by Fire*, 401; Foner, *Reconstruction*, 68–70.

4. *Illustrated History of Whitman County*, 344–45; "Judge W. A. Inman, Pioneer, Passes," *Colfax Gazette*, August 15, 1924, 1; Nazzal, "Judge William Inman of Colfax."

5. For a history of the Anderson Cavalry Troop see Stevens, "Forty-ninth Ohio Volunteer Infantry."

6. Snowden, *History of Washington*, 5:272–73.

7. Evans et al., *History of the Pacific Northwest*, 2:527.

8. See U.S. Bureau of Land Management, *History of the* BLM.

9. Evans et al., *History of the Pacific Northwest*, 427–29; Snowden, *History of Washington*, 270–73.

10. ETT Journal, May 25, 1882, and William F. Prosser to ETT, December 7, 1882 both in Tannatt Family Papers, MASC.

11. *Illustrated History of Whitman County*, 344–45; "Judge W. A. Inman, Pioneer, Passes," *Colfax Gazette*, August 15, 1924, 1; Snowden, *History of Washington*, 270–73; Evans et al., *History of the Pacific Northwest*, 527–28.

12. See McConnell, *Glorious Contentment*; Dearing, *Veterans in Politics*; Knight, *Brief History*.

13. See *Military Order of the Loyal Legion of the United States*.

14. Taylor, *Turner Thesis*, 3.

15. Doyle, *Social Order of a Frontier Community*, 3. See also May, *Three Frontiers*; Faragher, *Sugar Creek*; Hine, *Community on the American Frontier*.

16. Doyle, *Social Order of a Frontier Community*, 5.

17. Schwantes, *Pacific Northwest*, 128–29; McGregor, "Economic Impact of the Mullan Road"; Lyman, *History of Old Walla Walla County*, 1:126.

18. *Walla Walla Valley, Washington Territory*, 3.

19. "City Election," *Walla Walla Daily Statesman*, July 10, 1883.

20. Lyman, *History of Old Walla Walla County*, 1:257–58.

21. Lyman, *History of Old Walla Walla County*, 1:257–58.

22. "As We View the Result," *Walla Walla Union*, July 10, 1883.

23. "Sound Sense," *Walla Walla Daily Statesman*, July 30, 1883.

24. Bledstein, *Culture of Professionalism*, 121, 123–24.

25. Unidentified newspaper article, April 13, 1882, Tannatt Family Papers, MASC.

26. ETT Journal, January 11, 1882, Tannatt Family Papers, MASC. *Evergreen*, June 1898, 15.

27. ETT Journal, 1882; Lyman, *History of Old Walla Walla County*, 1:221–23; *Walla Walla Valley, Washington Territory*, 16–17.

28. "Sound Sense," *Walla Walla Daily Statesman*, July 30, 1883. In 1857, Fort Walla Walla made elementary school instruction available for the children of soldiers garrisoned there and those residing nearby. Walla Walla, however, made no educational provisions until the 1860s, though a superintendent of schools was elected in 1859. Dr. D. S. Baker donated a parcel of land in 1864, and the first Inland Empire public school opened to students in 1865. A second school was added in 1868, but education beyond primary levels was still unavailable in Walla Walla. Lyman, *History of Old Walla Walla County*, 1:210–11.

29. Lewty, *To the Columbia Gateway*, 33–41; Lyman, *History of Old Walla Walla County*, 1:165–70; Edwards, "Walla Walla," 39–40.

30. Lewty, *To the Columbia Gateway*, xvi.
31. Lewty, *To the Columbia Gateway*, 100–102; Villard, *Memoirs*, 2:309–12; Fahey, *The Inland Empire*, 30.
32. Unidentified newspaper article, Tannatt Family Papers, MASC.
33. Unidentified newspaper article, Tannatt Family Papers, MASC.
34. Unidentified newspaper article, Tannatt Family Papers, MASC.
35. Unidentified newspaper article, Tannatt Family Papers, MASC.
36. In January 1866, Henry Villard married Helen Frances Garrison, daughter of William Lloyd and Helen Benson Garrison and sister of William Lloyd Garrison Jr. The senior Garrison's abolitionist endeavors brought him into close association with Lewis and Arthur Tappan, Elizabeth Tannatt's New York cousins, and this relationship furthered the Villard-Tannatt ties. Villard, *Memoirs*, 2:268; Cain, *William Lloyd Garrison*, 7–8.
37. See Haarsager, *Organized Womanhood*; Jeffrey, *Frontier Women*; Jensen and Miller, "Gentle Tamers Revisited"; Jameson, "Women as Workers, Women as Civilizers"; Matsuda, "West and the Legal Status of Women"; Armitage, "Women and Men in Western History."
38. *Walla Walla, Washington Territory*, 24–26.
39. ETT Journal, February 16, 1882.
40. ETT Journal, January 11, 1882.
41. Zhu, *Chinaman's Chance*, 111–19. See also National Park Service, *Asian Pacific Pioneers along the Columbia River*; Washington State University, Center for Environmental Education, *Rock Lake, Kamiakin, and the Chinese Immigrants*.
42. Takaki, *Strangers from a Different Shore*, 110–12, 377–78; Zhu, *Chinaman's Chance*, 59–60.
43. ETT Journal, February 18, 1882, Tannatt Family Papers, MASC.
44. ETT Journal, May 8, 1882.
45. ETT Journal, May 9, 12, 1882.
46. ETT Journal, May 25, 1882.
47. ETT Journal, May 28, 1882.
48. ETT Journal, June 18, 1882.
49. Miscellaneous documents, Tappan Family Papers, MHS.
50. ETT Journal, January 29, 1882, Tannatt Family Papers, MASC.
51. Haarsager, *Organized Womanhood*, 98.
52. *Walla Walla Valley, Washington Territory*, 21.
53. Parker, *Washington Territory*, 4.
54. Susan English, "Settling Effect: The Women's Christian Temperance Union Fought for Women's Rights; and, Along the Way Helped Turn the Wild West into a More Mild West," *Spokane Spokesman-Review*, June 20, 1999, F4.
55. ETT Journal, February 4, 1882, Tannatt Family Papers, MASC.
56. *Union Signal*, August 3, 1883, 12.
57. Baker, *Moral Frameworks of Public Life*, 71.
58. For discussions on the benevolence and reform efforts of Wittenmyer and Willard see Leonard, *Yankee Women*, 51–103; "Annie Turner Wittenmyer";

Ginzberg, *Women and the Work of Benevolence*, 204–6; Willard, *Woman and Temperance*, 19–38; Gordon, *Women Torch-Bearers*, 1–18; "Frances Elizabeth Caroline Willard."

59. Ginzberg, *Women and the Work of Benevolence*, 5.

60. Abigail Scott Duniway endured humbler beginnings and a much harsher life than most high-profile female reformers. Born in 1834 into a large Illinois farm family, she received little formal schooling prior to the family's 1852 migration to Oregon. Her husband's ill-advised business dealings and subsequent disability left Abigail as the family's sole source of support, and in this capacity she operated a boarding school, worked as a teacher, and managed a millinery and notions shop. Through it all, her resentment concerning the lack of rights afforded American women grew. In 1871 she moved to Portland and established the *New Northwest*, and for the next decade and a half she traveled throughout the Pacific Northwest and lectured on the absolute necessity of woman suffrage. Although achieving this proved elusive in Oregon, Duniway's efforts are at least partly responsible for women's gaining the vote in Washington Territory in 1883 and in Idaho in 1896. Finally, in 1912, a successful suffrage campaign extended the ballot to Oregon women, though Duniway's frail health prevented her active participation. She died in Portland in October 1915. See Moynihan, *Rebel for Rights*; Ward and Maveety, *"Yours for Liberty"*; Haarsager, *Organized Womanhood*, 262–66; "Abigail Jane Scott Duniway."

61. Moynihan, *Rebel for Rights*, 137–38.

62. Moynihan, *Rebel for Rights*, 93–94; Edwards, *Sowing Good Seeds*, 67.

63. Edwards, *Sowing Good Seeds*, 69–70.

64. Ault, "Earnest Ladies," 127.

65. Frances Willard, "Across the Continent," *Union Signal*, August 23, 1883, 2.

66. McMillen, *History Of . . . East Washington's Woman's Christian Temperance Union*; miscellaneous newspaper articles, Tannatt Family Papers, MASC.

67. The issue of woman suffrage became particularly complicated in Washington, despite the fact that it was the fifth state in the Union to grant women the right to vote. Suffrage initiatives were introduced in the territorial and state legislatures quite regularly beginning in 1871; in fact, in 1883 the legislature granted Washington women the right to vote, only to revoke it in 1888. Finally, in November 1910, article VI of the state constitution was amended to read, in part, "there shall be no denial of the elective franchise on account of sex." See Pearce, "Suffrage in the Pacific Northwest"; Larson, "Woman Suffrage Movement in Washington."

68. Baker, *Moral Frameworks of Public Life*, 71.

69. Unidentified newspaper article, Tannatt Family Papers, MASC.

70. Unidentified newspaper article, Tannatt Family Papers, MASC.

71. T. R. Tannatt, "Communicated," *Walla Walla Statesman*, February 2, 1883, 2.

72. Unidentified newspaper article, Tannatt Family Papers, MASC.

73. Lyman, *History of Old Walla Walla County*, 1:294–95. While Walla Walla's early

prohibition efforts were defeated in 1884, the subjects of temperance and prohibition were not new to the Inland Empire. As early as 1855 territorial laws prohibited the sale of intoxicating substances to the Indians, and in 1879 the territorial legislature prohibited the sale of liquor within a mile of the Northern Pacific Railroad during construction. North of Walla Walla, the Whitman County Temperance League organized in 1883, the same year the WCTU came to Walla Walla. At midnight on December 31, 1915, Initiative no. 3 went into effect and closed all Washington saloons, three years before the national Prohibition Amendment went into effect. See Nuxoll, " 'Repent, Ye Boozers!' "

74. Ward and Maveety, *"Yours for Liberty,"* 268–69.
75. Ward and Maveety, *"Yours for Liberty,"* 268–69; Moynihan, *Rebel for Rights,* 185–86.
76. ETT Journal, March 11, 1884, Tannatt Family Papers, MASC.
77. *Union Signal,* August 18, 1884, 11.
78. Ault, "Earnest Ladies," 124–25.
79. Skocpol, "America's First Social Security System," 93.
80. McConnell, *Glorious Contentment,* 152.
81. McConnell, *Glorious Contentment,* 152. For further discussion of the Civil War pensions see Dearing, *Veterans in Politics*; McClintock, "Civil War Pensions"; Logue, "Union Veterans and Their Government."
82. Declaration for Original Invalid Pension, November 22, 1886, TRT Pension Records, file WC-774-T76, NARA.
83. J. C. Ainsworth, Asst. Surgeon, U.S. Army, February 14, 1887, War Department, Surgeon General's Office, TRT Pension Records, NARA.
84. U.S. War Department, *War of the Rebellion,* 1st ser., 40, pt. 1:184; O. Everts, Surgeon-in-Chief, Hospital 3rd Division, June 23, 1864, TRT Military Records, Co. F&S, 1 Mass, H.A., NARA.
85. Clayton McMichael to ETT, May 18, 1887, Tannatt Family Papers, MASC; R. S. Littlefield to ETT, 12 June 1887, Tannatt Family Papers, MASC.
86. Clayton McMichael to ETT, May 16, 1889, Tannatt Family Papers, MASC.
87. Frank Daulte, Affidavit, January 27, 1887, TRT Pension Records, NARA.
88. ETT to the United States War Department, March 17, 1892, Tannatt Family Papers, MASC.
89. Department of the Interior, January 15, 1898, January 14, 23, 1914, April 19, 1920, TRT Pension Records, NARA.
90. Miscellaneous documents, Tannatt Family Papers, MASC.
91. Lewty, *To the Columbia Gateway,* 117–20.
92. Lewty, *To the Columbia Gateway,* 106–12; Lewty, *Across the Columbia Plain,* xvi–xvii.
93. Lewty, *Across the Columbia Plain,* 27.
94. Lewty, *Across the Columbia Plain,* 30.
95. For a detailed discussion on the Farmington extension see Lewty, *Across the Columbia Plain,* 26–34.

96. TRT to Chief Saltees, July 30, 1886, Tannatt Family Papers, MASC.

97. DeSmet Mission [author unknown] to TRT, July 30, 1886, Tannatt Family Papers, MASC.

98. TRT to Hon. John H. Mitchell, April 27, 1888, Tannatt Family Papers, MASC. Thomas's disclosure is particularly relevant, as Elijah Smith was an ORN majority stockholder and among those ultimately responsible for Villard's separation from the companies and the sale of the ORN to the Union Pacific in 1889. Lewty, *Across the Columbia Plain*, 11–19.

99. J. D. C. Atkins, Commissioner, Office of Indian Affairs, to the Secretary of the Interior, April 30, 1888, Tannatt Family Papers, MASC.

100. Gayle Littleton, "Farmington—Past and Present," MASC; Maude Friedman, "History of Farmington," MASC; *Illustrated History of Whitman County*, 194–97.

101. Augusta [Hooper] to ETT, May 11, 1887, Tannatt Family Papers, MASC.

6. Retirement and Reflections on the Past, 1890–1920

1. TRT to Capt. William C. Rivers, June 1, 1902, Tannatt Papers, USMA.

2. In 1891 the Spokane Falls Chamber of Commerce voted to remove "Falls" from the city's name in an effort to project an image of modernity and progress and to remove any association with the "natural" landscape. Morrissey, *Mental Territories*, 60.

3. Fahey, *Inland Empire*, 40; Morrissey, *Mental Territories*, 42–43; Schwantes, *Pacific Northwest*, 232–35.

4. Gayle Littleton, "Farmington—Past and Present," MASC; Maude Friedman, "History of Farmington," MASC.

5. TRT to ETT, December 4, 1891, Tannatt Family Papers, MASC.

6. ETT Journal, May 6, 1893, Tannatt Family Papers, MASC.

7. TRT to ETT, n.d., Tannatt Family Papers, MASC.

8. TRT to ETT, December 6, 1891, Tannatt Family Papers, MASC.

9. TRT to ETT, February 14, 1892, Tannatt Family Papers, MASC.

10. TRT to ETT, n.d., Tannatt Family Papers, MASC.

11. TRT to ETT, December 8, 1891, Tannatt Family Papers, MASC.

12. N. P. Hill to ETT, June 25, 1891, Tannatt Family Papers, MASC.

13. ETT to N. P. Hill, July 27, 1891, Tannatt Family Papers, MASC.

14. N. P. Hill to ETT, March 28, 1892, Tannatt Family Papers, MASC.

15. Fahey, *Inland Empire*, 159–61.

16. That many middle-class newcomers to the West visited family and friends in distant locations sets them apart from those making up the earlier immigrant groups, whose members held little if any hope of ever reuniting with loved ones. See Faragher, *Women and Men on the Overland Trail*; Judson, *Pioneer's Search*; Schlissel, *Women's Diaries*.

17. Alice Ames to ETT, March 8, 1892, Tannatt Family Papers, MASC.

18. Alice Ames Evleth to ETT, November 16, 1899, Tannatt Family Papers, MASC.

19. William H. Tappan to ETT, August 1, 1900, Tannatt Family Papers, MASC. The baby to whom William Henry refers was probably named for her paternal grandmother, Elizabeth "Libbie" Sanford Tappan.

20. John G. Tannatt to Thomas and Elizabeth Tannatt, May 1, 1893, Tannatt Family Papers, MASC.

21. T. C. Tannatt to TRT, April 14, 1901, Tannatt Family Papers, MASC.

22. See *Morrill Act*; Schwantes, *Pacific Northwest*, 277; Fahey, *Inland Empire*, 80–82.

23. Bryan, *Sketch of the State College of Washington*, 4.

24. Schwantes, *Pacific Northwest*, 276; Bryan, *Sketch of the State College of Washington*, 75.

25. Bryan, *Sketch of the State College of Washington*, 75–81.

26. "Regents Are Out," *Pullman Herald*, March 10, 1893, 1.

27. "Declines the Honor," *Pullman Herald*, April 7, 1893, 1. Colfax's J. W. Arrasmith declined his appointment to the board due to the preexisting demands of his private business matters.

28. Frykman, *Creating the People's University*, 11–14.

29. *Evergreen*, March 1895, 15.

30. *Evergreen*, December 1896, 12.

31. Miscellaneous documents, "Thomas R. Tannatt" file, n.d., Regents' Biographies, WSU 140, MASC; TRT to E. A. Bryan, August 7, 1895, Enoch Albert Bryan Papers, 1843–1989, Cage 579A (Bryan Papers), MASC.

32. Bryan, *Sketch of the State College of Washington*, 105–7; TRT to ETT, November 20, 1893, Tannatt Family Papers, MASC. Blandford also served as Walla Walla County's prosecuting attorney from 1897 until at least 1904, and he was said to be a very articulate speaker. Lyman, *History of Old Walla Walla County*, 1:310–13.

33. TRT to ETT, November 20, 1893, Tannatt Family Papers, MASC.

34. Bryan, *Sketch of the State College of Washington*, 142–44.

35. TRT to ETT, January 30, 1895, Tannatt Family Papers, MASC; Frykman, *Creating the People's University*, 44.

36. TRT to ETT, January 30, 1895.

37. Bryan, *Sketch of the State College of Washington*, 166.

38. Hine and Faragher, *The American West*, 351.

39. Although the Populist movement fractured before its goals could be realized, many aspects of the Populist agenda reemerged as Progressive reform measures in the early twentieth century. For detailed works on the Populist movement see Clanton, *Congressional Populism*; McMath, *American Populism*; Goodwyn, *Democratic Promise*. For discussions on Populism specific to the American West see Schwantes, *The Pacific Northwest*, 262–68; Hine and Faragher, *The American West*, 350–52.

40. Frykman, *Creating the People's University*, 27–28; Bryan, *Sketch of the State College of Washington*, 177–88. Bryan received no "presidential" salary for his work at the Washington Agricultural College. Seventy-five percent of his pay

came as remuneration for teaching four courses and the other 25 percent for his work as director of the experiment station.

41. Bryan, *Sketch of the State College of Washington*, 186–87.

42. TRT to H. S. Blandford, September 17, 1897, Regents' Biographies, MASC.

43. Bryan, *Sketch of the State College of Washington*, 220.

44. TRT to Enoch A. Bryan, June 22, 1899, Bryan Papers, MASC.

45. Frkyman, *Creating the People's University*, 28.

46. R. C. Judson to TRT, June 3, 1899, Tannatt Family Papers, MASC.

47. TRT to E. A. Bryan, December 8, 1902, Bryan Papers, MASC.

48. Pettegrew, "'Soldier's Faith,'" 55.

49. TRT to Capt. William C. Rivers, June 1, 1902, Tannatt Papers, USMA. Captain Rivers, secretary of the Association of West Point Graduates, was involved in the task of bringing the biographical records of the academy's graduates up to date, and Thomas's letter is in reply to Rivers's request for information.

50. The story of the Steptoe Battle and the ensuing location of a commemorative monument is told here through Thomas's and Elizabeth's eyes and may, as a result, appear particularly sympathetic to the soldiers. According to the Indians, the army and the settlers who followed were largely unwelcome intruders to the Inland Empire, and the 1858 battle initiated a period of warfare in the region that lasted twenty years and ended with the surrender of Chief Joseph and the Nez Perce in 1877. For a more balanced account of the Steptoe Battle see Trafzer and Scheuerman, *Renegade Tribe*, 76–92.

51. See P. Anderson, *Daughters*; Gibbs, *The* DAR.

52. Daughters of the American Revolution, *History and Register 1924*, 71. Eben Tannatt held membership in the organization that would not admit his mother, and his membership in the Sons of the American Revolution is confirmed by an 1884 newspaper article inviting "all sons of veterans . . . to meet at Odd Fellows' Temple, G.A.R. rooms, . . . for the purpose of organization. All desirous of becoming members will please attend this meeting. E. T. Tannatt, Commander pro tem." Unidentified Walla Walla newspaper article, July 2, 1884, Tannatt Family Papers, MASC.

53. Unidentified newspaper clipping, Tannatt Family Papers, MASC.

54. ETT to State Regent, Washington DAR, June 12, 1903, Tannatt Family Papers, MASC.

55. For a more contemporary discussion on the role of women as "keepers of the past" see Brear, "We Run the Alamo, and You Don't."

56. "Reliable Report of the Late Indian Fight," *Weekly (Portland) Oregonian*, May 29, 1858, 1.

57. "Reliable Report of the Late Indian Fight," 2.

58. "Meet on Steptoe Battleground," *Spokane Spokesman-Review*, June 15, 1907, 1.

59. For detailed accounts of the Steptoe Battle see Anglin and Lindeman, *Forgotten Trails*; Trafzer and Scheuerman, *Renegade Tribe*; Glassley, *Indian Wars of the Pacific Northwest*; Peltier, *Warbonnets and Epaulets*; Manring, *Conquest of the*

Coeur D'Alenes; Hunt, *Indian Wars of the Inland Empire*; Kip, *Army Life on the Pacific*.

60. On May 10, 1907, an article in a Spokane newspaper reported a meeting of the Inland Empire Historical Society, "called principally for the purpose of making plans for the erection of a memorial monument on Steptoe battlefield, near Rosalia." It is unclear when the impetus for the coordination of this project shifted from the historical society to the DAR. Unidentified newspaper clipping, Tannatt Family Papers, MASC.

61. J. J. Rohn to T. J. Wilmer, May 4, 1902, T. J. Wilmer Papers, MAC.

62. Tannatt, *Indian Battles in the Inland Empire*, 2.

63. Tannatt, *Indian Battles in the Inland Empire*, 2.

64. "Dedicate Steptoe Monument Site," *Spokane Spokesman-Review*, June 16, 1908, 1.

65. ETT, paper presented to Esther Reed Chapter, DAR, on the 1858 Steptoe Battle, and justification for Commemorative Marker, 1907, Tannatt Family Papers, MASC.

66. "Meet on Steptoe Battlefield," *Spokane Spokesman-Review*, June 15, 1907, 1.

67. ETT Journal, June 14, 1907, Tannatt Family Papers, MASC.

68. *Congressional Record Containing the Proceedings and Debates of the Sixtieth Congress, First Session*, 511, 635.

69. TRT to Washington State legislators and other potential benefactors of the Steptoe Monument Fund, n.d., Tannatt Family Papers, MASC.

70. TRT to ETT, January 25, 1909, Tannatt Family Papers, MASC.

71. TRT to ETT, February 12, 1909, Tannatt Family Papers, MASC.

72. Miscellaneous newspaper articles, Tannatt Family Papers, MASC.

73. "To Visit Steptoe Battlefield," *Spokane Spokesman-Review*, June 14, 1907, 10.

74. "To Visit Steptoe Battlefield," 10.

75. "Hon. William Henry Tappan Dead," *Manchester Cricket*, January 26, 1907.

76. ETT Journal, 1909, Tannatt Family Papers, MASC.

77. ETT to Captain Braden, USMA, May 11, 1914, Tannatt Family Papers, MASC. It appears that "Te-hots-nim-me" was the Nez Perce translation for "Steptoe."

78. "At Monument Dedication 5000 Cheer Steptoe Heroes," *Spokesman Review*, June 16, 1914, 3.

79. "At Monument Dedication 5000 Cheer Steptoe Heroes," 3.

80. Wedding Announcement of Miriam Hooper Tannatt and Cyrus K. Merriam, Tannatt Family Papers, MASC.

81. "Lincoln Adviser in War Dies Here," *Spokane Spokesman-Review*, December 21, 1913, 1, 7; "Gen. Tannatt Is Buried," *Spokane Spokesman-Review*, December 24, 1913, 5; "Soldiers Will Attend Funeral," *Spokane Daily Chronicle*, December 22, 1913, 3; "General Tannatt, Pioneer Is Dead," *Walla Walla Union*, December 21, 1913, 1; *Pullman Herald*, December 26, 1913, 6; Washington State Board of Health, April 3, 1914, TRT Pension Records, NARA.

82. "Lincoln Adviser in War Dies Here," 7; Military Order of the Loyal Legion of

the United States, Commandery of the State of Oregon, Circular no. 1, Series 1914, Whole Number 243, February 5, 1914, Tannatt Family Papers, MASC.

83. ETT to Capt. Lewis G. Holt, January 31, 1914, Tannatt Family Papers, MASC.

84. Lewis G. Holt to ETT, February 12, 1914, Tannatt Family Papers, MASC.

85. ETT to Anna S. Tappan, June 15, 1913, SFTP.

86. "Mrs. E. F. Tannatt 82, Succumbs," *Spokane Spokesman-Review*, February 23, 1920, 6.

Epilogue

1. Charles W. Upham to New York Mining Conglomerate, February 22, 1865, Tannatt Family Papers, MASC.

2. Beckert, *Monied Metropolis*, 6.

3. May, *Three Frontiers*, 277–78.

4. May, *Three Frontiers*, 278–79.

5. *Walla Walla Weekly Statesman*, September 30, October 21, 1882.

6. Scheuerman, *Pilgrims on the Earth*, 101.

7. Doyle, *Social Order of a Frontier Community*, 18.

8. Doyle, *Social Order of a Frontier Community*, 257–58.

9. McGregor, "Economic Impact of the Mullan Road"; Fahey, *Inland Empire*, 39.

10. Doyle, *Social Order of a Frontier Community*, 157.

11. Doyle, *Social Order of a Frontier Community*, 157.

12. May, *Three Frontiers*, 257.

13. Archer and Blau, "Class Formation in Nineteenth-Century America," 35–36.

14. Blumin, *Emergence of the Middle Class*, 297.

15. Emerson, *Conduct of Life*, 259–61.

Bibliography

Primary Sources

1849 Advertisements and Announcements. http://www.bklyn-genealogy-info. com/Newspaper/Eagle/1849.Ads.html (accessed June 22, 2004).

1866 Denver/Auraria City Directory. http://www.archives.state.co.us/dcd/bd 2.htm (accessed February 6, 2000).

Bradley, Leverett. *A Soldier-Boys Letters, 1862–1865*. N.p., n.d.

Enoch Albert Bryan Papers, 1843–1989. Cage 579A. Manuscripts, Archives and Special Collections. Washington State University Libraries. Pullman WA.

Catalogue of the Teachers & Pupils, Chapel School, Manchester, Mass., for the Year Ending May 12th, 1855. Salem MA: Hutchinson's Printing Establishment, 1855.

Congressional Record Containing the Proceedings and Debates of the Sixtieth Congress, First Session. Vol. 42. Washington DC: Government Printing Office, 1908.

Manchester-by-the-Sea Town Records. Town Hall. Manchester-by-the-Sea MA.

The Morrill Act. Statutes-at-Large. Vol. 12 (1862).

Oregon Railway and Navigation Company Papers, 1876–1882. Cage 4545. Manuscripts, Archives and Special Collections. Washington State University Libraries. Pullman.

Regents' Papers Biographies. WSU 140. Manuscripts, Archives and Special Collections. Washington State University Libraries. Pullman.

Thomas R. Tannatt Military Records. Co. F&S, 1 Mass, H.A. National Archives and Records Administration. Washington DC.

Thomas R. Tannatt Papers. United States Military Academy Archives. West Point NY.

Thomas R. Tannatt Pension Records. File WC-774-T76. National Archives and Records Administration. Washington DC.

Tannatt Family Papers, 1813–1919. Cage 65. Manuscripts, Archives and Special Collections. Washington State University Libraries. Pullman.

Tannatt Family Papers. Northwest Museum of Arts and Culture. Spokane WA.

Samuel F. Tappan Papers. C. P. Weaver Private Collection. Manchester-by-the-Sea MA.

Tappan Family Papers. Manchester Historical Society. Manchester-by-the-Sea MA.

U.S. Army. *Missouri Infantry Regiment, Phelps's, Account Book, 1862—Infor-*

mation Sheet. http://www.umr.edu/ whmcinfo/shelf11/r272/info.html (accessed November 19, 2001).

T. J. Wilmer Papers. Northwest Museum of Arts and Culture. Spokane WA.

Secondary Sources

"Abigail Jane Scott Duniway." *Women in American History by Encyclopedia Britannica.* 1999. http://women.eb.com/women/articles/Duniway_ Abigail_Jane_Scott.html (accessed November 24, 2001).

Alexander, Thomas B. *Political Reconstruction in Tennessee.* 1950. Reprint, New York: Russell & Russell, 1968.

Anderson, Peggy. *The Daughters: An Unconventional Look at America's Fan Club—The DAR.* New York: St. Martin's Press, 1974.

Anderson, Virginia DeJohn. *New England's Generation: The Great Migration and the Formation of Society and Culture in the Seventeenth Century.* New York: Cambridge University Press, 1991.

———. "Religion, the Common Thread of Motivation." In *Major Problems in American Colonial History*, ed. Karen Ordahl Kupperman, 145–57. Lexington MA: D. C. Heath, 1993.

Andrist, Ralph K. *The Long Death: The Last Days of the Plains Indian.* New York: Collier Books, 1964.

Anglin, Ron, and Glen Lindeman, eds. *Forgotten Trails: Historical Sources of the Columbia's Big Bend Country.* Pullman: Washington State University Press, 1995.

"Annie Turner Wittenmyer." *Women in American History by Encyclopedia Britannica.* 1999. http://women.eb.com/women/articles/Wittenmyer_ Annie_Turner.html (accessed November 24, 2001).

Archer, Melanie, and Judith R. Blau. "Class Formation in Nineteenth-Century America: The Case of the Middle Class." *Annual Review of Sociology* 19 (1993): 17–41.

Armitage, Susan. "Women and Men in Western History: A Stereoptical Vision." *Western Historical Quarterly* 16 (October 1985): 381–95.

Arthur St. Clair Colyar. 2000. http://virtualmuseumofhistory.com/arthurst claircolyar/ (accessed July 15, 2001).

Association of Graduates of the United States Military Academy. *Annual Reunion, June 12th, 1914, Association of Graduates of the United States Military Academy.* West Point NY: The Association, 1914.

Athearn, Robert G. *The Coloradans.* Albuquerque: University of New Mexico Press, 1976.

———. *Forts of the Upper Missouri.* Englewood Cliffs NJ: Prentice-Hall, 1967.

Ault, Nelson A. "The Earnest Ladies: The Walla Walla Women's Club and the

Equal Suffrage League of 1886–1889." *Pacific Northwest Quarterly* 42, no. 2 (1951): 123–37.

Ayers, Edward L. *The Promise of the New South: Life after Reconstruction.* New York: Oxford University Press, 1992.

Baker, Paula. *The Moral Frameworks of Public Life: Gender, Politics, and the State in Rural New York, 1870–1930.* New York: Oxford University Press, 1991.

Bancroft, Caroline. *Gulch of Gold: A History of Central City, Colorado.* Boulder CO: Johnson Publishing, 1958.

Barber, John W., and Henry Howe. *Historical Collections of the State of New York; containing a General Collection of the Most Interesting Facts, Traditions, Biographical Sketches, Anecdotes, &c. Relating to its History and Antiquities, with Geographical Descriptions of Every Township in the State.* Port Washington NY: Kenniket Press, 1841.

"Bayard Taylor." *The Columbia Encyclopedia.* 6th ed. New York: Columbia University Press, 2001. www.bartleby.com/65/ (accessed July 15, 2001).

Beckert, Sven. *The Monied Metropolis: New York City and the Consolidation of the American Bourgeoisie, 1850–1896.* Cambridge: Cambridge University Press, 2001.

———. "Propertied of a Differed Kind: Bourgeoisie and Lower Middle Class in the Nineteenth-Century United States." In *The Middling Sorts: Explorations in the History of the American Middle Class,* ed. Burton J. Bledstein and Robert D. Johnson, 285–95. New York: Routledge, 2001.

Belissary, Constantine G. "The Rise of Industry and the Industrial Spirit in Tennessee, 1865–1885." *Journal of Southern History* 19, no. 2 (1953): 193–215.

Bernard, Gail A., MD, and Jeffrey K. Bennett, MD. "Vasospastic Amaurosis Fugax." *Archives of Ophthalmology, Journals of the AMA* 117, no. 11 (1999). http://archopht.ama-assn.org/issues/v117n11/ffull/epe90038–1.html (accessed August 5, 2001).

Bicentennial Committee for the Town of Manchester. *A Part of Manchester's Heritage.* Manchester MA: Cricket Press, 1998.

Blair, Karen J. *The Clubwoman as Feminist: True Womanhood Redefined, 1868–1914.* New York: Homes and Meier, 1980.

Bledstein, Burton J. *The Culture of Professionalism: The Middle Class and the Development of Higher Education in America.* New York: Norton, 1976.

Bledstein, Burton J., and Robert D. Johnson, eds. *The Middling Sorts: Explorations in the History of the American Middle Class.* New York: Routledge, 2001.

Blevins, Audie, and Katherine Jensen. "Gambling as a Community Development Quick Fix." *Annals of the American Academy of Political and Social Science* 556 (March 1998): 109–23.

Blumin, Stuart M. *The Emergence of the Middle Class: Social Experience in the American City, 1760–1900*. Cambridge: Cambridge University Press, 1989.

Bowman, John S., ed. *The Civil War Almanac*. New York: Bison Books, 1983.

Boynton, Edward, A.M., Adjutant of the Military Academy. *History of West Point, and its Military Importance during the American Revolution: and the Origin and progress of the United States Military Academy*. New York: D. Van Nostrand, 1863.

Bradley, Ian. *A History of Machine Tools*. Hemel Hempstead: Model and Allied Publications, 1972. http://www.turners.org/lathehistory.html (accessed July 15, 2001).

Brear, Holly Beachly. "We Run the Alamo, and You Don't: Alamo Battles of Ethnicity and Gender." In *Where These Memories Grow: History, Memory, and Southern Identity*, ed. W. Fitzhugh Brundage, 299–318. Chapel Hill: University of North Carolina Press, 2000.

Bright, Thomas R. "Yankees in Arms: The Civil War as a Personal Experience." *Civil War History* 19, no. 3 (1973): 197–218.

Brown, Dee. *Bury My Heart at Wounded Knee: An Indian History of the American West*. New York: Henry Holt, 1970.

Bryan, Enoch Albert. *Sketch of the State College of Washington, 1890–1925*. Spokane: Inland American Printing, 1928.

Cain, William E., ed. *William Lloyd Garrison and the Fight against Slavery: Selections from* The Liberator. Boston: Bedford Books of St. Martin's Press, 1995.

"Castles & Towers of Scotland, Craigmillar Castle." *Highland Traveller: The Travellers Guide to Scotland*. http://www.highlandtraveller.com/sites/castles/craigmillar.html (accessed June 14, 2001).

Chandler, Alfred D., Jr. *The Visible Hand: The Managerial Revolution in American Business*. Cambridge: Harvard University Press, 1977.

Christie, Jeanne Marie. "Performing My Plain Duty: Women of the North at City Point, 1864–1865." *Virginia Cavalcade* 46, no. 5 (1997): 214–24.

City of Black Hawk. *Black Hawk History*. http://www.cityofblackhawk.org/# (accessed July 8, 2001).

Clanton, O. Gene. *Congressional Populism and the Crisis of the 1890s*. Lawrence: University of Kansas Press, 1998.

Clodfelter, Micheal. *The Dakota War: The United States Army versus the Sioux, 1862–1865*. Jefferson NC: McFarland, 1998.

Clinton, Catherine. *Civil War Stories*. Athens: University of Georgia Press, 1998.

Clinton, Catherine, and Nina Silber, eds. *Divided Houses: Gender and the Civil War*. New York: Oxford University Press, 1992.

Coffin, Joshua. *The Toppans of Toppan's Lane, with Their Descendants and Relations*. Newburyport MA: William H. Huse, 1862.

"Common Welsh Surnames." *Celtic, Gaelic, Irish, and Scottish Names.* http:// www.crosswinds.net/ daire/names/welshsurs.html (accessed June 14, 2001).

Cooper, Constance J. "Tennessee Returns to Congress." *Tennessee Historical Quarterly* 37, no. 1 (1978): 49–62.

Countryman, Edward. *The American Revolution.* New York: Hill and Wang, 1985.

Cott, Nancy F. *The Bonds of Womanhood: "Woman's Sphere" in New England, 1780–1835.* New Haven: Yale University Press, 1979.

"Craigmillar Castle." *The World of Mary Queen of Scots.* 1998. http://www.ma rie-stuart.co.uk/Castles/craigmillar.htm (accessed June 14, 2001).

Cressy, David. *Coming Over: Migration and Communication between England and New England in the Seventeenth Century.* New York: Cambridge University Press, 1987.

Cullum, Bvt. Maj. Gen. George W., Colonel of Engineering, U.S. Army, Retired. *Biographical Register of the Officers and Graduates of the U.S. Military Academy at West Point, N.Y., from its Establishment in 1802, to 1890, with the Early History of the United States Military Academy.* Vol. 2. Boston: Houghton, Mifflin, 1891.

Cummings, Pamela J. "Worcester County Soldiers in the Civil War." *Historical Journal of Massachusetts* 20, no. 1 (1992): 32–52.

Custer, Elizabeth B. *"Boots and Saddles"; Or, Life in Dakota with General Custer.* Norman: University of Oklahoma Press, 1961.

Dahlie, Jorgen. "Old World Paths in the New: Scandinavians Find a Familiar Home in Washington." In *Experiences in a Promised Land: Essays in Pacific Northwest History,* ed. G. Thomas Edwards and Carlos A. Schwantes, 99–108. Seattle: University of Washington Press, 1986.

Daughters of the American Revolution. *History and Register 1924: Washington State Society Daughters of the American Revolution.* Seattle: Washington State Society Daughters of the American Revolution, 1924.

Dawley, Alan. *Class and Community: The Industrial Revolution in Lynn.* Cambridge: Harvard University Press, 1976.

———. *Struggles for Justice: Social Responsibility and the Liberal State.* Cambridge: Belknap Press of Harvard University Press, 1991.

Dean, Eric T., Jr. *Shook over Hell: Post-Traumatic Stress, Vietnam, and the Civil War.* Cambridge: Harvard University Press, 1997.

Dearing, Mary R. *Veterans in Politics: The Story of the G.A.R.* Baton Rouge: Louisiana State University Press, 1952.

Depew, Chauncey M. *My Memories of Eighty Years.* New York: Scribner, 1922.

Donnelly, Mabel Collins. *The American Victorian Woman: The Myth and the Reality.* New York: Greenwood Press, 1986.

Doyle, Don Harrison. *The Social Order of a Frontier Community: Jacksonville, Illinois, 1825–1870.* Urbana: University of Illinois Press, 1978.

Durham, N. W. *History of the City of Spokane and Spokane County Washington from Its Earliest Settlement to the Present Time.* Vol. 2. Chicago: S. J. Clarke, 1912.

Eckenrode, H. J., and Bryan Conrad. *James Longstreet: Lee's War Horse.* Chapel Hill: University of North Carolina Press, 1986.

Edwards, G. Thomas. *Sowing Good Seeds: The Northwest Suffrage Campaigns of Susan B. Anthony.* Portland OR: Oregon Historical Society Press, 1990.

———. "Walla Walla: Gateway to the Pacific Northwest Interior." *Montana: The Magazine of Western History* 40, no. 3 (1990): 29–43.

Emerson, Ralph Waldo. *The Conduct of Life.* Boston: Ticknor and Fields, 1860.

Enochs, James C. "A Clash of Ambition: The Tappan-Chivington Feud." *Montana: The Magazine of Western History* 15, no. 3 (1965): 58–61.

Evans, Elwood, L. F. Mosher, G. P. Kuykendall, and W. B. Lyman. *History of the Pacific Northwest: Oregon and Washington.* 2 vols. Portland: North Pacific History Company, 1889.

Evans, Sara. *Born for Liberty: A History of Women in America.* New York: The Free Press, 1989.

Fahey, John. *The Inland Empire: Unfolding Years, 1879–1929.* Seattle: University of Washington Press, 1986.

Faragher, John Mack. *Sugar Creek: Life on the Illinois Prairie.* New Haven: Yale University Press, 1986.

———. *Women and Men on the Overland Trail.* New Haven: Yale University Press, 1979.

Federation of American Scientists. "New York Naval Shipyard." *Military Analysis Network.* 1999. http://www.fas.org/man/company/shipyard/new _york.htm (accessed July 29, 2001).

Folmsbee, Stanley J., Robert E. Corlew, and Enoch L. Mitchell. *Tennessee: A Short History.* Knoxville: University of Tennessee Press, 1969.

Foner, Eric. *Reconstruction: America's Unfinished Revolution, 1863–1877.* New York: Harper and Row, 1988.

Fox, Joseph M. *The Story of Early Peekskill, 1609–1876.* Peekskill NY: Enterprise Press, 1947.

"Frances Elizabeth Caroline Willard." *Women in American History by Encyclopedia Britannica.* 1999. http://women.eb.com/women/articles/Willard_ Frances_ Elizabeth_ Caroline.html (accessed November 24, 2001).

Frykman, George A. *Creating the People's University: Washington State University, 1890–1990.* Pullman: Washington State University Press, 1990.

Games, Alison. *Migration and the Origins of the English Atlantic World.* Cambridge: Harvard University Press, 1999.

Gates, Charles M., ed. *Messages of the Governors of the Territory of Washington to the Legislative Assembly, 1854–1889*. Seattle: University of Washington Press, 1940.

Gibbens, Byrd. "A Virginia Family on the Colorado and New Mexico Mining Frontiers." *Pacific Historian* 30, no. 3 (1986): 39–53.

Gibbs, Margaret. *The DAR*. New York: Holt, Rinehart and Winston, 1969.

Ginzberg, Lori D. *Women and the Work of Benevolence: Morality, Politics, and Class in the Nineteenth-Century United States*. New Haven: Yale University Press, 1990.

Glassley, Ray Hoard. *Indian Wars of the Pacific Northwest*. 1953. Reprint, Portland: Binfords and Mort, 1972.

Godson, William F. H., Jr. *The History of West Point, 1852–1920*. Philadelphia: Temple University, 1934.

Good, Peter Peyto. *Family Records of James and Nancy Dunham Tappan*. Liberty, Union County IN: n.p., 1884. http://www.essexcountyma.org/new bury/toppana.htm (accessed January 15, 2002).

Goodwyn, Lawrence. *Democratic Promise: The Populist Movement in America*. New York: Oxford University Press, 1976.

Gordon, Elizabeth Putnam. *Women Torch-Bearers: The Story of the Woman's Christian Temperance Union*. Evanston IL: National Woman's Christian Temperance Union Publishing House, 1924.

Haarsager, Sandra. *Organized Womanhood: Cultural Politics in the Pacific Northwest, 1840–1920*. Norman: University of Oklahoma Press, 1997.

Hanscom, John. "Coal Company Town: Franklin and the Oregon Improvement Company." *Columbia* 8, no. 1 (1994): 13–18.

Hedges, James Blaine. *Henry Villard and the Railways of the Northwest*. 1930; Reprint, New York: Russell and Russell, 1967.

———. "Promotion of Immigration to the Pacific Northwest by the Railroad." *Mississippi Valley Historical Review* 15, no. 2 (1928): 183–203.

Hine, Robert V. *Community on the American Frontier: Separate But Not Alone*. Norman: University of Oklahoma Press, 1980.

Hine, Robert V., and John Mack Faragher. *The American West: A New Interpretive History*. New Haven: Yale University Press, 2000.

Hollenback, Frank R. *Central City and Black Hawk, Colorado: Then and Now*. Denver: Sage Books, 1961.

Hollister, Ovando J. *The Mines of Colorado*. Springfield MA: Samuel Bowles, 1867.

Howe, Thomas J. *The Petersburg Campaign: Wasted Valor, June 15–18, 1864*. Lynchburg VA: H. E. Howard, 1988.

Hoxie, Frederick. *Encyclopedia of North American Indians*. New York: Houghton Mifflin, 1996.

Humphrey, Grace. *Women in American History*. Freeport NY: Books for Libraries Press, 1968.

Hunt, Garrett B. *Indian Wars of the Inland Empire*. Spokane: Spokane Community College Library, 1908.

An Illustrated History of Whitman County, State of Washington. Spokane: W. H. Lever, 1901.

Jameson, Elizabeth. *All That Glitters. Class, Conflict, and Community in Cripple Creek*. Urbana: University of Illinois Press, 1998.

———. "Women as Workers, Women as Civilizers: True Womanhood in the American West." *Frontiers* 7, no. 3 (1984): 1–8.

Jeffrey, Julie Roy. *Frontier Women: The Trans-Mississippi West, 1850–1880*. New York: Hill and Wang, 1979.

Jensen, Joan M., and Darlis A. Miller. "The Gentle Tamers Revisited: New Approaches to the History of Women in the American West." *Pacific Historical Review* 49 (May 1980): 173–213.

"John M. Chivington" *New Perspectives on the West*. http://www.pbs.org/weta/thewest/people/a_ c/Chivington.htm (accessed June 30, 2004).

Johnson, Paul. *The National Trust Book of British Castles*. New York: Putnam, 1978.

Johnston, Robert D. "Conclusion: Historians and the American Middle Class." In *The Middling Sorts. Explorations in the History of the American Middle Class*, ed. Burton J. Bledstein and Robert D. Johnson, 296–306. New York: Routledge, 2001.

Jones, Jacqueline. "Men and Women in Northern New England during the Era of the Civil War." *Maine Historical Society Quarterly* 33, no. 2 (1993): 70–87.

Judson, Phoebe Goodell. *A Pioneer's Search for an Ideal Home*. Lincoln: University of Nebraska Press, 1984.

Kaufman, Polly Welts. *Women Teachers on the Frontier*. New Haven: Yale University Press, 1984.

Keniston, Bob. "Regimental History." *16th Massachusetts Volunteer Infantry*. 1998. http://members.aol.com/inf16mavol/history.html (accessed January 28, 2000).

Kenny, Herbert A. *Cape Ann: Cape America*. Gloucester MA: Curious Traveller Press, 1971.

Kerber, Linda K. *Toward an Intellectual History of Women*. Chapel Hill: University of North Carolina Press, 1997.

———. *Women of the Republic: Intellect and Ideology in Revolutionary America*. Chapel Hill: University of North Carolina Press, 1980.

Kerber, Linda K., and Jane Sherron DeHart. *Women's America: Refocusing the Past*. 4th ed. New York: Oxford University Press, 1995.

Kip, Lawrence, Second Lieutenant of the Third Regiment of Artillery, U.S.

Army. *Army Life on the Pacific: A Journal of the Expedition against the Northern Indians, the Tribes of the Coeur D'Alenes, Spokans, and Pelouzes, in the Summer of 1858*. New York: Redfield, 1859.

Knight, Glenn B. *Brief History of the Grand Army of the Republic*. http://suvcw. org/gar.htm (accessed November 25, 2001).

Koch, Fred C. *The Volga Germans in Russia and the Americas, from 1763 to the Present*. University Park: Pennsylvania State University Press, 1977.

Kunz, Jeffrey R. M., MD, ed. *The American Medical Association Family Medical Guide*. New York: Random House, 1982.

Lamson, Rev. D. F. *History of the Town of Manchester, Essex County, Massachusetts, 1645–1895*. Boston: Pinkham Press, 1895.

Land Department of the Oregon Improvement Co. *Eastern Washington Territory and Oregon: Facts Regarding the Resources, Productions, Industries, Soil, Climate, Healthfulness, Commerce and Means of Communication*. Portland: Oregon Improvement Company, n.d.

Larson, T. A. "The Woman Suffrage Movement in Washington." *Pacific Northwest Quarterly* 67, no. 2 (1976): 49–62.

Leckie, Shirley Anne. *Elizabeth Bacon Custer and the Making of a Myth*. Norman: University of Oklahoma Press, 1993.

———, ed. *The Colonel's Lady on the Western Frontier: The Correspondence of Alice Kirk Grierson*. Lincoln: University of Nebraska Press, 1989.

Lenzen, Connie. *Diseases of the Ancestors: How Do We Know What They Were?* 2001. http://www.oregonvos.net/ clenzen/diseases.html (accessed July 2, 2001).

Leonard, Elizabeth D. *All the Daring of the Soldier: Women of the Civil War Armies*. New York: Penguin Books, 1999.

———. *Yankee Women: Gender Battles in the Civil War*. New York: Norton, 1994.

Levy, JoAnn. *They Saw the Elephant: Women in the California Gold Rush*. Norman: University of Oklahoma Press, 1992.

Lewty, Peter J. *Across the Columbia Plain: Railroad Expansion in the Interior Northwest, 1885–1893*. Pullman: Washington State University Press, 1995.

———. *To the Columbia Gateway: The Oregon Railway and the Northern Pacific, 1879–1884*. Pullman: Washington State University Press, 1987.

Link, Kenneth. "Potomac Fever: The Hazards of Camp Life." *Vermont History* 51, no. 2 (1983): 69–88.

Livermore, Mary Ashton Rice. *The Story of My Life*. New York: Arno Press, 1974.

Logan, Mrs. John A. *Reminiscences of a Soldier's Wife: An Autobiography*. New York: Scribner, 1913.

Logue, Larry M. "Union Veterans and Their Government: The Effects of

Public Policies on Private Lives." *Journal of Interdisciplinary History* 22, no. 3 (1992): 411–34.

Lyman, W. D., MA, Lit. D., *Lyman's History of Old Walla Walla County, Embracing Walla Walla, Columbia, Garfield, and Asotin Counties.* 2 vols. Chicago: S. J. Clarke, 1918.

MacLean, Fitzroy. *Highlanders: A History of the Scottish Clans.* New York: Penguin Books, 1995.

Manchester-by-the-Sea, 1645–1970. Manchester MA: Cricket Press, 1970.

Manring, B. F. *The Conquest of the Coeur D'Alenes, Spokanes and Palouses: The Expeditions of Colonels E. J. Steptoe and George Wright against the "Northern Indians" in 1858.* Spokane: Inland Printing, 1912.

Marshall, John W. "Rockport." In *History of Essex County, Massachusetts, with Biographical Sketches of many of the Pioneers and Prominent Men,* 2 vols., comp. D. Hamilton Hurd, 2:1375–79. Philadelphia: J. W. Lewis, 1888.

Matsuda, Mari J. "The West and the Legal Status of Women: Explanations of Frontier Feminism." *Journal of the West* 24 (January 1985): 47–56.

May, Dean L. *Three Frontiers: Family, Land, and Society in the American West, 1750–1900.* Cambridge: Cambridge University Press, 1994.

McClintock, Megan J. "Civil War Pensions and the Reconstruction of Union Families." *Journal of American History* 83, no. 2 (1996): 456–80.

McConnell, Stuart. *Glorious Contentment: The Grand Army of the Republic, 1865–1900.* Chapel Hill: University of North Carolina Press, 1992.

McFarling, Lloyd, ed. and illus. *Exploring the Northern Plains, 1804–1876.* Caldwell ID: Caxton Printers, 1955.

McGregor, Alexander. "The Economic Impact of the Mullan Road on Walla Walla, 1860–1883." *Pacific Northwest Quarterly* 65, no. 3 (1974): 118–29.

McMath, Robert C., Jr. *American Populism: A Social History, 1877- 1898.* New York: Hill and Wang, 1993.

McMillen, Myrtle C. *History Of . . . East Washington's Woman's Christian Temperance Union, 1883–1953, Seventieth Anniversary.* N.p., n.d.

McNeill, William W., comp. and ed. *Gathering Gold: How They Did It In Colorado's First Gold Camp, the Central City–Black Hawk District.* Arvada CO: William W. McNeill, 1974.

McPherson, James M. *Battle Cry of Freedom: The Civil War Era.* New York: Ballantine Books, 1988.

———. *For Cause and Comrades: Why Men Fought in the Civil War.* New York: Oxford University Press, 1997.

———. *Ordeal by Fire: The Civil War and Reconstruction.* New York: Mc-Graw-Hill, 1982.

Military Order of the Loyal Legion of the United States. 2000. http://www.wali ka.com/mollus.htm (accessed November 26, 2001).

Mintz, Steven. *A Prison of Expectations: The Family in Victorian Culture.* New York: New York University Press, 1983.

Mitchell, Reid. *Civil War Soldiers.* New York: Penguin Group, 1988.

Morrissey, Katherine G. *Mental Territories: Mapping the Inland Empire.* Ithaca: Cornell University Press, 1997.

Moynihan, Ruth Barnes. *Rebel for Rights: Abigail Scott Duniway.* New Haven: Yale University Press, 1983.

National Park Service. *Asian Pacific Pioneers along the Columbia River.* 2001. http://www.nps.gov/laro/culturalvariations.htm (accessed December 6, 2001).

Nazzal, Jim. "Judge William Inman of Colfax." *Bunchgrass Historian* 25, no. 1 (1999): 4–19.

Nevins, Allan. *The War for the Union.* 4 vols. New York: Scribner, 1959–71.

Norton, Bettina A. "Tappan and Bradford: Boston Lithographers with Essex County Associations." *Essex Institute Historical Collections* 114, no. 3 (1978): 149–60.

Norton, Mary Beth. *Founding Mothers and Fathers: Gendered Power and the Forming of American Society.* New York: Knopf, 1996.

———. *Liberty's Daughters: The Revolutionary Experience of American Women, 1750–1800.* New York: Harper Collins, 1980.

Nuxoll, Jon. "'Repent, Ye Boozers!' Whitman County and the Liquor Question, 1855–1917." *Bunchgrass Historian* 13, no. 4 (1985): 3–31.

Oates, Stephen B. *A Woman of Valor: Clara Barton and the Civil War.* New York: The Free Press, 1994.

Order of Exercises of the Charlestown Female Seminary, for the Twenty-Sixth Anniversary, July 10, 1857. Boston: W. and E. Howe, 1857.

Parker, Frank J., ed. and comp. *Washington Territory! The Present and Prospective Future of the Upper Columbia Country, Embracing the Counties of Walla Walla, Whitman, Spokane and Stevens, with a Detailed Description of North Idaho.* Walla Walla WA: Statesman Book and Job Office, 1881.

Parsons, Eleanor C. *Hannah and the Hatchet Gang: Rockport's Revolt against Rum.* Canaan NH: Phoenix, 1975.

Pattee, John. "Reminiscences of John Pattee." *South Dakota Historical Collections* 5 (1910): 273–305.

Patton, James Welch. *Unionism and Reconstruction in Tennessee, 1860–1869.* 1934. Reprint, Gloucester MA: Peter Smith, 1966.

Pearce, Stella E. "Suffrage in the Pacific Northwest: Old Oregon and Washington." *Washington Historical Quarterly* 3, no. 2 (1912): 106–14.

Peltier, Jerome. *Warbonnets and Epaulets: With Pre- and Post Factor, Documented, of the Steptoe-Wright Indian Campaigns of 1858 in Washington Territory.* Montreal: Payette Radio Limited, n.d.

Petrik, Paula. *No Step Backward: Women and Family on the Rocky Mountain

Mining Frontier, Helena, Montana, 1865–1900. Helena: Montana Historical Society Press, 1987.

Pettegrew, John. "'The Soldier's Faith': Turn-of-the-Century Memory of the Civil War and the Emergence of Modern American Nationalism." *Journal of Contemporary History* 31, no. 1 (1996): 49–73.

Pomeroy, Earl. *The Pacific Slope: A History of California, Oregon, Washington, Idaho, Utah, and Nevada.* Seattle: University of Washington Press, 1965.

Reid, Brian Holden. "Another Look at Grant's Crossing of the James, 1864." *Civil War History* 39, no. 4 (1993): 291–315.

Reynolds, Terry S. "The Education of Engineers in America before the Morrill Act of 1862." *History of Education Quarterly* 32, no. 4 (1992): 459–82.

Roe, Alfred S., and Charles Nutt. *History of the First Regiment of Heavy Artillery Massachusetts Volunteers.* Worcester MA: Regimental Association, 1917.

Roe, Frances, MA. *Army Letters from an Officer's Wife, 1871–1888.* New York: D. Appleton, 1909.

Ross, Kristie. "Arranging a Doll's House: Refined Women as Union Nurses." In *Divided Houses: Gender and the Civil War,* ed. Catherine Clinton and Nina Silber, 97–113. New York: Oxford University Press, 1992.

Scheuerman, Richard D. "Germans from Russia: Pioneers on the Palouse Frontier." *Bunchgrass Historian* 11, no. 4 (1983): 4–23.

———. *Pilgrims on the Earth: A German-Russian Chronicle.* Fairfield WA: Ye Galleon Press, 1976.

Scheuerman, Richard D., and Clifford E. Trafzer. *The Volga Germans: Pioneers of the Northwest.* Moscow: University of Idaho Press, 1980.

Schell, Herbert S. *History of South Dakota.* Lincoln: University of Nebraska Press, 1968.

Schlissel, Lillian. *Women's Diaries of the Westward Journey.* New York: Schocken, 1992.

Schwantes, Carlos Arnaldo. *The Pacific Northwest: An Interpretive History.* Lincoln: University of Nebraska Press, 1996.

Sellers, Charles. *The Market Revolution: Jacksonian American, 1815–1846.* New York: Oxford University Press, 1991.

Shoepflin, Mariam Wagner, collector. Farmington Histories [ca. 1940–ca. 1961]. Cage 4138. Manuscripts, Archives and Special Collections. Washington State University Libraries. Pullman WA.

Sibbald, John R. "Army Women of the West." *The American West* 3, no. 2 (1966): 56–67.

Simon, John Y., ed. *The Personal Memoirs of Julia Dent Grant.* New York: Putnam, 1975.

Sizer, Lyde Cullen. "Acting Her Part: Narratives of Union Women Spies."

In *Divided Houses: Gender and the Civil War*, ed. Catherine Clinton and Nina Silber, 114–33. New York: Oxford University Press, 1992.

Skocpol, Theda. "America's First Social Security System: The Expansion of Benefits for Civil War Veterans." *Political Science Quarterly* 108, no. 1 (1993): 85–117.

Smalley, Eugene V. *History of the Northern Pacific Railroad*. New York: Putnam, 1883.

Smith, Duane A. *Rocky Mountain Mining Camps: The Urban Frontier*. Bloomington: Indiana University Press, 1967.

———. *Rocky Mountain West: Colorado, Wyoming, and Montana, 1859–1915*. Albuquerque: University of New Mexico Press, 1992.

Snowden, Clinton A. *History of Washington: The Rise and Progress of an American State*. 5 vols. New York: Century History Company, 1911.

Spencer, Elma Dill Russell. *Green Russell and Gold*. Austin: University of Texas Press, 1966.

Stansell, Christine. *City of Women: Sex and Class in New York, 1789–1860*. Urbana: University of Illinois Press, 1986.

Stevens, Larry. "Forty-ninth Ohio Volunteer Infantry." *Ohio in the Civil War*. 2001. http://my.ohio.voyager.net/ lstevens/49oh.html (accessed November 25, 2001).

Takaki, Ronald. *Strangers from a Different Shore: A History of Asian Americans*. New York: Penguin Books, 1989.

Tannatt, Elizabeth F. *Indian Battles in the Inland Empire in 1858*. Spokane: Shaw and Borden, 1914.

Tappan, Daniel Langdon. *Tappan-Toppan Genealogy: Ancestors and Descendants of Abraham Toppan of Newbury, Massachusetts, 1606–1672*. Arlington MA: by the compiler, 1915.

Tappan, William Henry. "Manchester." In *History of Essex County, Massachusetts, with Biographical Sketches of many of the Pioneers and Prominent Men*, 2 vols., comp. D. Hamilton Hurd, 2:1249–98. Philadelphia: J. W. Lewis, 1888.

Taylor, George Rogers, ed. *The Turner Thesis: Concerning the Role of the Frontier in American History*. 3rd ed. Lexington MA: D. C. Heath, 1972.

Temple, Wayne C., ed. "A Signal Officer with Grant: The Letters of Captain Charles L. Davis." *Civil War History* 7, no. 4 (1961): 428–37.

Trachtenberg, Alan. *The Incorporation of America: Culture and Society in the Gilded Age*. New York: Hill and Wang, 1982.

Trafzer, Clifford E., and Richard D. Scheuerman. *Renegade Tribe: The Palouse Indians and the Invasion of the Inland Pacific Northwest*. Pullman: Washington State University Press, 1986.

True, Marshall. "Middle Class Women and Civic Improvement in Burlington, 1865–1890." *Vermont History* 56, no. 2 (1988): 112–27.

Turner, Wallace B. "Frank Hall: Colorado Journalist, Public Servant, and Historian." *Colorado Magazine* 53, no. 4 (1976): 328–51.

U.S. Adjutant General's Office. *Records of the Office of the Adjutant General, Fort Randall, D.T., Post Returns, 1856–1892.* Washington DC: The National Archives, 1949, microfilm, reel 403.

U.S. Bureau of Land Management. *History of the BLM.* 2001. http://www.blm.gov/nhp/facts/index.htm#history (accessed November 25, 2001).

U.S. Census Bureau. *Sixth Census of Population: Westchester County, New York, 1840.* Washington DC: The National Archives, 1934, microfilm, reel 110.

———. *Seventh Census of Population: Essex County, Massachusetts, 1850.* Washington DC: The National Archives, 1934, microfilm, reel 310.

U.S. Geological Survey. *Major Hydrologic Features in the Mount St. Helens Region.* 1999. http://vulcan.wr.usgs.gov/Volcanoes/MSH/Maps/map_ msh_ hydro_ features.html (accessed November 9, 2001).

U.S. War Department. *War of the Rebellion: A Compilation of the Official Records of the Union and Confederate Armies.* 128 parts in 70 vols. Washington DC: Government Printing Office, 1880–1901.

Villard, Henry. *The Early History of Transportation in Oregon.* Ed. Oswald Garrison Villard. Eugene OR: The University Press, 1944.

———. *Memoirs of Henry Villard, Journalist and Financier, 1835–1900.* 2 vols. Westminster: Archibald Constable, 1904.

———. *The Past and Present of the Pike's Peak Gold Regions.* 1860. Reprint, Princeton: Princeton University Press, 1932.

Vinovskis, Maris A. "Have Social Historians Lost the Civil War? Some Preliminary Demographic Speculations." *Journal of American History* 76, no. 1 (1989): 34–58.

———. "Stalking the Elusive Middle Class in Nineteenth-Century America: A Review Article." *Comparative Studies in Society and History* 33, no. 3 (1991): 582–87.

Walla Walla Valley, Washington Territory: Its Resources, Climate, River and Railroad Systems, Cities and Towns, Land and Land-Laws, and General Advantage as a Place of Residence. Walla Walla WA: Statesman Book and Job Press, 1879.

Walters, George J. *Wir Wollen Deutsche Bleiben: The Story of the Volga Germans.* Kansas City: Halcyon House, 1982.

Ward, Jean M., and Elaine A. Maveety, eds. *"Yours for Liberty": Selections from Abigail Scott Duniway's Suffrage Newspaper.* Corvallis: Oregon State University Press, 2000.

Washington State University. Center for Environmental Education. *Rock Lake, Kamiakin, and the Chinese Immigrants.* 2000. http://ceed.wsu.edu/

wsu_ StudentProjects/Northern_ Borders/rock_ lake.htm (accessed December 6, 2001).

Watson, Harry L. *Liberty and Power: The Politics of Jacksonian America.* New York: Hill and Wang, 1990.

Weatherford, Doris. *A History of the American Suffragist Movement.* Santa Barbara CA: ABC-CLIO, 1998. http://www.suffragist.com/timeline.htm (accessed October 6, 2001).

Weaver, C. P. *The Tappans of Manchester.* Tappan Family Papers. Manchester Historical Society. Manchester-by-the-Sea MA.

Welch, James. *Killing Custer.* New York: Norton, 1994.

Welter, Barbara. "The Cult of True Womanhood: 1820–1860." *American Quarterly* 18, no. 2 (1966): 149–74.

Wiebe, Robert H. *Businessmen and Reform: A Study of the Progressive Movement.* 1962. Reprint, Chicago: Ivan R. Dee, 1989.

———. *The Search for Order, 1877–1920.* New York: Hill and Wang, 1967.

Wilentz, Sean. *Chants Democratic: New York City and the Rise of the American Working Class, 1788–1850.* New York: Oxford University Press, 1984.

Willard, Frances. *Woman and Temperance; Or, The Work and Workers of the Woman's Christian Temperance Union.* Chicago: The Temple, 1897.

Willard, Frances, and Mary A. Livermore, eds. *A Woman of the Century: Fourteen Hundred-Seventy Biographical Sketches Accompanied by Portraits of Leading American Women in All Walks of Life.* Buffalo: Charles Wells Moulton, 1893.

Williams, Hattie Plum. *The Czar's Germans: With Particular Reference to the Volga Germans.* Denver: World Press, 1975.

Wilson, Frederick T. "Old Fort Pierre and Its Neighbors." *South Dakota Historical Collections* 1 (1902): 263–380.

Wolle, Muriel V. Sibell. *Ghost Cities of Colorado: A Pictorial Record of Central City, Black Hawk, Nevadaville.* Denver: Smith-Brooks, 1933.

Woloch, Nancy. *Women and the American Experience.* 2 vols. New York: McGraw-Hill, 1994.

"Wright's Indian Vegetable Pills 1901–1933." *History Wired.* http://historywired.si.edu/object.ctm:ID=18 (accessed June 22, 2004).

Yeager, Willard Hayes. *Chauncey Mitchell Depew—The Orator: His Education in Oratory, His Early Speeches, His Views on the Theory of Public Speaking, and a Collection of His Hitherto Unpublished Addresses.* Washington DC: George Washington University Press, 1934.

Zebley, Kathleen R. "Samuel Mayes Arnell and Reconstruction in Tennessee." *Tennessee Historical Quarterly* 53, no. 4 (1994): 246–59.

Zhu, Liping. *A Chinaman's Chance: The Chinese on the Rocky Mountain Mining Frontier.* Boulder: University Press of Colorado, 1997.

In the Women in the West series

When Montana and I Were Young:
A Frontier Childhood
By Margaret Bell
Edited by Mary Clearman Blew

Martha Maxwell, Rocky Mountain
Naturalist
By Maxine Benson

Front-Page Women Journalists,
1920–1950
By Kathleen A. Cairns

The Art of the Woman: The Life
and Work of Elisabet Ney
By Emily Fourmy Cutrer

Emily: The Diary of a Hard-
Worked Woman
By Emily French
Edited by Janet Lecompte

The Important Things of Life: Women,
Work, and Family in Sweetwater
County, Wyoming, 1880–1929
By Dee Garceau

The Adventures of the Woman
Homesteader: The Life and Letters
of Elinore Pruitt Stewart
By Susanne K. George

Flowers in the Snow: The Life of
Isobel Wylie Hutchison, 1889–1982
By Gwyneth Hoyle

Domesticating the West: The Re-creation
of the Nineteenth-Century American
Middle Class
By Brenda K. Jackson

Engendered Encounters: Feminism
and Pueblo Cultures, 1879–1934
By Margaret D. Jacobs

The Colonel's Lady on the Western
Frontier: The Correspondence of
Alice Kirk Grierson
Edited by Shirley A. Leckie

A Stranger in Her Native Land:
Alice Fletcher and the American Indians
By Joan Mark

So Much to Be Done: Women Settlers
on the Mining and Ranching Frontier,
second edition
Edited by Ruth B. Moynihan,
Susan Armitage, and
Christiane Fischer Dichamp

Women and Nature: Saving the
"Wild" West
By Glenda Riley

The Life of Elaine Goodale Eastman
Theodore D. Sargent

Moving Out: A Nebraska Woman's Life
By Polly Spence
Edited by Karl Spence Richardson